THE *Anne Rice* READER

By Katherine Ramsland

PRISM OF THE NIGHT: A BIOGRAPHY OF ANNE RICE

THE VAMPIRE COMPANION: THE OFFICIAL GUIDE TO ANNE RICE'S THE VAMPIRE CHRONICLES

THE WITCHES' COMPANION: THE OFFICIAL GUIDE TO ANNE RICE'S LIVES OF THE MAYFAIR WITCHES

THE ANNE RICE TRIVIA BOOK

THE ANNE RICE READER (EDITOR)

THE ROQUELAURE READER: A COMPANION TO ANNE RICE'S EROTICA

THE ART OF LEARNING

ENGAGING THE IMMEDIATE: APPLYING KIERKEGAARD'S INDIRECT COMMUNICATION TO PSYCHOTHERAPY

THE *Anne Rice* READER

EDITED BY

KATHERINE RAMSLAND

BALLANTINE BOOKS • NEW YORK

 Published in the United States by Ballantine Books, a division of Random House, Inc., New York, and simultaneously in Canada by Random House of Canada Limited, Toronto.

Grateful acknowledgment is made to Alfred A. Knopf, Inc., for permission to reprint excerpts from *The Witching Hour* by Anne Rice. Copyright © 1990 by Anne Rice O'Brien.
Grateful acknowledgment is made to Stan Rice for permission to reprint an excerpt from the poem "Anne's Curls" from *Some Lamb* by Stan Rice. Copyright © 1975 by Stan Rice.

http://www.randomhouse.com

Library of Congress Cataloging-in-Publication Data
The Anne Rice reader / edited by Katherine Ramsland. — 1st ed.
p. cm.
Includes bibliographical references and index.
ISBN 0-345-40267-7
1. Rice, Anne, 1941– —Criticism and interpretation. 2. Women and literature—United States—History—20th century. 3. Fantastic fiction, American—History and criticism. 4. Erotic stories, American—History and criticism. 5. Horror tales, American—History and criticism. 6. Witchcraft in literature. 7. Vampires in literature. I. Ramsland, Katherine M., 1953– .
PS3568.I265Z54 1997
813'.54—dc21 96-49831

Text design by Ann Gold
Cover design by Carlos Beltràn
Cover photo by Karen O'Brien
Manufactured in the United States of America
First Edition: February 1997
10 9 8 7 6 5 4 3 2 1

Contents

CONTENTS

ACKNOWLEDGMENTS

Many thanks to the following people for their contributions to this book. Some sent material or helped to locate sources, while others offered comments and assistance, or made themselves available for interviews. In some instances, enthusiastic support was the greatest help of all.

I'm grateful to Kimberly Barker, Tom Cruise, Kirsten Dunst, Mary Farrelly (my beloved and indispensable New Orleans assistant), David Geffen, Lee Anne Haigney, Donna Johnston, Jim Kerr, Jerry Kirsch, Danny Manning, Susie Miller, Ruth Osborne, Michael C. Reindel, and Barbara Trimmer.

Of course, this book would not have been possible without Anne Rice, who gave me the short stories included within, and whose support and encouragement over the years have provided the information and resources that helped me develop the proper perspective for editing a collection like this.

Thanks also to each and every one of the contributors, to my agent, Lori Perkins, to my husband, Steve, and to my coeditors at Ballantine, Joanne Wyckoff and Andrea Schulz.

PART ONE

Anne Rice

Introduction

Anne Rice, the person, is as fascinating as Anne Rice, the writer. For the past several years, I have had the privilege of an intimate association with her while I wrote a biography and four companion guides to her novels. Although it's not easy to condense a full biography into a succinct overview, I have done so to provide a historical perspective for the novels discussed later in this book. Readers who would like more detail on Rice's life are referred to my *Prism of the Night: A Biography of Anne Rice*.

I invited Rice's longtime friend Kathleen Mackay to write a piece on their relationship. Mackay provides a detailed perspective on a pivotal time in Rice's life, beginning with the conference where Rice acquired the agent who sold her first novel, *Interview with the Vampire*, to Vicky Wilson at Alfred A. Knopf. Mackay witnessed Rice's exciting career in its early stages and offers a look back at those first steps. As a writer herself, she gives this friendship a very special place in her life.

In addition, New Orleans native Kenneth Holditch addresses Rice's relationship with the "city that care forgot."

One of my most interesting interviews with Rice was the one I did for *Quadrant*, a journal of analytic psychology, for their popular culture issue. In the interview, Rice talks about a number of subjects, both personal and philosophical, that cast light on her approach to her work. I include that interview here in full.

To round out this section, I asked Rice if I could reprint

two stories from her college days, which she graciously permitted. They were first published in the mid-1960s in her college literary journal, *Transfer*. I'll never forget the serendipity of running across them while I was looking at articles in a San Francisco library. I hoped that someday I'd be able to give them more exposure, and now I am able to do so.

I like "October 4th, 1948" and "Nicholas and Jean" for the way they display Rice's sensual style a full ten years before she published her first novel. The first story, which reveals what it was like for Rice to grow up in New Orleans, takes place on her own seventh birthday and shows her fascination with the spooky old houses of that city.

Anne Rice

AN OVERVIEW

Katherine Ramsland

Anne Rice made her publishing debut in 1976 with her first novel, *Interview with the Vampire*. She was thirty-four. Since then, she has authored fifteen novels, five of them under other names.

Born Howard Allen O'Brien in New Orleans on October 4, 1941, Anne (the name she adopted in reaction) lived in that exotic city until she was fifteen. Her father, Howard, who had given Anne his name, worked for the post office while Katherine, Anne's mother, set out to raise her four daughters to be geniuses. Well educated for a woman in those times, Katherine had great aspirations for her family, and she viewed her children as brilliant and talented. This encouragement made a strong impression on Anne. "She gave me so many wonderful things," she says about Katherine, "but above all, she gave me the belief in myself that I could do great things. She gave me a sense of limitless power."

Anne was the second of four girls (she later gained a half sister with her father's second marriage). Katherine allowed all her daughters a great deal of freedom, encouraging them to follow their whims, and through that to discover their strengths. If Alice, Anne's older sister, wanted to dance, then the furniture was moved to see what she could do; if the girls wanted to draw, they could draw on the walls. Unfortunately, the family had little money for lessons, so the children often found their ambitions stymied. Thus, they learned to rely on their imaginations for entertainment.

Katherine fed their imaginations with the detailed stories she told in her own special style. She memorized whole segments of films and novels and related them to her children. She also read poetry to them, introduced them to Dickens (Anne's favorite author), and told vivid ghost stories. Young Anne often walked past the large, deteriorating mansions of New Orleans, peering inside to catch sight of a female ghost with flaming hair or the Devil himself—said to keep a residence there. She wrote about these childhood fantasies in her first published short story, "October 4th, 1948."

Anne also resonated to stories of vampires, particularly those told from the vampire's perspective. One such tale, Richard Matheson's "Dress of White Silk," was about a child vampire. "I never forgot that story," Anne says. "I wanted to get into the vampire." Later she saw the movie *Dracula's Daughter* with Gloria Holden and admired its tragic sensuality. Such images left a deep impression on her.

With Katherine's encouragement, Anne and Alice developed a complex fantasy life for their entertainment. Anne wrote original plays in which all of her sisters participated. She also lost herself in complicated daydreams that often lasted many years. There is no doubt that this early exercise of her imagination influenced the elaborate nature of her novels.

Another aspect of Anne's childhood that affected her later work was her healthy sense of the physical world. In the humid and colorful city, she noted the abundant colors, fragrances, architectural styles, and interesting personalities that she encountered on her long walks to and from school.

She also found stimulation in the daily ceremonies of her parochial education. Raised Catholic, she learned early to envision union with God through the sacrifice of Christ. "You sit there and you imagine what Christ felt as he walked down the street carrying the cross," she recalls, "what the thorns felt like going into his forehead and the nails into his hands."

Stories about the suffering and transports of the saints were the ones that most captivated her. In them she recognized a spiritual payoff for self-sacrifice. In her private oratory, an unused bathroom in the back of her home on St. Charles Avenue, Anne prayed fervently. She wanted to experience the stigmata, the bloody imprints that mark unusual devotion, because she needed to be special in the eyes of God. "Anne's temperament was such," her father said, "that when she embraced something, she had to exercise real restraint not to become a fanatic." Life meant intensity. "I am an excessivist," she agrees, "and I'll be that to the last day of my life." To her young mind, a deeply devoted religious practice offered a way to become extraordinary, so she decided to become a nun.

Secretly, however, Anne also had strong erotic feelings. Told that sexual desire was sinful, she felt that she was different from other children. She was ashamed over what she eventually identified as masochistic fantasies, and those feelings were expressed later by the character Lisa in *Exit to Eden*. "I had dark, strange sexual feelings when I was very little," Lisa admits. "I wanted to be touched and I made up fantasies."[1]

To make matters worse, her mother's urgings to view herself as having unlimited potential came up hard against the expectations of her church. As much as she wished to abide by Catholic standards of goodness and obedience, she could not ignore what she soon discovered: girls did not receive the same status and privileges as boys, and to be in a relationship with a boy was to lose some of one's own power. Socially, girls were scorned for the same sexual desires that were tolerated in boys.

Awareness of such inequities made Anne impatient with a religious faith that stipulated repressive behavior. Her confusion and anger from that period eventually flowed into her second novel, *The Feast of All Saints*. Although set in antebellum times, its central characters are adolescents whose development into young adults plays havoc with their lives and relationships.

Unfortunately for Anne, when she most needed her mother's guidance during this tumultuous time, Katherine was deep into alcohol addiction. Howard's three-year hitch in the navy, begun in 1942, had left Katherine alone with the responsibilities for two young children, Alice and Anne. She began to drink to stave off loneliness and fear. Yet, even after Howard's return, she was unable to control her drinking, because her vision of what life should be—social status, artistic accomplishments, financial comfort—had outdistanced her economic means. Having buffered her disappointments and thwarted ambitions with alcohol, she could not stop bingeing. As Anne neared the age of fifteen, Katherine died. The loss devastated Anne. She had to learn to take care of herself while also taking care of her younger sisters, Tamara and Karen.

TRANSITIONS

Just over a year later, Howard remarried and moved his daughters to Richardson, Texas, near Dallas. For the first time, Anne found herself in a secular school. She no longer had to wear uniforms or attend to other aspects of strict

Catholic etiquette. The freedom to think for herself and to read books that had been forbidden throughout her childhood planted seeds for rejecting her faith altogether when she reached college. Against her father's wishes, she read existential philosophy and writers such as Hemingway and Woolf, and was thrilled by the new worlds opening up. She also fell in love.

The day Stan Rice sat next to her in class, she found herself instantly under his spell. She thought he looked like James Dean. They dated briefly, but Stan showed no real interest in her, so rather than wait around for him, Anne decided to go on to college.

After her freshman year at Texas Woman's University, she dropped out and moved to San Francisco with her college roommate, Ginny. They set up house together in the low-rent Haight-Ashbury district, and Anne got a job as a claims processor for an insurance company.

In the meantime, Stan Rice was wondering where Anne O'Brien was. He remembered her as a young woman with real intensity and wanted to see her again. When he discovered that she'd gone to California, he was stunned. He got her address and wrote her a letter. Anne was delighted and wrote back; this was the start of their torrid romance by correspondence. Stan eventually proposed by mail. Anne accepted and returned to Texas, and they were married shortly after her twentieth birthday, in 1961. When Stan finished his first sophomore semester at North Texas State, they packed up everything they owned—which was very little—and set out to make their home together in the liberal city of San Francisco. There they worked and went to school while Stan began to make a name for himself as a poet.

Although Anne knew she wanted to write, she majored in

political science at San Francisco State College (later University). She took literature courses as well and wrote stories for a select group of friends. Stan exposed her to contemporary poetry, broadening her appreciation for the pliability and richness of language. She eventually published her short story "October 4th, 1948" and the first chapter of the novella "Nicholas and Jean" in *Transfer*, the school's literary journal.

During the late sixties, after getting her degree, Anne set herself the task of writing one short story per day to develop her skills. One of them, written in 1968, was about a vampire telling a reporter what it was like to live as one of the undead. Anne put that story aside to work on other more promising ideas, taking it out to revise only after one of the most pivotal and tragic events of her life.

INTERVIEW WITH THE VAMPIRE

In 1966, Anne and Stan had a daughter, Michele. Blond and precocious, she became the center of their lives. Stan was teaching in the Creative Writing department at San Francisco State University, while Anne was taking graduate courses. She often brought Michele with her to the library, where she explored subjects for potential novels, studied for her courses, or just read. Michele was only four when she first complained of a strange fatigue. A trip to the doctor brought a shocking diagnosis: acute granuleucytic leukemia.

Anne and Stan threw themselves into exploring every possibility for a cure, from vitamin C to experimental drugs, but over the next two years Michele's health declined. Finally, she was hospitalized. Early one morning, just weeks before her sixth birthday, she slipped away.

The Rices then entered the darkest period of their lives.

They drank to numb their grief, staying drunk from one day to the next to stave off their despair. Having lost her mother and now her daughter made Anne feel vulnerable and terribly alone. She wanted to die, too. For many months, she could not get through the day without several six-packs of beer.

As time passed, Anne realized that she had to pull herself together and find some direction. Although she did not stop drinking until a few years later, she knew she had to do something now to turn the tide. While Michele was ill, Anne had gotten her master's degree and had taken a job as a copy editor at a company that published law books. Still, she believed her only real talent was writing. She was torn between quitting her job to go all out as a full-time writer or just trying to write part-time. When Stan encouraged her to quit, she grabbed the opportunity and pulled out all her previous work to look for possibilities. The story that caught her eye was called "Interview with the Vampire." She decided to revise it.

She named the vampire narrator Louis and delved further into his early background as a mortal. When she came to the part where his brother dies, she tapped into her own grief over Michele, and started to write with great emotional fervor. She knew intimately Louis's loss and regret.

"Seeing though Louis's eyes allowed me to write about life in a way I hadn't been able to do in a contemporary novel," Anne explains. "I couldn't make my life believable in that form. I didn't know how to use it. When I abandoned that struggle and wrote *Interview with the Vampire*, it all came together for me. I was able to describe reality through fantasy."

In five weeks, working mostly at night, she finished the novel and knew that with this book she would be published. "I dream, hope, imagine that this will be my first published work," she wrote in her diary. "I feel ashamed of nothing in it—not even what I know to be flaws. I feel solidly behind it as though Louis's voice were my voice and I do not run the risk of being misunderstood." Despite several rejections, she eventually found an agent who sold her novel to Knopf, which published it in 1976.

Interview found a phenomenal reception, earning within the first year nearly one million dollars from hardcover and paperback sales and movie deals. With its lush language and existential questing, this novel hit a nerve with the seventies' culture and found a large audience. Young people seeking alternatives to traditional religion or craving unique, deeply subjective ways to view human experience resonated to Louis's spiritual lament. As one reader remarked: "Rice goes into the darkness and illuminates it for us."

The story captured another audience as well, which Anne gradually realized with the emergence of a large gay following: She was writing with great sympathy about people who did not fit in with normal society and who suffered over it. "I see the vampires as outsiders," she affirms, "creatures outside of the human sphere who can therefore speak about it the way Mephistopheles could speak about it to Faust. I gave them conscience and intelligence and wisdom so they could see things humans aren't able to see."

One of the most poignant aspects of this novel is the child vampire, Claudia, whom Louis and Lestat make from a five-year-old. Clearly there was some connection between this character and Anne's deceased daughter, although Anne insists that she was unaware of it as she wrote *Interview*: "I never consciously thought about the death of my daughter when I was writing it. . . . The child vampire, Claudia, was physically inspired by Michele but she ultimately became something else—a woman trapped in a child's body, robbed of power, never knowing what it's like to really be a woman and to make love. She became a metaphor for a raging mind trapped in a powerless body."

Interview became a cult favorite, gaining momentum as millions of copies were sold. Yet it took nearly twenty years for this novel to reach the silver screen. When the movie came out in November 1994, with a script that Anne had written, she felt a great sense of satisfaction and completion. "It's about us as well as about vampires. It's about those who feel deeply, who have lost faith in a meaningful universe, and [who] find an immoral or amoral existence impossible."

HISTORICAL FICTION

After her initial success, Anne resisted pressure to write a sequel and turned to historical novels that satisfied her appreciation of the richness of more romantic eras. Having already done research on Louisiana, she decided to pursue a novel about *les gens de couleur libre*, the class of the Free People of Color in antebellum New Orleans. In *The Feast of All Saints*, where adolescents from this class find their way in a confusing world of ambiguous racial and sexual issues, Anne gave her main character, Marcel, more of a sense of personal freedom and power than she had allowed Louis. She used one character, Dolly Rose, to affirm female power, even as the women Anne knew in the San Francisco area were reaching for liberation, equality, and respect.

While Anne was at work on this novel, she became pregnant again. In 1978, nearly six years after losing Michele, she had a son, Christopher. Her hope for having a family was renewed.

She followed *The Feast of All Saints* with another rich

historical novel, *Cry to Heaven*. Set in Italy, where Anne had explored Rome and Venice in 1977, this tale featured the celebrated castrated opera singers of the eighteenth century. The central character, Tonio, has been forced into this neither-male-nor-female existence and struggles with issues of gender, self-expression, art, and power.

Neither of these novels was as successful as *Interview*, so Anne decided against another story in the historical milieu. She opted to return to the type of erotic writing to which she had devoted herself in the sixties.

THE EROTICA

Although friends warned her against such a career move, she insisted on writing authentically and wanted to give voice to what was pressing for expression. "The idea was to create a book where you didn't have to mark the hot pages," she says, "where every page would be hot."

To gain maximum freedom, Anne elected to write under a pseudonym. She chose the name A. N. Roquelaure, from the French word for "cloak." Loosely basing her novel on the fairy tale of Sleeping Beauty, Anne created erotic adventures for a young princess and her prince. *The Claiming of Sleeping Beauty* begins with Beauty's awakening from her hundred-year sleep into a fantasyland of shocking S&M scenarios. The prince who revives her becomes her master and takes her to his mother's castle, where they train her to be a love slave.

Rice followed this novel with *Beauty's Punishment*, which exposed Beauty to even more extreme discipline (within safe parameters). In the third novel, *Beauty's Release*, Beauty finds yet greater enhancement. Anne then tired of the repetition inherent in such books and decided to end the series there.

The Roquelaure novels were written during the mid-1980s, when a conservative backlash from many feminists denounced pornography, but Anne insisted that women should have the freedom to read, think, and write whatever they pleased. For her, the books were a political statement about integrity and liberation. "I'm proud of the Beauty books," she declares, "and happy with them. I did what I wanted to do."

Although Anne had set out to explore female sexuality in this series, her most fully developed character is male. His name is Prince Laurent. He is the only one able and willing to play the roles of both slave and master and who truly understands the complexity of human experience. In him, Anne found a resonant male voice. He became a model for a character about whom she was writing simultaneously under yet another pseudonym.

While developing the Roquelaure novels, she adopted the name Anne Rampling for the erotic love story *Exit to Eden*. She felt she needed another pseudonym because this novel was so different from the Roquelaure trilogy. The story is told from two alternating points of view: that of Lisa, a dominatrix who runs a pleasure club on a private island, and that of Elliott, a bisexual man who signs up to become a pleasure slave for The Club's wealthy patrons. "My intention was to write a pornographic novel," Anne recalls, "but the characters of Elliott and Lisa came alive for me. I fell in love with them right away." Elliott and Lisa explore the psychology of S&M as a safe way to vent the innate violence in human nature, then fall in love and opt for marriage.

With Lisa, Anne felt that she had made the breakthrough she had desired in her Roquelaure series by presenting a developed female perspective, although it was somewhat dark and humorless. She had reached for authentic feeling and given Lisa her own beliefs about sexual outlaws, transgender experiences, and the inability to view sexual play between consenting adults as deviant or wrong. She felt that *Exit to Eden* was a bold novel and was proud to have it published in hardcover in America. In addition, while creating Elliott, she found the voice that took her back to her vampires.

THE VAMPIRE LESTAT

In 1985, nine years after *Interview with the Vampire*, Anne published the long-awaited sequel, *The Vampire Lestat*. This was her eighth novel. Having initially experienced trouble writing it, she had at last developed the protagonist she had envisioned. No longer in deep mourning for Michele, she wished to avoid echoing Louis's despair. Now she had a hero, a man of adventure, and her exploration of the psychology of males who were both dominant and submissive had made that possible. Reading fast-paced American detective fiction by James M. Cain and Raymond Chandler, Anne deepened her sense of how Lestat should tell his side of the story.

"Lestat grew as a character almost beyond my control," Anne admits. "He spontaneously appeared in the corner of my eye when I was writing *Interview*, and then he took on great strength and had experiences that went into the second novel."

Having been abandoned by Louis and gone into a deep trance, Lestat awakens in the late twentieth century and decides to become a rock star. Adventurous and feisty, he exhibits a greater range of sensuality and bisexual capacity than did Louis, while being more assertive. He quickly became Anne's favorite among all her characters. "If I were a vampire, I would certainly want to be Lestat," she says. "His strength, his penchant for action, his lack of regret, his lack of paralysis, his ability to win over and over again, his absolute refusal to lose—I love to write from that point of view. Lestat is the dream of the male I would love to be."

Lestat explains how he became a vampire and then pursued a much older vampire, Marius, to learn of the vampires' origins. He finds that their progenitors, Akasha and Enkil, were possessed by an immense spirit during early Egyptian times that had fused with their hearts and created an unbearable blood thirst. To diffuse the spirit's craving, they had made more vampires. As they aged, they had experienced a decreased need for blood. Nevertheless, their many "children" killed to survive and made even more of their own kind. Lestat is their descendant.

He turns all that he learns into rock videos, identifying himself with the Greek god Dionysus and using his music to waken Akasha from her centuries-long trance. By this brash act, he ushers into both the mortal and vampire worlds a menace that nearly alters human destiny.

This story concluded in 1988, in the third vampire novel, *The Queen of the Damned*, wherein Akasha decides to kill 99 percent of the male population. She plans to set up a new Eden formed from feminine perspectives, believing that this will transform the world into a peaceful place. She forces Lestat to help, but after much slaughter he defies her and joins a gathering of vampires who resist Akasha's tampering with human evolution. They risk their lives, but in finally destroying Akasha, they discover an effective new way to preserve the spirit that animates them. Thus, The Vampire Chronicles could continue.

This third vampire novel was one of Anne's most abstract,

relying on philosophy rather than her experiences or fantasies to carry the plot. She has expressed a mixed reaction to it, from feeling that it was her most accomplished work to date, to viewing it as the one novel that she dislikes. Yet she had wanted to develop the theme of how an idea that sounds good can be evil, and that not all evil is found in dark archetypes like Satan or Hitler. To her mind, writing about pure abstractions like the traditional notions of good and evil hinders real understanding. "To me, what's fascinating in art is to get inside evil and see the good inside it. I don't think you can understand evil until you do that. That doesn't for a moment mean that one excuses evil or sympathizes with it. I just want to understand what it's about and so I go into the complexity."

In *QD*, Anne also introduced the Talamasca, a fictional worldwide organization of people who study supernatural phenomena. Many of the group possess paranormal abilities themselves, and they track stories about witches, ghosts, and vampires. Two members of this ancient and elite establishment, David Talbot and Aaron Lightner, would go on to play important roles in future novels.

OTHER EXPERIMENTS

Between *Lestat* and *QD*, Anne wrote *Belinda*, published in 1986 under her Rampling pseudonym. Set in her house in San Francisco's Castro district, *Belinda* is about an artist in his forties who falls in love with a sixteen-year-old runaway. The girl, Belinda, had grown up with an alcoholic mother who depended on her child to take care of her, just as Anne's mother had. Through Belinda, Anne addresses many of her concerns from adolescence; but, like the artist, Jeremy Walker,

Anne was reaching for artistic freedom, and she seemed to identify more with his character. Jeremy wanted to stop writing the children's books that had earned him much success and do something wild and unusual, just as Anne wanted to explore unusual fictional subjects other than vampires. Anne's forays into erotica had brought her the kind of success for which she had hoped and none of the problems. Jeremy, too, gets to transcend his previous work. Despite dire warnings of disgrace and demise as he unveils his controversial nude portraits of Belinda, he actually triumphs.

With *Belinda*, the experiment with pseudonyms came to an end. Since Anne had been revealed as the author of both the Rampling and Roquelaure novels, she saw no reason for hiding behind other names. She decided to write all future books under her own name.

Her next novel after *QD* was *The Mummy Or Ramses the Damned*. Although she wrote it as a plot for a television miniseries, she had disagreements with the producers, so she turned it into a novel instead. Viewing this tale as a "romp" in the tradition of grade-B horror movies, Anne brought to life a beautiful immortal man, Ramses, the ancient Egyptian king. She placed him in Edwardian England and had him fall in love. "It was fun evoking that atmosphere and doing outrageous things that I wouldn't do in other books," she insists. This paperback was a runaway success.

THE WITCHES

Anne's next novel was *The Witching Hour*, a saga about thirteen generations of a family of witches who reside in New Orleans. She was still living in San Francisco when she started it, but in 1988 she decided to return to New Orleans to reestablish her connection with the sights, sounds, smells, and accents that would make the details in her novel authentic.

Anne wandered her old neighborhoods to collect background detail for her character Michael Curry, who grew up in the Irish Channel where her father's family had settled. "I discovered hundreds upon hundreds of buried memories," she recalls, "triggered by things I saw and heard." Michael's life story borrowed much from Anne's. "He's more like me than any other character," she admitted when the novel was published in 1990. Michael shares with Rice a love of Dickens and architecture, a Catholic and a secular education, an alcoholic mother, an aversion to liberal hypocrisies, a desire to learn, and the ability to teach himself.

Through Michael, Anne expressed her feelings about returning to New Orleans and walking along the streets and into the churches that had been so central to her youth. She also talked about her fading religious sentiment (and when she regained her sense of God, she gave this experience to Michael as well, in a sequel). When Michael and Rowan decide to restore their mansion, Anne used details from her own renovations, and when they throw a large family party, the food, music, and decorations came from Anne's family reunion. More significant, the house in which they live is Anne's home. She spotted it for sale one day while wandering in the Garden District.

Setting *The Witching Hour* in her new house, she went from room to room and out to the yard to experience scenes that she was writing: Deirdre's bed was one she owned; Lasher was "born" in her parlor; Michael nearly drowned in her pool; Antha died from falling onto her flagstone walkway; and Stuart's ghost appeared on the impressive twenty-seven-step staircase. The real settings added powerful sensual detail, and haunting her own house with her witches, ghosts, and malevolent characters fueled her momentum. This house "belongs" to the many generations of the Mayfair family who have occupied it as part of the legacy of wealth settled on designated Mayfair females—always witches. The incubus that haunts it has influenced its design in anticipation of the day he will be born into flesh via the thirteenth and most powerful witch, Rowan Mayfair. His symbol is the Egyptian keyhole doorway—a genuine architectural feature of the First Street house that Anne eagerly incorporated into the plot. Through it, Lasher finally enters the physical realm.

One of the primary themes that inspired *The Witching Hour* and its sequels was family connection. "The theme of family runs all through my work," Anne admits, "and it will continue to figure in my writings." As a child, she took a strong interest in the members of her extended family. "I don't remember a time when I didn't care about family," she admits. "I was very hungry to have a family and I was envious of kids who had large families." However, there were many relatives about whom she knew little. When she returned to New Orleans, she set about rectifying the situation. She invited over two hundred aunts, uncles, and cousins to get reacquainted with one another. Simultaneously, she expanded the characters and relationships in her novels: As Anne learned more about her own kin, the Mayfair family swelled in size and history. She listened to dialects, dug up family stories, and studied character traits even as she reveled, like Rowan, in the feeling of being connected with so many people. "Kinship. Could they guess how indescribably exotic that was . . . ?"[2]

The Witching Hour was Anne's most ambitious novel to date and, although she believed it was finished with Lasher's birth and Rowan's defection, it was not long before she devised a sequel.

THE VAMPIRE CHRONICLES

Before that, however, another vampire novel demanded to be written. Her vampire community was still intact, and Lestat still held her attention. While on a book tour, Anne was particularly taken with the seamy milieu of Miami, so that was the city in which she started Lestat's new adventure in *The Tale of the Body Thief*.

As the story opens, he is being tracked by an unusual type of vampire hunter, Raglan James, who offers Lestat a temporary body exchange. Intrigued by the idea, Lestat agrees to switch, then gets duped as James makes off with his powerful vampire body. With the help of his friend David Talbot from the Talamasca, Lestat retrieves it, and in the process he tempts his morally upright friend to join him in immortality. David refuses but Lestat does not give up. Lestat recognizes that he likes being a vampire despite the evil it entails, and, acting on his nature, he makes David into a vampire against his will.

As Anne wrote *Body Thief*, she entered a dark period. Life seemed especially fragile and she felt terribly fatigued. "It was an awful time," she admits, "a black, black period. I don't know how the novel got written. I just did it."

A few months later, she gave another family party to celebrate her fiftieth birthday. Her father attended, although his health was deteriorating, and that night he had a bad fall that put him in the hospital. Anne wondered if the spell of depression she had experienced earlier that year had been a foreboding. A similar portent had preceded her daughter's fatal illness. Organizing continuous care for her father, Anne spent long hours in the hospital with him, musing over how Lestat had worried about the fragility of his mortal friend David Talbot, who was the same age as her father. Shortly after Thanksgiving 1991, Howard died as she held his hand. "I felt grateful to fate that I was there at the moment he died," she says.

When she went back to look at the novel, she was amazed by the prescience it seemed to express: "Anyone reading this book," says Anne, "would think it had been written after my father's death. It was almost as if it had been written in a state of premonition."

TALTOS

Lasher, the sequel to *The Witching Hour*, was Anne's first venture into science fiction. She proposed a DNA basis for the sort of creature that Lasher turned out to be—a Taltos—and devised a story to explain his presence in the Mayfair history.

At the same time, Anne developed more characters in the Mayfair family and in the Talamasca. Her favorite was Mona Mayfair, a precocious, sexually charged thirteen-year-old genius who embodies the adventurous spirit that Anne wished for herself. Mona lives in a house on St. Charles Avenue that Anne had recently purchased for renovation. An entire branch of the Mayfair family came to be associated with that mansion before Anne eventually sold it.

Another feisty character, nineteen-year-old Mary Jane Mayfair, shows up in *Taltos*, the novel that succeeded *Lasher*. One thread of the plot follows the adventures of Mary Jane and Mona as they assert their right to make decisions for themselves despite their youth, and includes Mona giving birth to a child. The other thread presents the full story of Lasher's nearly extinct race.

This series of three novels was named Lives of the Mayfair

Witches, and there might be a fourth installment in the future.

MEMNOCH THE DEVIL

This, the fifth vampire novel, takes Lestat on his ultimate adventure. He accompanies the Devil, whose name is Memnoch, to Heaven and Hell to hear the story of creation and the origin of evil.

Anne wrote *Memnoch* in a month and felt drained by the effort. Nearly a year later, when she read the page proofs, she had the experience that Lestat had receded from her imagination: What they had done together was finished. She felt that as he walked down St. Charles in the last pages of the book, he looked into the window of an abandoned Mercedes dealership and disappeared. "He left me. He just left me. He said, 'Anne, no more for now.' And off he went."

When fans protested on her book tour, she had a few second thoughts.

GHOSTS

Lestat may yet return, since he embodies all the qualities of Anne's archetypal hero, but for her next novel she turned her energies in a new direction. Researching Jewish lore, she came up with the idea of an angry and bitter ghost named Azriel telling his story to Jonathan, a Jewish scholar. In *Servant of the Bones*, Azriel explains that he was born in ancient times. When Cyrus the Great conquered Babylon, he chose Azriel for his youth and beauty to become the new god for his own people. Azriel explains how he was killed and how he became a spirit. Like a genie, he served many masters over the centuries, until he discovered that he could take control of his own will. He then became a renegade spirit. Eventually he enters into the lives and fates of a contemporary Jewish family, one of whom has set up a dangerous worldwide network with the intent of becoming a messiah. His power and ambitions are built on malice and deception, so Azriel stands against him. Like Louis before him, Azriel wonders, throughout the novel, about the possibility of his own redemption. He has learned from examples of self-sacrifice and kindness how to conquer his anger. Although this tale ends with his modern-day adventure, his existence over the centuries offers possibilities for sequels.

Deciding to write yet another ghost story that would be part of a series but *not* be a sequel to *Servant of the Bones*, Anne was inspired by the films *Amadeus* and *Immortal Beloved* to create *Violin*. She traveled to Brazil and Vienna for settings. She read Romantic poetry. She recalled her own youthful struggle to master the violin, which ended in utter frustration. "*Violin* contains a new kind of language overflow," she says, "a ferocious abandon, somewhat like the excess of *Interview with the Vampire*."[3] Consistent with the vision of her supernatural universe, populated by her witches and vampires, this novel presents new characters who still struggle with issues of goodness, mortality, and inner darkness.

Anne has noted that her novels draw together along similar themes. All of them are about the rich existence of people considered outsiders by normal social standards, and all emphasize the wisdom of experience over abstract ideas. "We've lost faith in imaginative fiction, and many of our finer writers have turned away from it," she laments. "Deeply embedded in our culture is the idea that truth lies in the familiar, the ordinary. But I refuse to believe that fantasy cannot be enormous in scope and profoundly valid and meaningful.

"I think people are hungry for imagery and hungry for the deeper truths that fantasy and myth give them. They crave the really flamboyant characters and flights of imagination. I believe the popularity of my work is related to that. It never really goes away."

Anne constantly evolves and renews herself with her writing. The way she develops her plots and characters reveals much about the person behind the authorship. Because she includes authentic feeling from her own life, her work will continue to affect her readers deeply. Beyond that, the sophisticated moral themes that interest her will no doubt inspire serious interest among critics.

NOTES

1. Anne Rice, *Exit to Eden* (New York: Arbor House, 1985), 193.
2. ———, *The Witching Hour* (New York: Knopf, 1990), 682.
3. ———, "Commotion Strange," No. 5, July 5, 1996.

Novels by Anne Rice

Interview with the Vampire (Knopf, 1976)
The Feast of All Saints (Simon & Schuster, 1979)
Cry to Heaven (Knopf, 1982)
The Claiming of Sleeping Beauty (Dutton, 1983)
Beauty's Punishment (Dutton, 1984)
Beauty's Release (Dutton, 1985)
Exit to Eden (Arbor House, 1985)
The Vampire Lestat (Knopf, 1985)
Belinda (Arbor House, 1986)
The Queen of the Damned (Knopf, 1988)
The Mummy or Ramses the Damned (Ballantine, 1989)
The Witching Hour (Knopf, 1990)
The Tale of the Body Thief (Knopf, 1992)
Lasher (Knopf, 1993)
Taltos (Knopf, 1994)
Memnoch the Devil (Knopf, 1995)
Servant of the Bones (Knopf, 1996)
Violin (Knopf, 1997)

A Literary Friendship

LIFE IS NOT A FOOTRACE

Kathleen Mackay

"I remember what you were wearing," Anne said recently, recalling our first meeting in August 1974. It was the first night of the weeklong writers' conference at Squaw Valley, California, and we were at a party welcoming us to the writers' community. The party, held in a wooden A-frame off the dirt road that leads to the ski slopes, was hosted by George Plimpton, Blair Fuller, and others who were running the conference. I was a twenty-five-year-old Harvard graduate pursuing a journalism career in San Francisco. I noticed a young woman with long, dark hair sitting quietly on the sofa, wearing a serious, thoughtful expression. I went up and introduced myself. Anne, then thirty-two, explained that she had with her an unpublished manuscript about a vampire telling the last two hundred years of his life to a radio DJ in a Victorian house on Divisadero Street. That evening, our friendship began.

Anne was Fiction, I was Nonfiction. We met between writing workshops and played literary word games with other writers in the huge post-and-beam dining room of the old Squaw Valley Lodge, at the foot of the ski slopes.

At the conference, Anne met literary agent Phyllis Seidel, who accepted Anne as a client. I was watching a literary career take off, and witnessed Anne's excitement as she said, "I have to go call my husband again."

Since Anne doesn't drive, I gave her rides in my old navy Volvo to other cocktail parties, and to dinners at The Bear Pen, one of the writers' hangouts, which was a diner/restaurant near the wide, sloping entry road to Squaw Valley. There, Johnny Cash sang "Wheel of Fire" on the jukebox, and everyone danced to country music. When I drove Anne back to our rooms in the lodge, she asked me to check several times to make sure that I had locked all the doors of my car. "You don't think I'm crazy for asking you to check again, do you?"

"No, not at all," I said, each of us escalating the other's paranoia about what might happen to us in this deep, dark, empty ski resort, high in the mountains, on a summer night.

I drove Anne back to Berkeley from Squaw Valley at the end of the conference. As Elton John softly sang "Daniel" on the radio, we talked about what we wanted to do as writers ("and I was drinking beer the whole time," Anne recalled). When I dropped her off at her Bonita Street apartment, Stan opened the door to greet her, and the look of joy on his handsome, young face was unparalleled. He hugged her tightly. His wife now had a literary agent: her career was at a turning point. This was my first glimpse of this extraordinary marriage.

Knopf editor Victoria Wilson had been at the writers' conference, and Phyllis Seidel had given her the *Interview with the Vampire* manuscript to read. When Vicky, then twenty-four, returned to New York, she convinced Knopf president Bob Gottlieb that she wanted to buy it. ("This is either the most insane or most brilliant book I've ever read, but it's definitely the strangest, and we have to publish it," she said.) When Anne learned that the distinguished Alfred A. Knopf publishing house would pay her a $12,000 advance for the novel, we were all ecstatic. Subsequently, when *Interview* was published to great acclaim and a big movie sale followed, I wrote articles about Anne and her writing for the *San Francisco Chronicle* and the *Examiner* and later for *People* and the *Los Angeles Times*.

As our friendship grew, I was close at hand for the publication of *The Feast of All Saints* and *Cry to Heaven*. With the success of these books, Anne and Stan moved from their book-cluttered two-bedroom Bonita Street apartment in Berkeley to a Georgian house on Claremont Avenue, and from there to a big white house with an elevator in the Oakland hills. With each move, the Rices' New Year's parties grew bigger, but many of their friends were the same: Berkeley writers and intellectuals, drinking beer, smoking joints, and arguing about the Spanish Civil War, Henry James, and Norman Mailer. Aside from the annual Christmas and New Year's gatherings, though, Anne and Stan were often reclusive.

The only exception was when they would emerge to join the book parties at Minerva's Owl, a bookstore on Union Street. The locus of San Francisco literary parties in the 1970s, Minerva's Owl was tiny, and during book parties fifty to seventy people would crowd into the aisles of the store, juggling white wine in plastic cups and copies of the latest book by the local author being honored. Squaw Valley organizer Blair Fuller, who had founded *The Paris Review* in the 1950s with George Plimpton, was a co-owner of the popular store. There we celebrated the publications of books by many authors who had taught at Squaw Valley: Herbert Gold, Evan S. Connell, Curt Gentry, and Don Carpenter.

The San Francisco literary scene in the seventies was quite male-dominated, and Gold, Gentry, and Carpenter had their rituals: liquid lunches at Enrico's, swimming at a downtown club, weekends at Esalen—swapping stories about agents, women, wives. Sometimes they also swapped agents and women (wives? I don't know). When Anne and her hugely successful *Interview* burst upon this group of macho, elite authors, they didn't quite know what to make of it. Vampires? And a movie sale? Her first novel?

Anne and Stan were invited to many of the A-list literary parties, as I was, but I remember that the core group of writers had drawn their wagons warily, unwilling to let anyone in. We circled them tentatively, not yet belonging, not quite fitting in. We were treated respectfully, but without the immediate bonding that cemented the male authors' friendships. There were also distinguished women writers in San Francisco at that time who made the literary scene—Alice Adams, Diane Johnson—but I never saw them reach out to embrace Anne, either. Their reluctance could have been generational (they were older), or it could have been that they felt little affinity for the topics Anne favored (Anne's work was more dramatic and excessive than theirs).

Yet the insularity of the San Francisco literary scene never detracted from what I viewed as the immense creativity of San Francisco in the seventies—a creativity that I felt nourished and inspired Anne's work. I saw her influenced by the world around her: San Francisco's sparkling city, all hills and bridges; the green, gentle, bohemian Berkeley hills; the ex-hippies who had never quite left the sixties; the former radicals who had never let go of the Left. It seems like a fantasy now, looking back, but the creative atmosphere was one that never really forced you to grow up. I certainly didn't. Drawn to San Francisco by its music, and writing for *Rolling Stone*, I lived at Winterland

and at the Fillmore when I wasn't involved in the more mundane pursuit of earning a living.

If I was nourished by its music, Anne drew inspiration from San Francisco's neighborhoods. She shared some of her love of the city with me in "Literary Hangouts," a piece I wrote for *Travel & Leisure*:

"San Francisco is special to me because it is truly a cosmopolitan place where neighborhoods can become whole worlds unto themselves. The Castro district is an example. People can transform or resurrect a neighborhood through their love of the architecture.

"San Francisco has a way of remaining flexible to the creative nature of its residents. It fills me with hope that no amount of overcrowding, crime, or neglect has been able to defeat them. . . . This is a city of artists on all levels. We live in an atmosphere of art that permeates the city, from the facades of the Victorian buildings to the poetry readings going on constantly at places like Intersection."

When the San Francisco literary scene failed to embrace Anne with boundless enthusiasm, their coolness seemed to make her all the more determined to succeed. After parties at Minerva's Owl, Anne, Stan, and I would have dinner at Yet Wah, drenched with fog. Over a Chinese feast of almond pressed duck, curry chicken, and shrimp in lobster sauce, we would dissect those parties, the personalities, and a tone of detachment would set in, removing us from the place. Our ambitions were so big that seen in their light, San Francisco seemed so small.

I was writing about the entertainment industry regularly, and L.A. beckoned. Anne stayed true to course—the frosty reception from the male literary establishment in S.F. did not dissuade her from thinking big. She was very clear about what she wanted to do. She talked about having the impact that

Dickens had. She recalled how eagerly Dickens's readers had awaited each sequel, how Hemingway, Shakespeare, and Dickens had cut through all classes with their work. And she would, too. She and Stan saw few people; Anne dug in to her writing. And in 1980, I moved to L.A.

As I reflect on Anne's development as a writer in the 1970s, when she broke in to the world of best-sellers, I am struck by how important I believe Stan Rice was to Anne's success. Never had I met a kinder, more noble, more courtly man than Stan Rice. In the 1970s, when I was in my twenties, none of my friends had "husbands." The word harkened back to the 1950s, when Mom was at home and Dad was at work. Since Anne and Stan had married in 1961, and had fallen in love in the late 1950s, theirs was more a relationship of another era. But never had I been exposed to a more perfect partnership, a blending of two souls who were meant to be together, and whose lives and ambitions totally supported each other's. Because I was writing about Anne for many national publications in the late 1970s, I was always sensitive to how my accounts of her success would affect her husband. Would he be jealous? Should I write more about him? But Stan, secure in his tenured position in the creative writing department at San Francisco State, was fine. Stan was thrilled by his wife's success. As for the money, Anne told me, "Stan took to the money like a cat takes to cream." In fact, I remember Anne saying that after big chunks of money came in, Stan loved to go out and buy shirts. (I trust he has a closetful now, one in every color.)

My admiration for Stan's devotion to Anne was equaled only by my respect for him as a father. In 1979, I saw him happily take a sabbatical and stay at home, changing Christopher's diapers, so that Anne could focus on writing. His poetry is testimony to his adoring relationship with Mouse (Michele) and the excruciating pain he and Anne suffered when she died. His poems in *Some Lamb* are so moving, so touching; the tragedy of Mouse can paralyze one with sadness. But what is uplifting in *Some Lamb* is Stan's clear, strong, true love for his wife. My favorite poem is "Anne's Curls," which speaks of sex, love, anger, fighting, reconciliation, and trust. To me, the final verses and images epitomize their marriage:

On the street outside the post office
& before in the alley between Penney's
and the parking lot we
struggle with it. "Would you like to walk with me
from here *to* there? *I ask insultingly.*
I come back & find you are sitting on the steps,
really alone. You refuse my arm.
Two hours later we are really married.
To die of fear of revealing yourself
*to the person who loves you is murder.**

The tension of this scene, its resolution, and its vulnerability testify to the strength and resilience of the Rices' marriage. What I witnessed in the seventies was Stan's constant support for Anne, and that was highly, highly unusual. This was 1976, after all. Usually it was the wife who supported the husband's success. But here was a husband supporting his wife as her stellar career soared, and it didn't ruin their marriage. He wasn't competitive; he was cheering her on every step of the way. They also shared common values. I remember Anne telling me a story I found wryly ironic, that they once had a huge fight over "what is a sense of humor." A big fight. Slam-

*Used by permission of the author.

ming doors, not speaking. The works. Not your typical American marriage.

In her novels, Anne has written often that the greatest romances are the love between equals (bringing to mind Shakespeare's "Let me not to the marriage of true minds/ Admit impediments. Love is not love . . ."). The romance between Anne and Stan is truly a love of equals, and they have remained on equal footing in every way that I can tell in the twenty-two years I have known them. While I am hardly an expert in such matters, I will say simply that they have the best marriage I have ever seen. In the seventies I used to joke that I wanted to get a T-shirt printed with CLONE STAN RICE.

The realization that Anne had an unusual marriage also affected the way I viewed her as a writer. When Anne and I first met, many women writers were voicing the aspirations of women, and my female friends flocked to readings by Erica Jong, Betty Friedan, and Germaine Greer. My friends and I gave each other gifts of books by Sylvia Plath and Lillian Hellman. As our friendship grew, Anne's voice and work inspired me. She was a writer who happened to be a woman, not a Woman Writer like those revered by the female English Lit students crowding into bookstores in Palo Alto and Berkeley wearing Birkenstocks and backpacks. She transcended gender. She had a beautiful marriage. She wasn't angry at men. (Or, to be more specific, her anger didn't impede her ability to have a happy relationship with a man.) She loved literature. These aspects of her life and work were a terrific inspiration to me. Her advice strengthened and comforted me in my darkest moments. If you were true to your commitment as a writer, Anne felt, you would fulfill your destiny and be a success. She recognized that success did not have to be defined in purely material terms.

She saw any person of character, of integrity and strength, as a success. By her example she offered the inspiration that fuels creativity. I still remember how fragile Anne was in 1974, recovering from the devastating loss of her daughter. How I admired her courage as she just kept going, overcoming this tragedy in her life. We have shared our deepest fears and sorrows, our greatest joys, and Libra and Scorpio birthdays, holidays, and the premiere of the film *Interview with the Vampire*.

Some friendships fall apart when one friend is more successful than the other, but this has not happened with our relationship. Not only have I been thrilled by each of Anne's successes, but her success has helped strengthen my resolve at times when forging ahead seemed difficult or tricky. I have many friends who have been blessed by wealth, but in most cases it came from their mates or from inheritances. But Anne has earned every penny she has. This is one reason why I respect her so, and I have always admired the businesswoman in her. In turn, she has advised me about taking the great leaps of faith that must accompany serious risk-taking and that often accompany deal-making that leads to big money. I trust her guidance on issues of finance, getting paid what you are worth, and being taken seriously in a business context. Because she has done well in the publishing world, she encourages her friends to do so, but she doesn't hold her talent out as a marker that others must equal. She recognizes and respects the differences in writers' styles, tastes, and talents and, as a friend, is extremely generous in her praise, moral support, honesty, and faith. There are very few people in whom I can confide about matters, whether literary, romantic, or financial, and have such confidence that the advice offered will be from the heart, genuine.

Though our lives may seem very different, Anne and I have common goals. The essence of this is captured in a long letter I faxed to her several years ago. (Our reunions, which occur twice a year, are not as frequent as we would like because of the demands of our careers. But we fax each other long letters regularly, and these letters cover many of the intimate, salient details of our lives.)

My letter said, "As we enter the twentieth year of our friendship I'm grateful for your loyalty, inspired by your talent, and comforted by the fact that you know from experience that we have within us the ability to rise above our hurt and suffering to create something beautiful, that lasts."

The Landscape of Childhood Memories

NEW ORLEANS IN THE LIFE AND WORK OF ANNE RICE

W. Kenneth Holditch

"Place," Eudora Welty says, "is one of the lesser angels that watch over the hand of fiction,"[1] and for Anne Rice, that place is, of course, New Orleans. There are many novelists who conceivably could write about any area, but Rice, like William Faulkner, is integrally linked with the place of her birth. "I always felt more alive and less isolated when I was writing about New Orleans," she says. Characters in most of her works either originate in the city or migrate there in the course of the narrative. Only two novels to date (excluding the erotic-fantasy Roquelaure series), *Cry to Heaven* and *The Mummy*, have no New Orleans associations, and even *Cry to Heaven*, Rice acknowledges, "is pretty much infused with a longing for New Orleans."[2] There is no doubt that the city has had a profound effect on the way Rice writes. A look at its culture, landscape, and architecture offers an important perspective on how to interpret her work.

New Orleans provided Rice not only with settings but history, myths, legends, customs, mores, characters, and, perhaps most important, the ambience of a place unique in the United States; it is the most European of all American cities. Rice refers to it as "not a city of acquired lifestyles, trendy shops, and cutesy ice cream parlors," but rather "a rich city" that has slowly evolved over time, retaining much of its "endless, incorruptible charm." Nevertheless, she wonders, "How can anyone ever really capture the city? Who can ever do justice to the spell it exerts over those who linger there?"

It was in San Francisco, where she lived for more than twenty-five years, that a homesick Anne Rice, hungry for "the landscape of my youth," attempted for the first time to write about New Orleans. So much of her life had been infused with aspects of the city, such as the constant sight and sound of the famous uptown streetcar, that, living away, she would "wake in the night and think I hear the streetcar passing as it did always, every fifteen minutes or so, on St. Charles Avenue, in front of the house where I grew up." Having read all the books she could find about her hometown, she tried to capture its unique quality in fiction with a contemporary setting, but friends who read her stories could not understand. Why, they asked her, did she insist on writing about mansions and live oaks? She was unable to convince them that "those are the streets I walked through as a child." Her descriptions were real, not the trappings of romantic fiction.

When she began work on the manuscript that would become *Interview with the Vampire*, she first identified with the young interviewer, then suddenly with the vampire, who, as a Creole, had lived in New Orleans in the eighteenth and nineteenth centuries. As Louis talked sadly about Louisiana and the past, Rice found herself seeing things through his eyes and touching "the reality of the strange texture and glamour of New Orleans." Her new point of view converted her childhood memories, along with the historical material she had collected, into sensuous experiences rather than mere words.

In her supernatural fiction, Rice employs the standard

trappings of the gothic—old and crumbling buildings, entities of one kind or another, exotic sexuality, and mystery—but, with her unique style, she invests them with readily identifiable local elements such as the swampy surroundings, the sultry climate, the patchwork ethnic blend of population, and countless bizarre events and customs that make up New Orleans history. This atmosphere adds much to the grotesque aspect of her fiction. For example, the doctor in *The Witching Hour* remembers his experiences with the ominous Mayfair clan when he "had tasted real horror in those damp, dark New Orleans days, and his view of the world had never been the same."[3] Similarly, Father Mattingly wonders if the Mayfair women are involved in voodoo or devil worship, convinced as he is that "evil had thrived" in their uptown mansion.[4]

Which elements of the city have particular appeal for Rice? One of the qualities that has always made New Orleans different from other southern cities, and has intrigued authors since the eighteenth century, is its amazingly diverse and multicultural population, which resulted in the establishment of several discrete neighborhoods where certain ethnic groups chose to dwell: the French, the Spanish, the Irish, the Germans, the Creoles of color. Residents of these neighborhoods continue to relish the mystery and the myth over that which can be explained; fact often bores them, and the more far-fetched and exotic the legend or fantasy surrounding the local characters, locales, or customs, the more intense their enjoyment of it. Since modern science has seized as its manifest commitment the dismissal of all that is inexplicable and mysterious, New Orleans has become almost an anachronistic city.

Inseparable from its history are the romantic figures, either mythic or historical: the French Ursuline nuns, Laffite and other privateers, the mysterious Spanish priest Père Antoine, the *voodoienne* Marie Laveau and her daughter, the quadroon courtesans, the prostitutes of Storyville, as well as musicians, authors, and an abundance of those in politics and business who operate beyond the law. Rice relishes the fact that history always surrounds one in the area known as the French Quarter, as well as in the Garden District, bringing with it the "ghosts of all those high-toned personalities" who helped to shape the place and its mystique. The stories of real people who lived there are as intriguing as those of witches and vampires.

After *Interview*, Rice turned to a more realistic portrayal of the city, "to float into the world" of the nineteenth-century quadroons and produce *The Feast of All Saints*. The world of the Creoles of color was a strange and haunting one she had discovered during her New Orleans research. She was fascinated by the people, the culture, and the system called *plaçage*, in which white Creole men established mistresses of color in residences on the outskirts of the Vieux Carré and produced second families. The descendants of these mistresses and the wealthy men who kept them were essentially trapped in that system, living, as in Rice's words, "in the midst of life" in the city and yet "completely shut out of it by laws," able to prosper and gain prestige but not permitted to enter professions or to vote. On the surface, at least, theirs was a glamorous world, filled with intrigue, secrecy, and the legendary quadroon balls where men met the young free women of color from whom they would choose their lovers. At the same time, Rice realized, despite the glamour—or perhaps because of it—"there was the potential there for tragedy."

In this subculture, which existed nowhere else in the South, were hundreds of young men, offspring of these strange unions. Often they were educated in Paris, but returned home to live in the insulated world of the quadroons. Among these young men, perhaps overeducated for their station in life, were artisans, artists, and authors, many of whom yearned for something more out of life than that which the caste system provided. Among them were several poets who, hungry to have their work in print, published the city's first literary journal, *Les Cenelles*—an "incredibly romantic" endeavor, Rice realized—and filled its pages with romantic poetry. Fascinated by the pathos of these aspiring authors, Rice knew instantly that she must capture them on paper, and the result was the creation of her characters Marcel and Christophe. So intense was her empathy for these "lost souls" that she remembers walking along the city streets "feeling that I was one of them."

Clearly, they fit the pattern she had established in *Interview* and to which she returned in subsequent novels: the plight of the individual who is an outsider amid the clannish and caste-structured New Orleans society and culture. The quadroons "left their imprint on all different aspects of the city and yet nothing was known about them." *The Feast* filled that vacuum in the public awareness of New Orleans history.

Set in the 1840s in the part of the French Quarter, which "was then as forever a small town," where the quadroon mistresses lived with their children and waited for their white protectors, the novel provides readers not only with a glimpse into the tragic lifestyle of these alienated people but also re-creates vividly the city during that era. Rice's depiction of the Vieux Carré before the Civil War is romantic and even melodramatic, yet it is probably as close as anyone will ever come to capturing that world. It is, like most of her work, a kind of love letter from the author to the place that holds for her an endless fascination.

Other aspects of the city have affected Rice's depictions of it. One is its weather. The subtropical climate of New Orleans figures strongly in the lives of the residents and in literature, and Rice, perhaps more than any of her contemporaries, has a clear perception of, and an ability to recreate, the unusual weather there. The young doctor in *The Witching Hour* says of the oppressive New Orleans heat, "You start out fine, and then your clothes just get heavier and heavier."[5] Rice remembers from her childhood "what it was like to sit on an old screen porch during a rain storm," and insists that "there is no rain like rain in New Orleans, coming down softly through the immense trees, something heard and felt before it is ever seen." The image of rain recurs often in her work, as when the doctor in *The Witching Hour* thinks that "rain in New Orleans is so beautiful."[6] Rice recalls as well the ever-present threat during the summer months, hurricanes, one of which, when she was a child, "upended the magnolia tree on Jackson and St. Charles and left it lying across the old streetcar tracks."

Another feature of the city is its lowlifes. New Orleans has from its early days been infested not only with myriad varieties of insects and vermin—flying cockroaches and termites, for example, and the rats that appear frequently in Rice's novels—but with criminals. Since the eighteenth century, fugitives from the law, or those seeking escape from illegal, immoral, or otherwise unsavory pasts, have flocked to the French Quarter to lose themselves as if it were a sort of Foreign Legion. The streets of many of the older neighborhoods are unsafe, with muggings, burglaries, rapes, and murders increasingly commonplace. The city has always been dangerous, and residents often regale visitors with accounts of notorious crimes from the old days when the waterfront—an area Rice depicts in *The Feast*—was as lawless as the Wild West, or the years when the infamous Storyville purveyed every sort of vice under the protection of the law. Although the romance has to some degree worn off that prevalent threat to safety and sanity that is part of the city's texture, a certain degree of fascination with it persists.

The noted tolerance of New Orleans residents for eccentricity to some extent emanates from the love of being entertained, having fun, partying. To the outsider, the city must at times appear to be a menagerie of grotesqueries, for traditionally its inhabitants have provided shelter and understanding for more than its share of the strange and even the infamous. The streets of the French Quarter swarm with bizarre individuals who seem, given the exotic atmosphere through which they move, perfectly at home and are surprising only to the unsophisticated tourist. Even Rice's character Louis notes how easy it is for a vampire to pass through the city streets unnoticed. In the 1980s, there was the small, wizened Latin American woman who was often seen carrying an enormous cross or a statue of St. Joseph in her arms as she walked to grocery stores that provided her with meat scraps for her large pack of dogs. A stranger to her neighbors, her background unknown, she lived her lonely and isolated life on Chartres Street; when she died at an advanced age, she left a small fortune to the Catholic Church. Even now, in this more prosaic age, if you stroll through the Vieux Carré almost any day of any week you will likely encounter Ruthie the Duck Girl, a local eccentric who has moved through the narrow streets for close to half a century, sometimes wearing an ancient and tattered wedding dress and accompanied by whatever her current companion may be, a duck or a dog; or the mysterious and sometimes disturbing Bead Lady, clad in various unusual costumes, including a hard hat, a football helmet, voluminous scarves, plastic capes, bedsheets, metal plates, or garishly colored leisure suits; walking and muttering in what seems to be a foreign language, importuning passersby to buy old carnival beads she has retrieved from gutters. Such an assemblage in such an atmosphere would surely inflame the imagination and spur on the creative urge in an impressionistic writer like Anne Rice.

It is, of course, not only the people that intrigue Rice and provide the inspiration and material for her best work, but the background against which they live, the old French and Spanish town houses of the Vieux Carré, some of them two hundred years old, and the even more opulent mansions of the Garden District and St. Charles Avenue. Rice was born and grew up near the Irish Channel, part of the Faubourg Ste. Marie, one of the city's oldest suburbs. Her family had lived there since the large influx of the Irish in the mid-nineteenth century. The area was in marked contrast to the Garden District, where earlier the wealthy Anglo-Americans had settled, and the variance between the two is reflected in her novels. Walking from her home on St. Charles Avenue to school or church, the young girl could not help noting the "almost unreal" Garden District's beautiful Greek Revival houses with their large front yards surrounded by cast-iron fences, set amid magnolias, crape myrtles, and towering oak trees. When she crossed into the Irish Channel, it was like moving into another world, for there she observed an essentially treeless landscape and much smaller, though nonetheless distinctive, dwellings, including the Victorian shotgun houses decorated with gingerbread molding.

Many of her early experiences in uptown New Orleans went into the creation of the character Michael Curry in *The*

Witching Hour. While living in San Francisco, Michael remembers the Irish Channel, in which he grew up and which he loathed, along with the double houses and small yards, the loud bars, the unattractive matrons and their offspring, the "stench of Magazine Street," the layer of dirt that covered everything, and "the harsh accent that marked you as being from the Irish Channel," an accent remarkably similar to those found in "Brooklyn or Boston or anyplace where the Irish and Germans settled." Garden District boys taunted him for going to Redemptorist School: "We can tell by the way you talk."[7]

When he returns to New Orleans after a long absence, he recognizes the accent in his cabdriver and mentions it, only to be told that his is the same, but by now Michael has forgotten his animosity toward the Irish Channel. He thinks of himself as part of the Garden District, which he considers the *real* landscape of his youth, the "only paradise he had ever known," that "warm sweet place he'd left when he was seventeen, that old great square of some twenty-five-odd city blocks known in New Orleans as the Garden District."[8] So intensely did he love that area with its "darkly beautiful" streets,[9] the heavy "fragrance of the night jasmine," the sky catching fire and illuminating the live oaks "so that each tiny leaf was suddenly distinct,"[10] that he early developed an interest in architecture, learned to recognize the "Greek Revival, Italianate, late Victorian," the "side hall houses and raised cottages," and to distinguish the Corinthian from Doric columns,[11] a knowledge that only intensified his devotion to the place. As a boy, gazing at the mansions "slumbering behind their massive oaks and broad gardens," he determines that someday he will own such a white-columned house with blood-red azaleas around the porch, with a piano, elegant curtains framing the tall windows, and chandeliers hanging from the ornate ceilings.[12]

While still living in San Francisco, Michael Curry thinks of the past in New Orleans, "a city of characters," outstanding among them "the old Irish Channel storytellers," including his grandfather, who related how as a child he had sneaked into St. Mary's "just to hear what German Latin sounded like."[13] Rice, too, grew up with the myths and legends related by Irish relatives, a heritage that gave her a love of words and helped transform her into a writer. Whatever the event, she recalls, the storytellers would dramatize it, at home, at parties, at wakes and funerals. The Irish had a bent toward poetry, the tendency to use "language to the hilt," to create phrases with "real bite." Rice wonders if some chemical in the makeup of the Irish character is responsible for the ability to spin a good yarn. Whatever it is, she says, "When you get the Irish down here in the South, you get a double dose." In her youth, Rice not only listened to the storytelling but delighted in reading all the material she could find on such things as the local ghosts, searching for the houses in which various apparitions had supposedly been sighted. Most of what she discovered finds its way into her novels.

Another quality of the New Orleans Irish is their religious devotion, and unquestionably growing up a Catholic there in the 1940s and 1950s exerted a strong influence on Rice. In *Belinda*, Jeremy Walker remembers, decades after the experience, "those long lush church ceremonies" of his childhood in New Orleans, with the masses of "white gladiolus on the altars, the satin vestments so carefully embroidered," and the colors, all of which had a "liturgical meaning."[14] Rice comments on the prevalence of "spectacular churches" in the city, including two in which she worshiped as a child, the Romanesque St. Alphonsus, where the Irish congregated, and across the street, the German St. Mary's; two buildings, both dedicated to the same religion, filled with stained-glass windows, murals, and religious statues, for two ethnic groups that were incompatible with each other at that time. The interior of St. Alphonsus, she recalls, was like a "fantasy world," and she describes hers as an "old-fashioned Catholic childhood drenched in old-world ceremony—the Latin Mass, the Tre Ore services in Lent, the weekly novena service, and so many special Feast Day Masses," each with its own "special New Orleans quality, a love of excess," and an amalgam of foreign traditions, Irish, German, French, and Spanish, manifested "in little customs, even sometimes words," all of it part of "the day-to-day texture of my life." There was a certain Puritan quality about such a life, of course—for example, Rice and her peers were forbidden to see movies based on plays by Tennessee Williams—but it was a life lived amid an extremely sensuous and sensual, even erotic environment. In The Vampire Chronicles and the Mayfair novels, the reader can feel the brooding presence of the Church, an institution that was, and to some extent still is, a major influence in the city.

The Irish Channel and the Garden District, their ethnic groups, and their churches figure significantly as settings in all of Rice's work. At the conclusion of *Interview*, we learn that Lestat is living uptown, "off St. Charles Avenue. Old house crumbling . . . shabby neighborhood. Look for rusted railings."[15] Later, in *Lestat*, his residence is described as a mansion on Prytania in the Garden District, a block from Lafayette cemetery, through which, Rice recalls, she "used to roam as a child." When she came to write the novels about witches, Rice employed her own First Street mansion as the home of the Mayfair family, and the home of Jeremy Walker in *Belinda*, a "gigantic old rose-colored house" with dark shutters, a picket fence, and massive oleander bushes, was inspired by a now-demolished house on St. Charles, "around Conery Street."[16]

Rice also draws extensively on one of the most startling aspects of the cityscape of New Orleans—the European-style cemeteries with their seemingly endless rows of stark white tombs, a sight that often disturbs tourists with its evocations of mortality. In *The Witching Hour*, Father Mattingly stands beside the gates of Lafayette Cemetery at twilight, acutely conscious of the beauty of the moment, "the golden time of evening when the sun is gone and everything gives back the light it has absorbed all day long," but he is also struck by "how forlorn it was, the old whitewashed walls, and the giant magnolia trees ripping at the pavement."[17] These cities of the dead are at once comforting to observers and at the same time somehow menacing, especially since many of the older graveyards have been vandalized, exposing human remains to public view. In some instances the desecration involves not only the monuments and their ornate decorations but the removal of parts of the corpses—fingers, skulls, and other bones. In the oldest, Saint Louis Number One, for example, crime has long been prevalent, with robberies, assaults, and even murder not uncommon. Evidence of the practice of voodoo is to be found in the older cemeteries, especially on the Glapion tomb, in which the Widow Paris, believed by many to have been Marie Laveau, the famed *voodoienne*, is buried. That monument, located in Saint Louis Number One, is always covered by marks made with broken bricks or colored chalk, while candles, food items, and more arcane objects are assembled at its base. One enters these old hallowed places with an eerie feeling and with full knowledge that lurking behind one of the tall whitewashed tombs may be an attacker, so that even seeing a vampire would seem, in retrospect, no more unusual than the reality of the place.

One of the images that remained strong in Rice's memory during her time of "exile" was of the "crumbling whitewashed walls of the Lafayette Cemetery with its little templelike graves," through which she wandered as a child. In *The Witching Hour*, Rowan Mayfair is startled when for the first time she enters that uptown graveyard, "a veritable city of peaked-roof graves, some with their own tiny gardens," with paths beside them on which one can walk "past this tumbling down crypt or this great monument" dedicated to the memory of firefighters of the past, to children who died in various orphanages, and "to the rich who had the time and money to etch these stones with poetry. . . ."[18] Later, dining with her aunt and uncle at the well-known Commander's Palace, across the street from the graveyard, Rowan can see through the window of the restaurant the white tombs, and she thinks, "The dead are so close they can hear us." When Ryan Mayfair replies, as if able to read Rowan's mind, "Ah, but you see, . . . in New Orleans, we never really leave them out,"[19] he voices a common sentiment of natives, many of whom religiously attend to the graves of their forebears, whitewashing them at regular intervals and visiting them on All Souls Day. Walker Percy, in his novel *Lancelot*, attributed to New Orleanians "a gift for the trivial," including "scrubbing tombs,"[20] and in his essay "New Orleans, Mon Amour," he observes that the cemeteries are more cheerful than the hotels and wonders "why two thousand dead Creoles should be more alive than two thousand Buick dealers."[21]

Anne Rice is certainly not the first author to be inspired by the exotic, erotic, and grotesque aspects of life in New Orleans, and to recognize its gothic ambience, which requires no imaginary evils, à la Stephen King, to make it frightening. Both George Washington Cable and Lafcadio Hearn in the nineteenth century wrote about the mysterious settings, bizarre local characters, and ghosts, real or imagined, that haunted the streets of the old Quarter and uptown. More recently, in his play *Suddenly Last Summer*, Tennessee Williams envisioned a Garden District mansion inhabited by a strong woman who, although she exhibits no supernatural powers, seems somehow outside the human realm as she lives among her carnivorous plants and exerts control over her family. But Anne Rice has put her distinctive stamp on the material of the city, the beautiful and the strange, what Poe called the Arabesque and the Grotesque, and the result has been a unique fiction about the place.

When I asked Rice in 1980 if she agreed with the often expressed belief that it is difficult to write *about* New Orleans while living *in* New Orleans, she wasn't sure. She thought about the question—for *ten* years—and then replied, surprisingly, in the middle of another conversation: "Perhaps you were right, when you said that maybe it was not a tragedy that I had to leave, because during my exile in California, twenty-five years or so, I would have dreams about New Orleans. I was obsessed with it." Much of that longing for her native place "went into making the chapters of my books about New Orleans particularly vivid for me." So real was her evocation that she could sit at the typewriter and "go home," not as a conscious act, not deciding, "I'm going to the city where I want to be"; rather, such an intensity would develop that "I always felt more alive and less isolated when I was writing about New Orleans."

Like Lestat, who returns home after a long, long absence, Rice felt, "I had to go home. And home was New Orleans, where the warmth was, where the flowers never stopped blooming. . . ."[22] When she returned to live in the New Orleans landscape of which she had dreamed for many years, first buying the house on Philip Street, then several mansions on First Street and St. Charles Avenue, and finally St. Elizabeth's, an enormous complex that covers much of one block, she was able to traverse that landscape again in the flesh. She saw the church in which her parents had married and she had been christened, the houses where various relatives had resided, and she professed to have been "just overwhelmed" by the experience. As she listened to the "sound of the rain falling on the banana trees" and could smell "the river breeze coming off the river," she could work more effectively on *The Witching Hour*. Although she had feared that memory might have enhanced the landscape of her youth, she found it still the "intense place" that she recalled, with an "otherworldly quality" so strong that being there was "like being in the Caribbean or the Mediterranean."

The young girl who experienced the powerful and distinctive images of the city grew up to convert them, through her creative gift, into the material of novels. Those memories are re-created in the thoughts and speech of her characters and constitute a sort of lyrical refrain in her fiction, in which certain strong, colorful sensory impressions recur often. She is thankful that New Orleans has provided her with "the atmosphere and richness I think Europe gave to the Lost Generation in the twenties," and as a result, whatever subject she chooses to "write about is interwoven, psychologically or philosophically, with the city."

In the mid-1980s, I called Rice in San Francisco to ask for any new impressions she might have about New Orleans. At the time she was busy, but told me that she would write to me in a few days. When the letter arrived, it was filled with keen impressions. Her concluding statement not only let me know what she had been busy with when I called but made a telling comment about the extent to which she missed her beloved New Orleans: "I was cooking red beans and rice when you called. I am so homesick!" Anyone who knows the city will understand from this statement the depth of her longing for the place that gave her birth.

NOTES

1. Eudora Welty, *The Eye of the Story* (New York: Random House, 1970), 166.
2. This and subsequent uncited material in this essay is drawn from five interviews between the author and Anne Rice from 1980 to the present.
3. Anne Rice, *The Witching Hour* (New York: Knopf, 1990), 3.
4. Ibid., 21.
5. Ibid., 79.
6. Ibid., 25.
7. Ibid., 40–41.
8. Ibid., 36.
9. Ibid., 192.
10. Ibid., 168.
11. Ibid., 44.
12. Ibid., 38.
13. Ibid., 57.
14. Anne Rice, *Belinda* (New York: Arbor House, 1986), 106.
15. ———, *Interview with the Vampire* (New York: Knopf, 1976), 372.
16. ———, *Belinda*, 52.
17. ———, *The Witching Hour*, 96–97.
18. Ibid., 622.
19. Ibid., 624.
20. Walker Percy, *Lancelot* (New York: Farrar, Straus, Giroux, 1977), 58–59.
21. ———, "New Orleans, Mon Amour," *Harper's*, September 1968, 88.
22. Anne Rice, *The Vampire Lestat* (New York: Knopf, 1985), 508.

Let the Flesh Instruct the Mind

A *QUADRANT* INTERVIEW WITH ANNE RICE

Katherine Ramsland

Quadrant: What has been your exposure to Jung or Jungian ideas?

Anne Rice: I've heard his name and basic words that he invented all my life, but my specific knowledge of Jung is pretty vague. I remember friends in California talking about the collective unconscious. They said it was like each of us possessing the memory of the entire race, so that we respond sometimes as though we remember things that didn't actually happen to us, but in fact had happened to other people. I think that's probably true.

Q: In your novel *Exit to Eden* you talk about there being a racial memory of the erotic and erotic paraphernalia. Were you using the term *racial memory* in the sense that you just described it?

AR: I guess, but I wasn't thinking about Jung at the time. In *Exit to Eden* I was suggesting racial memory as an explanation for the attraction we have to suffering—the primitive desire to achieve intimacy through violation, for the attraction we have to suffering. What I was trying to say is that sadomasochism has almost nothing to do with the way one is brought up or one's religious background or any particular incident in one's childhood. People from all different walks of life and all different kinds of backgrounds enjoy masochistic fantasies. If we look for a cause, we would have to think about something like racial memory—something encoded in the genes, some way in which, after thousands of years, we've turned experiences of violence and violation into something erotic.

Q: You've definitely generated a strong collective response with your Vampire Chronicles. How did you start writing about vampires?

AR: I wrote about vampires as a whim. I was sitting at the typewriter wondering what it would be like to be a vampire. I wanted to see through his eyes and ask the questions I thought were inevitable for a vampire to ask who'd once been human. I was just following my imagination and my instincts. At first it was a short story, but I kept rewriting it, and during one of the rewrites it became a novel.

Seeing through Louis's eyes allowed me to write about life in a way I hadn't been able to do in a contemporary novel. I couldn't make my life believable in that form. I didn't know how to use it. When I abandoned that struggle and wrote *Interview with the Vampire*, it all came together for me. I was able to describe reality through fantasy.

Q: Do you use your fantasy life for writing your novels?

AR: No. Writing is part of my fantasy life. It's one level of it. I think of my fantasy life as having three levels. One of them is a kind of ongoing imaginary world with people who have always been there since I was a small child. That world is always with me and it's a great source of enjoyment. And of course, it evolves as I do and mirrors my immediate interests. My earliest memories of it are about children and parents and great big houses and lavish interiors—a kind of fairy-tale kingdom. When I was twelve and very interested in being a nun, all the characters were going into a convent or they were religious brothers and priests. It's just a world of imagination in which I'm probably working out psychological problems in some way; but I never write down what goes on at that level. Nobody from that imaginary world has ever evolved into characters in my novels. My writing is another level of my fantasy life. Another is sexual fantasy, very similar to what I wrote in the Roquelaure novels.

Q: Do you pay attention to your dreams?

AR: I do to some extent. I just used a dream in the vampire novel I'm writing now. I had the dream years ago: A tiger was coming up to my neck; I thought it was going to kill me, but instead it ate the necklace I was wearing. Without question, I'm as much influenced by a dream like that in terms of feeling and mood and symbolism as by things I read or see on other levels. And it happened to fit very well with the book I'm working on.

Actually, I don't remember dreams that often, but the very intense ones leave me feeling that I was almost transported to another place. I remember those. They echo. But I have them very rarely. I can go for months or years without remembering dreams at all.

I've had only maybe three profound dreams—dreams that felt like something other than dreams. One I had as a little girl, at about age four. This was very influential on my writing *The Queen of the Damned*. In the dream I saw this woman who was completely white, like marble, and she was walking with a prayerbook in her hand. Someone said to me, "That's not your grandmother. That's your Regis grandmother." I didn't know the meaning of the word *Regis* and I had never heard of it. I never forgot that dream. It was very frightening to me.

And I had a dream about my daughter, Michele, being sick—of something being wrong with her blood and her withering and dying. She was turning blue and collapsing because of the fluid in her veins. It was awful. That dream was before she was diagnosed with leukemia.

Q: You said that *Interview with the Vampire* was a way for you to describe the reality of your life through fantasy. Do you see a connection between the experience you had with Michele's illness and the vampire image?

AR: I never consciously thought about the death of my daughter while I was writing it. I wasn't conscious of working anything out. When I wrote it, it was like dreaming. The book had a life unto itself. Of course I was shaping it, doing the things that have to do with craft, but the images were spontaneous and arbitrary.

The child vampire in *Interview*, Claudia, was physically inspired by Michele, but she ultimately became something else—a woman trapped in a child's body, robbed of power, never knowing what it's like to really be a woman and to make love. Actually, she became a metaphor for a raging mind trapped in a powerless body. I've had blind readers who have heard the book on tape tell me they identify with that character. I've also had people who are very small call me because they identify with her. That's really how I see her—as having been ripped off.

Q: Are all of your books "like dreaming"?

AR: To some extent, yes, but *Interview* was really the most unconscious book I ever wrote. I just started to write and let it lead me wherever.

The only other novel that was like that was *Exit to Eden*. That novel was totally unplanned. In fact, my intention was to write a pornographic novel, but the characters of Elliott and Lisa came alive for me. I fell in love with them right away. Something started to happen for me and it ceased to be just pornography, or it became a heightened form of pornography, because the people who were involved in the sex scenes were so real—people who had personality and history. It just got sexier and sexier, and when I finished, I felt terrific. I felt that something terrific had happened in the book.

Q: Jung often spoke about the erotic in terms of the archetypal interplay of opposites. Can you comment on the importance of using elements of opposition in your novels?

AR: What interests me is really the *mixture* of those opposed elements—the transcendence of dramatic extremes. The reason I like to write about people who are bisexual is that I see them as transcending gender. I don't see my characters as homosexual; I never have. I think their reception in the gay world has been due to the fact that they aren't stereotypes. My characters are simply people who have homosexual relationships; I don't see them through some kind of guilt overlay. That's why the movie scripts I've seen of my novels are so defective—they tend to make these characters decidedly and rather negatively homosexual. It's such a tragic misunderstanding.

I don't usually create pure opposites who interact as

such. The tension between opposites, as I see it, is not a violent clash of objects so much as a mixing in each individual character—masculine and feminine, good and evil. That's why I love the *Godfather* movies. They devote such attention to showing the good and hopeful side of the Corleones—the ways in which these are ordinary men who happen to kill people for a living. So many of the images of real evil in Hollywood are broad and stereotypical. Hitler, for example, always comes off as a one-dimensional monster, and you never get a sense of who he was as a human being, what his motivations were. I'm not talking about creating sympathy for an evildoer, and I'm not maintaining that understanding evil will eradicate it. I don't think any amount of understanding would have made Ted Bundy redeemable. I'm speaking as a writer about being fascinated by evil—about the need to go into its complexity, to know what makes men like Bundy tick.

Q: Is this why you've changed the conventions of the vampire tale to make the vampire more fully developed as a character?

AR: I always saw vampires as romantic and abstract. In *Dracula* they're presented as closer to animals—feral, hairy, foul-smelling. But I always saw them as angels going in another direction—not toward goodness necessarily, but they had become finely tuned imitations of human beings imbued with this evil spirit. Since the spirit is not material, what actually happens is that they become refined and abstract rather than animalistic and materialistic.

This idea probably stuck with me from childhood, when I saw the movie *Dracula's Daughter*. I loved the tragic figure of Dracula's daughter—the regretful creature who didn't want to kill but was driven to it. It had that tragic dimension. The vampire myth is at its fullest, most eloquent, and most articulate in this movie because the vampire herself was articulate and eloquent. I never forgot that film. It has the best seduction scenes I've ever seen—very subtle. You don't see her come into contact. She lifts the ring and hypnotizes the victim.

Also, when I was a child, we would talk about books in my house. There was a story going around called "Dress of White Silk." It was told in the first person, from the point of view of a child vampire. I thought it was quite wonderful. I wanted to get into the vampire. I've always been interested in the point of view of people right in the center of it all.

Q: In a sense, you've humanized the vampire—made him into a tragic romantic figure. You've also given him consciousness; he's not an animated corpse bent on satiation, but a different order of human. This shifts the conscious/unconscious drama from living people versus the vampire to something going on inside the vampire himself. What has this shift accomplished?

AR: Actually, I don't see the vampire story in terms of conscious or unconscious. I see the vampires as outsiders, creatures outside of the human sphere who can therefore speak about it—the way Mephistopheles could speak about it to Faust. I gave them conscience and intelligence and wisdom so they could see things humans aren't able to see.

Q: How did the vampire Lestat evolve as a character?

AR: Actually, Lestat grew as a character almost beyond my control. He spontaneously appeared in the corner of my eye while I was writing *Interview*, and then he took on great strength and had experiences that went into the second novel. I was focusing so totally on Louis and Claudia when I was working on *Interview* that I didn't realize Lestat was developing such coherence. He started out as just a bad guy. You never know who's going to take over a novel.

Q: Would you say that you identify with Lestat in some way?

AR: If I were a vampire, I would certainly want to be Lestat. What fascinates me about him is that he knows right from wrong and he still does what he has to do. His strength, his penchant for action, his lack of regret, his lack of paralysis, his ability to win over and over again, his absolute refusal to lose—I love to write from that point of view. Louis is exactly the opposite character—passive, defeated, disappointed. Lestat is undefeatable, and it was great fun to write about that. I feel that I'm more like Louis and that Lestat is the dream of the male I would love to be.

Q: You've taken the erotic qualities typical of vampire fiction and heightened them. Can you say something about that?

AR: Vampire fiction is erotic because the vampire is an erotic image to begin with. Religions used to have sensuous gods and goddesses, like the old lusty vegetation gods, but they're gone now, and what lingers in our imagination is the vampire. He demands a sacrifice from us, but in that sacrifice is great rapture, and we respond unconsciously.

Q: How did you make the link between vampires and the old vegetation gods?

AR: I was halfway through the second novel before I hit on that connection. It was like turning something over and seeing the other side, and it all fell into place. I was reading Sir James Frazer and Joseph Campbell and books on myth by Robert Graves, and suddenly I happened on the Osirian myth. I thought, "This is it! It's perfect!"

But I do think the connection between the vampire and the vegetation gods is already there. I see myself as exploring that relationship, not creating it. I think if you keep mining the unconscious, if you write and you constantly drive for IT—that feeling of intensity and connection—those things always get discovered. Only after it was all rolling did I see that Lestat was a Dionysian figure. And then I saw the way to make the mythology of the vampires. It was almost like a sort of joke for me. Lestat finds this ancient Roman, Marius, and Marius tells him, Well, guess what? We were vegetation gods. It was like an in-joke. *The Vampire Lestat* was a novel of wandering and discovery.

Q: You speak of the drive for IT, the essence. What do you mean by that exactly, and what brings you closest?

AR: IT is the moment of really important truth—what you would want to utter on your deathbed; what you would say if someone came and asked, "Do you have one thing to tell us?" You keep trying to boil it down, really get to it, this moment of truth that makes your hair stand on end, the most important thing you can say about our struggle in the world—a moment of exploding truth.

Q: Did the erotica get you to IT?

AR: Very much so. The idea was to create a book where you didn't have to mark the hot pages, where every page would be hot, and so I was trying to get right to the very heart of that fantasy—to reach the moment of pounding intensity and to take away everything extraneous, as much as could be done in a narrative. To do that you have to be absolutely alive to what you're writing, and it's very hard to achieve a consistent contact. You get swept up in building a scene and you have to keep trying to get through that to make the book more totally IT.

Q: Do you see a connection between the vampire books and the erotica you've written in the Roquelaure and Rampling books in terms of the union of spirit and flesh?

AR: I wasn't conscious of a connection between the vampire books and the erotica, but yes, they certainly involve the same themes—dominance and submission—and there's an erotic tone to everything that happens.

I know that the books are always talking about truth being in the flesh. Claudia says to Louis, "Let the flesh instruct the mind," and I do feel that very strongly. In *The Queen of the Damned*, when Maharet makes Jesse into a vampire, she says she is anchored to the flesh forever, and during the transformation she has a vision in which Maharet says, "Beware the pure idea." Certainly erotica insists that experience of the flesh is not evil. It isn't a mandate to act out our fantasies. It just says that what the flesh desires is not necessarily bad, but requires exploration, attention. Beyond that, I don't know. I'm sort of listening to my own advice. I'm pretty immersed.

Q: Do you see a connection between the erotic and the horror genres in general?

AR: Yes, I think the connection is profound. There's something about the excitement of ghost stories that's like sexual excitement. The victim in these stories is always forced into submission. The vampire story in particular involves a kind of seduction, a taking of the victim.

Q: You mentioned wanting to become a nun. Do you see a connection between the popular fascination with the vampire and the denigration of the sacraments as magical by the Protestant Reformation?

AR: The vampire does appear in literature right at the time the Reformation is gaining ascendancy, and he certainly does represent the old Catholic Europe. I'm sure my own vampires are seen as embodying the magic of my childhood Catholicism. They have the power of the saints: They can work miracles and transcend time.

Q: Do you think the reforms of the Second Vatican Council were a mistake?

AR: It wouldn't be fair of me to say much about this. I left the Church in 1960. My feeling is that the Catholic Church destroyed the very traditions that people so desperately need. Many people left.

Q: Does the vampire have something to offer in the way of spiritual transformation?

AR: I think the vampire represents somebody who's transcended time and transformed himself into an immortal and becomes like a dark saint—a being with all the powers that transcend the corruptible. He represents the longing for immortality and freedom. Admitting that can be quite beautiful.

Q: Does our culture deny us that?

AR: Yes, our culture tells us to be practical and to face the fact that nothing lasts forever. We're very much a Protestant culture in that respect. There's a terrific emphasis on practicality. When people say to me, "Why don't you write about what you know?" or, "Why are your novels so different?" what they're really saying is, "Why aren't you writing the typical Protestant novel—a story about hardworking people who are taking stock of their lives and trying to develop an individual moment of illumination or insight?" Even people in books tell writers to write about what they know, to keep a lid on their imaginations.

Take a look at a story like *The Wizard of Oz*. Dorothy goes off into Oz, which is like my fiction, full of witches and curses and castles and shadows, but it all turns out to be a fraud and a nightmare. Dorothy winds up back in Kansas and realizes that "happiness is in your own backyard." Do you remember that backyard? The pigs and the farm? That's what our culture is teaching people. You stay right here on the farm; don't go running off to the big city; you'll just find corruption and sin and wickedness.

And what has Dorothy got at the end of *The Wizard of Oz*? The comfort of mediocrity. She'll be with Auntie Em and the pigs for the rest of her life. I'm interested in something else—that leap of the imagination into another order of being, the reinvention of self. My work is filled with moments where people are shattered and broken and have to reinvent themselves, like Tonio in *Cry to Heaven* when he's castrated or Louis when he's made a vampire. As religion loses its hold for people in a really magical way, people have to reinvent themselves in terms of new ideas.

I suppose I think of this as a Protestant/Catholic dichotomy because I've just been reading a book by Ioan P. Couliano, *Eros and Magic in the Renaissance*. He points out that Ignatian spiritual exercises, which were part of the Counter-

Reformation, encouraged the sensual imagination. You were to imagine yourself as Jesus, bent under the cross; how it felt to have nails going into your hands. Some of what my vampires are struggling with—questions of good and evil and whether God exists—are unquestionably the preoccupations of my childhood religion.

Q: Are your books a form of mythmaking?

AR: I don't know how to answer that. We can't escape myth. Even if we're nonreligious or nonemotional, we experience moments when we're aware of myth, whether we can describe it or not. We're aware that we're in an archetypal moment. For example, when I go to a wedding and a man turns to his daughter and lifts her veil, then turns to the young man, that's an archetypal moment that gives me chills.

The vampire image is powerful in that way. It calls up something in us that goes right back to the gods of ancient times. The image is seductive, alluring—a being who drains the life from us so that he or she can live. In some inchoate sense, the idea of being sacrificed to such a god becomes romantic.

Q: Is writing "what you know" necessarily pedestrian and without mythical resonance?

AR: No. My objection to the well-meaning advice to "write what you know" is not that ordinary knowledge is pedestrian, but that what you know in your fantasy life is also "what you know." The dichotomy is false. Telling a young writer today to write what you know instead of writing fantasies is just as absurd as telling Shakespeare he should have written about his relationship with his wife instead of

Hamlet. What the Brontës knew were their fantasies, and their books are as legitimate and powerful as any novel based on experience.

Q: Do you think high fantasy is the only place to find large questions and intense passions?

AR: No, but I'll tell you, it's hard to beat. Fantasy for thousands of years has been the medium for people talking about the very meaning of life itself. It is no accident that the words "To be or not to be" appear in a play that begins with a ghost. Banquo's ghost speaks of guilt and love and loss and cruelty, all of the major questions. It's difficult to ask these questions in "realistic" novels, because they are so often cynical and overly sophisticated. If you're writing the well-made novel about a woman's divorce in suburban Connecticut, you're not going to have her sit at the kitchen table and say, "Why do I exist?" She's going to speak in veiled terms about alienation. That kind of fiction has worked itself into a corner. It caters to the belief that nobody talks about the meaning of life. The meaning of life becomes the kind of question people ask in their "fantasies." I keep using the word *fantasy*, but that's not really right.

Q: What word would you use?

AR: Imaginative fiction. *Macbeth* has witches in it but it isn't a fantasy. I mean works that have characters larger than life, mythic, battling forces. Deeply embedded in our culture is the idea that truth lies with the familiar, the ordinary, the middle-class, even. We've lost faith in imaginative fiction, and the finer writers have turned away from it. But I refuse to believe that "fantasy" cannot be enormous in scope and profoundly valid and meaningful. I insist on writing the way people wrote two hundred years ago. I think this is a terribly sterile age. We don't even have a Faulkner or a Hemingway to turn the natural into cultural mythology. We've got people running to the theaters to see *Silence of the Lambs* because Hannibal Lecter is the closest thing we've got to a dazzling character. Today's literature takes us no further; it leaves us with a woman in Berkeley who has an abortion and experiences a small moment of illumination, makes up with her boyfriend, and cooks dinner.

Q: Do you think this is a masculinized culture?

AR: I would say no, but this is a tricky question. Our culture is terribly influenced by domesticity and women, but women, by and large, are doing what men have forced them to do. I read a book once about how the female scribblers of the nineteenth century took over literature and finally drove out people like Hawthorne and Melville. I mean scribblers like Harriet Beecher Stowe. The word *scribbler* is a denigrating term for women who wrote pious books that conformed exactly to what ministers believed people should read. I think this sort of atmosphere is still with us—women conforming to men's ideas about domestic propriety, even as their husbands make a show of not being forced into a tamed domestic environment.

Q: I asked the question because you were talking about the culture losing faith in all but objective realism. A rational culture is usually considered masculinized.

AR: I don't think being rational has anything to do with being masculine. Men are utterly irrational—they go to war, they rape, they kill, they beat people with clubs. Crime is irrational and most of the crime in the United States is committed by men. To say that it's a masculine culture because it's rational is ludicrous. You might even say that it's women who are providing the rational weight to the culture.

Q: Do lesbians respond as enthusiastically to your books as gay men do?

AR: I do have a very large gay audience of both men and women and I'm very proud of that. The women in my novels are androgynous and strong. They defy convention and reach for freedom. I think the whole gay audience responds to the fact that these characters are not defined by their sexual orientation, but are quite genuinely bisexual; they love regardless of gender. These characters are totally alive for me when I write about them. Men and women are equally attractive to me when I'm writing. I can't *not* see things that way.

Q: Are you familiar with the misogynist conventions of traditional vampire stories?

AR: I don't really see traditional vampire stories that way. The men in the original *Dracula* don't hate women; in fact, they direct all their hatred toward the male figure of the vampire. They are repulsed by the vampire's bestial masculinity—the hairy palms, the animal drive. They're Victorian prudes who can't stand their own sexuality and want to protect women from it.

Q: You're talking about Bram Stoker's version of the story.

AR: Yes, what I've managed to read of it. To tell you the absolute truth, I can't get through the whole book.

I've read the first chapters with Jonathan Harker and some stuff in the middle and the end, and I've read plot descriptions.

Q: You don't think the women in Stoker's book are described as weak and stereotypical?

AR: I don't think those women are presented as any weaker than Jonathan Harker. In the scene where he's in the room with the female vampires, he's a total sexual victim. Vampire literature always turns gender considerations on their head. That's not new with me. Renfield and Harker are as much victims as Mina and Lucy. In fact, when Lucy is transformed into a vampire, the scene is filled with vitality and dark magic.

Go back to Lord Ruthven and Le Fanu—vampire literature always says that gender doesn't matter. What matters is a much deeper desire to be dominated and a response to that domination and terror of the one who will fulfill that desire.

Q: Are there other symbols in Western culture besides the vampire that you have explored and amplified?

AR: I think I've explored one aspect of the mother goddess with the queen in *The Queen of the Damned* and with Gabrielle, Lestat's mother: the heartless cold goddess who leaves—how did Robert Graves put it—"the bones of the poets all around her." I was also exploring in that book the entire figure of the father and teacher—the paternalistic wise man. I saw that more in Marius than in anyone else. Marius believes in authority and he has a great sense of his own authority.

Q: You also describe in Marius a hunger for a sense of continuous consciousness. How do you think that hunger is part of who we are?

AR: I've always found the idea of continuous consciousness very seductive—someone who knows everything that ever happened and why. I'm afraid there's no such thing, but it was an idea I took for granted as a child. I thought at the final judgment there would be a moment of great illumination—when everyone would be gathered together and the truth of every moment would be told. It's very comforting to me to read about near-death experiences where people say they undergo a kind of life review and really see how their actions affected other people. But this isn't continuous awareness as I imagined it. I always felt as a child that whatever you were doing, someday, whatever the misunderstanding was on the playground, it was all going to be straightened out. There would be a moment of recognition and justice and harmony.

Q: What makes that idea so seductive?

AR: It's seductive because it carries the promise of order, of all suffering and pain and confusion being redeemed. Of everything being redeemed in a moment of great illumination and understanding. I find misunderstandings excruciating. It must be interesting to grow up without the idea of continuous consciousness—to believe that your actions are happening in private. I'm still not sure my actions are happening in private. I still pretty much live my life as if somebody is going to be told everything at the end of the week. That's what happens when you go to confession regularly. I think I still kind of live like that.

Q: Do you think your writing does anything to heal or redeem culture?

AR: That's too large a question for me to know. Sometimes the only thing that keeps me going is the fact that I'm happiest when writing and there are people who totally understand. Beyond that, I don't know.

Q: Is your writing a healing experience for you?

AR: Oh, yeah. I feel complete and alive when I write.

October 4th, 1948

Anne Rice

The rain had threatened for hours. When they were gathered on the banks of the lagoon in the park, a loosely connected group of brightly colored summer clothes with easels and boxes of paints, the thunder had rattled behind the sky and teacher had ordered the class indoors. So that, even though it was chillingly beautiful outdoors, they had to paint under the artificial light in the shadows of bad plaster copies of minor Renaissance works. Dalia had dawdled, accomplishing nothing until twelve o'clock, when they were freed, with orders not to linger in the park but to go straight to their bus stops . . . she then, full of ideas for sketches and rich combinations of colors, ran to meet Lucy on the bridge, and together they distributed their sack lunches, finely crumbled, to the swans, and then oblivious to the chides of the thunder walked up the lagoon to places in the park where they had never been, to trees they had never climbed, to a neatly kept shrine to William Shakespeare, the existence of which had previously been unknown to them . . . where they sat on the stones watching the bees circle over the roses, Dalia sketching the bronze profile of William, and Lucy squinting in loyal silence at the Bard not fully comprehending what he was or what they were doing. Dalia then asked Lucy to carry the sketchbook, while she explored the recesses of a brick archway that bounded the shrine on the north and led to a flagstone path overgrown with weeds and slick with algae.

They followed, Lucy obediently holding the sketch pad above the tall grass until they reached the lagoon again, where the sky appeared as the trees grew farther apart . . . and it was obviously gray and damp.

But the rain did not come. They took the St. Charles car together, Dalia waving good-bye after her stop to Lucy, who stood next to the driver at the front window by the door . . . their favorite place . . . a little dangerous when the door swung open, but a delightful vantage point from which to watch the tracks disappear under the car, and to pretend one was driving the car. Dalia walked slowly, dragging the tip of the sketch pad on the ground behind her, trying to make a journey of the block that was growing disappointingly shorter each year or epoch of her childhood. First she walked across the brick sidewalk before the Nellie Fallwell place, pigeon-toeing her steps to conform with the braided rows of bricks, and then hopped from flagstone to flagstone before the Episcopalian bishop's house, and paused for a moment before the giant pine trees that sprang from the strip of lawn that ran along his curb, to bend her head back until her neck tingled and the pine seemed to be falling suddenly down on top of her. Then dizzy with a catch in her throat that tasted like nausea she walked slowly down the deserted cement that measured the last lap to her own front walk. The yard was empty, the swing stirred over the beaten dirt beneath the oak tree that darkened their front porch with its abundant foliage. The walk itself was dusted with footprints. The ivy spilled from the patches near the picket fence over the cement squares and rustled in the wind that was growing colder as the thunder gurgled louder over the top of the house. Behind the screen porch Dalia could just trace with her narrowed eye the shape of her grandmother as tiny specks of white light filtered through the screen from her gray hair. She moved jerkily from one side of the porch to the other, and as Dalia approached, she heard the scraping of her grandmother's everworking broom. She rounded the porch and went up the side steps into the house, which was warm and smelled of cabbage and ham. A piano, or rather the recording of a piano, tinkled in the front room. A sewing machine churned the air in the back. She listened to the thunder crackle on the roof, and went into her room, laid her sketch pad down, and went to her favorite window, which only became accessible to her for a reasonable view after she had pushed a rocker up to the wall and stood upon the bed (after first removing her shoes). From this point she watched the pecan tree across the street lash at their neighbor's house . . . a large yellow Victorian house whose thick rectangular body tapered to a gingerbreaded arm of servants' quarters and utility porches over the side garage, which had been no doubt a stable or carriage house at one time. A thick brick wall hid the lower porches of the house and the pecan's great dry branches hid the upper stories except for the easily perceivable broad outline, and occasionally chimneys, long since plugged like Dalia's chimney, never belching smoke, just clinging to the sloping roof and tempting the ivy to climb over the windows to choke their round mouths. The wall itself had sagged in many places, and was badly blistered where the pecan tree root had risen under the sidewalk, making it into a steep little mountain over which it was very exciting to skate fast since an open crevice at the peak through which the knots of roots protruded, threatening to trip a child not completely familiar with the street. In the summer, delicate wisteria hung in the shade along the wall dropping waxy violet blossoms to the ground that made old ladies and running children slip and fall. But now in the early autumn chill the blossoms were gone and the branches clung with grim persistence like bones frozen to the brick. For the flash of a second Dalia thought she heard the rain, but the tar street remained a dusty black, and the sidewalks showed no specks. She waited to discover if it had been the rustle of pecan leaves on the other house or the dry hiss of a car in the avenue in front. The wind picked up a beer can and rolled it angrily into the gutter. The leaves roared against each other. Dalia's grandmother banged the French doors shut and clumped gently back down the hallway to the kitchen. Dalia leaned forward against the screen, her elbows aching on the sill, shifting to a new point of flesh and bone and beginning to ache again . . . hoping they would not ask her to come or go or do some dull and irritating errand.

The piano tinkle faded off and rose again with orchestral accompaniment. The melody was easily singable, and Dalia sang softly to herself, hardly able to hear herself over the wind and the leaves and the finally tinny thrash of the beer can as it fell to rest against the telephone pole that cut the tranquil scene in half.

This type of day pleased Dalia very much. She could never understand how her mother could say that it was a gloomy day when it rained; or how she could label a monotonously sunny day with boring expanses of blue sky as a beautiful day. A day with grays and gusts and rustles of turbulent weather was to Dalia a much more exciting interval in time than those days that tumbled one upon another all summer each as blue and as hot as the other. On gray days the house across the street was deepened to a burnt ocher and silver secrets sparkled in its opulently high-arched windows. The tree bowed to make the most curious shadows on the sidewalk, and the cold sting of the air on one's face and ears, the gentle lift of one's hair off the back of the neck by the wind . . . these were the very precious pleasures that held their own dark charm . . . much like the smell of flowers at a funeral, or the glow of a candle in a shadowy shrine in the rear of the church. It was not a kind of charm easily explained by Dalia. She could only think of comparable things, realizing that in naming similarly attractive objects and places, she was expecting the names of these objects to explain the charm for her . . . and they could not, if the day could not. And at times she sounded morbid and her grandmother condemned it gently with the warning . . . "When you have seen your loved ones go, you won't care so much for calla lilies then." But in the meantime Dalia loved them and had often sketched with richly soft pastels in art class three calla lilies nestled on a simple effect of black velvet. Another favorite item was the candle, preferably the candle lighting a shadowy doorway, a candle set in a heavy bronze holder taller than herself. There were such candles in their parish church that sent enchanting flickers up the marble walls and sent bizarre expressions over the faces of the plaster saints and chalk virgins. Dalia loved the smell of the wax and the aroma of the incense that rose from the altar at the Benediction that followed the Stations of the Cross.

Distracted from the street by momentary considerations of candles and their warm wax, she climbed down from the rocker and went to see if everything in the many rooms of the house was as she had left it that morning. In the kitchen her grandmother and mother were drinking tea from thick white cups without saucers, her mother pouring milk into the steam that rose from the brim, and her grandmother eating a piece of burnt toast saved from breakfast. "You're a storyteller, Catherine," she said busily, which Dalia's mother protested quickly, "No, Mama, it was fifty-seven dollars. Why, Alice would never have bought it if it had been more than that. It was fifty-seven dollars. I remember it well." And Dalia passed unnoticed to the kitchen door, where she watched through the dusty screen the banana trees in Mrs. Sersy's yard lap her porches and her garage roof tops. One of Mrs. Sersy's boarders hurried along the porch with a heap of freshly dried linen ripped from the lines, obscuring his face. The wind turned the clothesline like a jump rope.

"It's going to rain," her grandmother said. And her mother raising her voice, "Oh, Dalia, before it rains, dear, go to the store. Hurry dear, don't go to Hills but to Piggly Wiggly. I need some soap and a head of cabbage." There was the tinkertink of change on the galvanized table top, the spoon clinked into the cup. "Go on dear, before it rains." And Dalia, thinking it over as though she had a choice, concluded, it wouldn't be too bad, walking in the wind, it might be pretty . . . especially to go to Piggly Wiggly and pass the Nellie Fallwell place and look beyond the broken banisters to see if she could again see the bizarre sight of a tree reaching its branches through the place where fine furniture once sat behind French doors. With one eye fixed upon a patch of thick black cloud moving over Mrs. Sersy's chimney, she recorded quickly the names and brands, and the prospective prices, and without losing the cloud she tucked the change into her blouse pocket, and her mother pushed wide the screen door and she clattered down the steps, skipping down the alley to the front yard and running into the street, she came quickly with a dry hot mouth to Nellie Fallwell's broken gate. She hung there catching her breath, her cheek perilously near the buckling rusted sculpture of the gate post with its ivy-rimmed holes through which the fence posts once were rigged, but which were empty now except for the nets of spiders and fragments of their stuck victims. The path that led to Nellie's gate went deep into the block before it broke into bamboo stalks and the wild lace rose-of-montana and the dried skeleton of wisteria. Where the shrubbery broke or was occasionally broken through by workmen of unknown origin and intent, Dalia could see the banisters of the old porch, dark wrought iron webs of leaf and grape clusters always kept a shining black on newer Garden District houses . . . but in Nellie's ruined house they had rusted to a colorless grime, which Dalia remembered was soft to touch like the broken end of a piece of chalk. Behind the stiff blanket of stone, once a living room wall, which now left only jagged patches searching in the cold air for the lost upper floors, Dalia saw branches of an oleander tree, its white flowers flapping back and forth in the gap of silence created by their distance. What utter enchantment it would be, she thought, to climb beyond the chicken coop stretched over the gate, and go up the flagstone path to probe among those rooms without their tops . . . to see the fallen oleander petals clogging places where perhaps there was still left a panel of Nellie Fallwell's hardwood floor, or to find in the tall grass a lady's mirror with a silver handle and curious initials carved in its back. But if the neighbors saw . . . but the truth really was, which Dalia wouldn't tell Lucy or anyone else . . . that she was frightened to go that far . . . for from the gate she could enjoy the ruins in perfect safety, but there inside the yard among the crumbling walls where Nellie Fallwell had walked and talked and dined she couldn't bring herself to walk alone or even with another child her own size.

A hush fell over the street, the air was clammy on her ears

and hands. Clutching her pocket closed and the change still against her breast, she ran the long blocks to Piggly Wiggly, and thinking of the Nellie Fallwell house she got the groceries and carried them easily with one arm . . . just soap and a head of cabbage and the candy bar her mother had added for her, for which she realized she had forgotten to say thank you. Dalia thought she felt a drop of water on her shoulder, and on her cheek. She looked but saw no rain. She walked slowly until Nellie Fallwell's lot loomed a long stretch of jungle in back of the corner street, and then cautiously she walked off her own avenue down the side of Nellie Fallwell's property, to several feet before the old carriage house leaned out over the sidewalk. The picket fence was good, she reflected, for keeping out men, but she was small enough to slide with ease between the rods of rusted iron. The wind was gone. The street was still. She gazed in the crystal gray at the long side porch with its massive Corinthian columns . . . the best preserved of which were on the west side, and then she tipped the grocery bag inside the yard over the cement ledge in which the fence was rooted and quickly without giving herself a chance to waver she slid between the pickets and fell in on her feet, smoothing her skirt down in Nellie Fallwell's front yard.

If Nellie Fallwell had been very rich, she pondered, walking through the weeds, her eyes alert to broken glass or bugs, surely the money had gone to someone . . . and why didn't they come to take care of the house? Most people wanted little houses now, and houses up and down St. Charles Avenue were being broken daily into rooms and apartments. Before her eyes the shape of an iron bench emerged in the tall greenery, its curlicues thick with moss and spiderwebs. It had rusted to a dingy red. Dalia touched it gingerly as she inspected the empty frame where the seat had been and studied the lower part of the legs where they had rotted right into the mud and growth. A house goes fast when no one lives in it, her mother had said . . . and resolutely with a heave of courage she turned to confront the house and let her eyes soar upward, pushing her head backward to the top of the great columns which now stood only a few feet from her outstretched arms. A bird flew down from where Nellie's roof had once rested, a resplendent twenty-five feet above the stone foundation. The column wavered against the cloud-banked sky, and Dalia felt the dizziness in her throat that came from inspecting palm trees. She wanted to look down again, but suddenly she knew with all her heart that if she turned she would find, must find, amid the rocky blueprint of the rooms a terrible spectre, and only after her neck was numb did she dare to look . . . to see only the heavy doorframes filled with glass and the vacant spaces between the heavy piles and the fragment of an orange crate and of course the inevitable empty whiskey bottle that turned up in every deserted place. Nellie Fallwell wasn't there. A bumble bee quizzed up the column trunk. The bird returned to its pinnacle. And Dalia slipped gracefully through a circular window in the high foundation . . . it had been a shallow cellar window once . . . through which plumbers passed to crawl beneath the rooms to fix the pipes . . . and Dalia stood up again inside Nellie's house, calmly assured that Nellie wasn't coming. There was in fact no one and nothing there, but Dalia. She sat down on the orange crate and let her head roll from west to east, her eyes touching briefly on the curls atop each column . . . floating greedily over the last traces of violet wallpaper on the last slabs of walls . . . resting on a crooked door that buckled its walnut veneer under the gray sky . . . the sound of traffic had been swallowed by the high grasses, the oleanders subtracted the street from her vision. A tall magnolia tree made her unsure that the bishop's house had ever been to the east of that lot, and she sat apart from the world in the center of the old house . . . her heart pounding as very gently, without even a pitter of warning, the rain began to come.

Nicholas and Jean

Anne Rice

This young man whom I was telling you about . . . this young man whose arms were white bones, whose eyes were violet . . . a very willy-nilly color for the eyes of a boy, this young boy who had been told on many occasions that he was willy-nilly, had a passion for velvet, for the feel of things that were rare. He had been bred on the moldings in fine houses, on the champagne that is brought out of the cellars of those houses like fine fish from the sea, and he was without a penny when my flashlight, which was going before me, a searchlight, fell on him at the end of the hallway, filling the archway as though he were the final word of the prayer. I thought that he was a spectre in that house, the last remnant of the age that had made those walls possible; when approaching, which was no easy task because the sea was diffusing itself into a fog that was almost rain, a slow-motion rain that threatens to kill you, to lead you off into the water itself, I had contemplated on the road the hundreds of unfortunates that had built those walls, that had quarried those stones, perhaps chipping them from another house, perhaps lifting them already squared to put in those places until they reached the sky, until the house itself became as ominous as the cliff from which it grew, until the windows when lighted must have hung so high that they were stars.

Well, this boy of course was very much alive, and as it was later discovered lived off the floor in one of the spacious rooms of the lower floor. There was a perilous dampness shimmering on the floor. His clothes lay in moist hovels, a very precious mirror hung from the ceiling on a long cord which might have been a lady's stocking, and the boy who wore a very dirty velvet coat had a hand as fine as the hand of a virtuoso violinist. He turned the mirror so that it held the moon in one full-bodied glance and then he let it spin.

"At night, why?" I think he asked me, as we were driving back to the town.

Because I could not resist; I was impatient. The Count, who was my best customer, adored having himself photographed, loved even the bad pictures that I reluctantly developed knowing the money was always good, had offered it to me tonight; and I had seen it in the day once from his yacht and once from a helicopter coming in from the airport . . . those towers green with moss, those windows which the sun would fill with gold . . . the waves banging on those cliffs I knew must fill the rooms with a backdrop of roar.

Yes, yes, he agreed and laughed as though I were the boy with the enthusiasm. He asked for one thing, a glass of champagne.

"The Count knows me," he said. "Intimately! Didn't he warn you that I was there?" And when he said this the words seemed to take a strange trip in my mind, to wander to the very back of it and drop down, down . . . didn't he warn me that at the end of that hallway in the darkness in which I was so sure that I was alone I might have committed some unforgettable little physical sin, that this boy would blossom at the end of the flashlight, would blaze against that frosted wall, this boy would clasp with his spider hand the end of the beam so that the light would show the veins in fluorescent red, and laugh with delight?

I noticed in the restaurant that his shirt was silk, and that the whites of his eyes were riven with red lines, and that he shivered as though from force of habit.

"Why there all alone?"

"He told me I might, when I had no place to go. We were going along fine until we fought about something, and out out out on the street I went again. He begged me to go back with so many ideas, so many rules, it was like offering the bird the cage, so I said no, even though it was cold and I had nothing; the whole scene smacked of morality! But! There was a ballet dancer who was offering to take me away . . . it happened later that he died."

"How old?"

"Oh, seventy or so, he really didn't dance, he was always at the theatre sponsoring one of the young ones, he took me to only the finest restaurants, and bought me only the finest clothes." He smiled. "A painter?"

He drank his champagne and let his lips glow with it.

"And you are going to take the house?"

How could I not take it? Wandering there, among those stones, in the night, letting my flashlight find this spectre . . . "But you may still sleep there," I said. There were so many rooms, and I needed only a darkroom, a studio, the walls for my pictures.

"A painter?" he asked.

"A photographer."

The food he ate without grace, the game was up for grace because he was so hungry, and I watched him devour everything with the enthusiasm of a bird, I watched him settle in the chair, and the violet eyes flicker on his face, and the red lines close in until the violet itself seemed to be almost extinguished, and then as though he had been taught from long years, like those women I remembered so well, he reached across the table and said: "And you? Are you always so serious?" and gripping my hand in his tremble, "Are you sometimes gay?"

My apartment has gas heat, has a thick carpet and tight windows so there is no hint of dampness, and lying under the sunlamp at two o'clock in the night it is like a beach without the smell of the waves; but with the coldness of the beer against your hand, and he with his eyes closed, folded under the light like a delicate blossom, said: "When I was ten I went away with my tutor. He was insanely jealous, would not permit me out of the house. He would not teach me anything after we went away . . . I ran away from him in a big city. I was thirteen and I looked even younger I guess, so I took all his money with me and ran, ran, ran. I wanted badly to travel. All over the place."

"And did you?"

"Yes, all over; the first time, the very first time with our Count. I met him at the opera where I got a job as an usher; I was supposed to be serving wine and I dropped everything and when I looked up from the floor he was leaning over me, winking his eye, and smiling."

"Did he send you to school?"

Laughter.

"Oh, of course not. He kept me in his rooms, most of the time; in one place he told them I was his son, another place his nephew. He bought me this ring, do you see, it's a real diamond, and so many clothes. Then I left him that time, I left him, in some place where I didn't speak the language, and found a young man who was a millionaire. It was rumored he was one of the richest in the world."

And the story ended because the words which were then

traveling so slowly that they echoed, died on his lip, and fell into my hand, and he went to sleep; he tumbled into me like a gentle hot bundle of soft and hard things; he folded into me like my mother part, and his long thin leg caught the sunlight of that lamp and was turned to metal.

Split into one hundred fragments by the crystal door, I saw him, the violet eyes, the red velvet jacket, the black leather glove, and those delicate features of which a girl might have been proud.

"I am going away," he said, pacing up and down the floor. "I'm most grateful that you let me sleep here." He sat down at my invitation. I who was heaped with photographs could only stare.

"With Regie; he is going to take me to Madrid, to which I have never been. He has a show there. He is so kind, so generous."

"He is a performer?"

"A manager. Well, he used to be a performer when he was young." And I pictured those eyes wandering like beams of light over rotting flesh, and I saw the very firm arm reach out for my photographs; the black glove discarded hit the ground silently without weight. "He is a darling." A darling, a darling, a darling, a darling . . .

And then he disappeared. One night a month later, when I had cleaned out several rooms, had hired a servant, had found a man who would deliver wood for the fireplaces, had gotten a gas refrigerator and a gas stove, I was in my darkroom under the red light when I heard the steps on the staircase, and opening the door and stepping out into the cold air, I looked up and saw the little head again at the end of the hallway, which was an open window still without glass, a gaping mouth to the sea, saw the gentle slope of the little bird shoulders, felt the little hands then on my lapels, and put my arms under those little arms, drew the iridescent eyes close to my cheek where I could listen to the lashes rising and dropping, kissed him, held him, and heard him say with a slight giggle: "The man died."

There were a thousand pictures of him taken in the next few months, and a visit from the Count: "Oh yes, Jean, I meant to tell you about Jean, did you let him stay? My wife so hated Jean, wanted me to do something foul to him, but he's not a bad boy, oh no, not a bad boy . . ."

But Jean, who was drunk for a while after his homecoming, who was delirious to find the rooms heated, who rolled over and over on the warm stones, on the animal skins, Jean was very slim and prone to vomiting . . . it was unusual food, or too much wine, or too much sex; he would convulse, shiver, fall over the toilet and crack his head on the porcelain . . . and I would carry him into bed, a cough cracking his little chest. So I took him to a doctor, and there was an immense diet written out, for my "nephew," and shots, and Jean, who was sick of it all, who hated broccoli, and pitched the glass of milk across the room, went away within a few days afterward.

He took fifty dollars from my wallet and my suitcase, and on the third day when I was sick and could only force myself to work without feeling or sight, I got a letter from him in which the spelling and punctuation defied the imagination, a letter of thanks and tears, and promises to send back the fifty dollars, and he was going out of the country with a man he had known before who was powerful and rich. I rolled over in my bed, and saw far below the mighty car of my friend Larry Haller crunching into the large drive before the house, and running down the steps I found him wiping the dampness from his pink sunglasses, and smiling in the misty shadows.

Let me say briefly of Larry Haller that he appeared shortly after Jean returned to the house. Jean had a picture of him in his room, at the top of the mirror, but had not woven him into his lengthy confessions. Haller was a banker who had survived every old and recent trick of economic change; he had a distinguished pedigree but married a young working girl, and in the last three years since that marriage he had embroiled himself in the building of a museum, a school that was without tuition for the talented poor, a shipping company, a radio station, and numerous other enterprises which kept him forever in the news, an attention he not only did not avoid but seemed to enjoy. He wore bright colored sports jackets and had introduced the summer before the wearing of pink sunglasses, which had now become somewhat of a fad. He came to me shortly after Jean, and asked me to photograph his wife, who was beautiful, and I did it with a relish that was rare, and we were friends after that, and he sent a string of other wealthy clients. Well, this morning I ran to meet him and after he had wiped his glasses he told me that he had seen Jean the night before, it must have been three o'clock, running through the streets downtown as though he was being pursued. So when it was dark I went downtown. I spent the evening inquiring about him where Haller had seen him. He was not unknown. But he was nowhere. I went again the following night, and I found as I moved across the city into the older section where the bars boast histories as well as fine liquor that he was indeed well known. One bartender: "The fairy, of course I know him. I know who you mean. He was here. Not so much this year as last year." And another: "The beautiful boy, who is looking for him now? Yes, I saw him but not lately," and then finally a waitress, her tray aching with bottles and glasses: "Oh, Jean, Jean, Jean . . . yes, gone away with the bat to the bat cage."

Gone away with the bat to the bat cage, gone away with the bat to the bat cage; I called Larry Haller. He told me to call him again in twenty minutes.

Be brave, he said to me, the Bat Cage was only a few blocks from where I was standing; I must go to a restaurant with a bright red door and a gold knocker; I must demand to sit in the back; I must ask for roast beef but not with natural gravy: "Say that you do not like natural things."

This restaurant was in itself a difficult place to find and to enter, but I paid a large amount to the waiter and insisted, furiously insisted to be seated in the back, and so was given a table in the rear and there forced to wait an interminable amount of time among paintings too dark to see, among pieces of chaotic sculpture allowed to layer with dust while the waiters of assorted sizes and shapes moved among the far-flung clientele. They attended finally, and I gave my order and the waiter appeared not to notice the tremble in my voice. I ate the food, paid him, and then he directed me to a door beyond the kitchen.

Here the scene changed. It was a fire door made of metal that I entered. And the hall inside was of a former age, an age of wallpaper and high ceilings, and gas light fixtures. I went down the long hallway. I paused finally among the wooden doors and I said clearly: "There is someone knocking at your door," and one of the doors opened and a man came forward with something in his hand that was black and glittered with sequins. He escorted me into a little bedroom furnished in tasteful delicate antiques. There was a piano there with heavily carved legs, and a little desk littered with notes. He lifted the object in his hand. It was a mask. He tied it around my face, and I fitted it comfortably over my nose.

"I am particular," I said. "He is a little boy, with bright violet eyes and very white skin. His name I think is Jean."

He smiled and nodded his head. He let his fingers play with the gold medallion that hung around his neck. Then he ran them lightly over the waves of his thick black hair and jerked his head like a bird.

"You have a gentleman's taste," he whispered. "You must expect to pay a gentleman's price." I handed him a fifty-dollar bill and he placed it on the desk. He opened the door and led me down to the hallway into a large room. It was sumptuously furnished though as I inspected the details I saw that in many respects it was like a stage set, much drapery, gold fringe, and paint where there should have been gold dust. But it was a closed and effective atmosphere and the windows looked onto faded murals just behind the sparkling panes. He led me through this place to a stairway and into another hallway where mirrors alternated with doors. I watched us traveling together, himself a small birdlike man with a gleaming medallion, myself tall, dark in my raincoat and anonymous with the curious black sequined mask. Finally we found our door, and he inserted a key in a large lock. He opened the door partially and the air that seeped out was like warm water. There was not much light; he withdrew his birdlike head and then stood behind me. I went in, my heart pounding, and as the door shut behind me with a very definite click, I saw through the bright brass posts of a large bed, his little legs twisted, his chest so thin with heaving the breath that barely escaped the lips, the circles under his eyes so tender and blue that I dared not think of touching them, my Jean white on the cream-colored lace bedspread. His lashes barely moved; then they fluttered and he smiled as he saw me, but without recognition. He rose slowly and I realized that even had I been stripped bare of my coat and mask he would not have known because his eyes were gray with sedatives, the balls barely not drowning in his head. I walked lightly to the bed shivering on the brass rods; leaning over him, I heard him whisper: "And what would you prefer?" and then he sank back into the pillows of cream lace and stretched so that the long lines of his body were tight. His hair the color of which no sedative could dull burned in the bed. He closed his eyes, and his face seemed to draw in with the effort of breath. I sat by his side and slid my hands under his back and gently lifted him. He remained with eyes closed, laughing silently, folding against my body: "Anything you desire?" he whispered.

"That you come home," I answered. He opened his eyes and looked at the ceiling and then he turned as though the weight of his head were too much for him, and pressing him close to me, I said: "Jean, Jean, why did you do this," and lifting the mask I kissed him. He tightened around me and began to cry. "Nicholas, I love you. Please take me away from this place or I'll die."

The man with the medallion was furious. I had dressed Jean only in my coat and he lay against the wall as we argued. I threatened to phone the police and insisted that he was my nephew, and finally we were on the street where the boy collapsed completely.

Larry Haller's doctor was awakened without complaint in the middle of the night. My friend Jean had been given a ridiculous amount and mixture of drugs. He slept for at least fifteen hours, in which time I made frequent trips to my bed where he lay like a small child of my own. When he awoke the spell had not quite left his eye; he ate a soft-boiled egg and drank some water. He insisted that champagne would settle his stomach, but I insisted that it would not. I wiped his forehead and straightened the bedclothes and brought the lamp down to a mellow gild. I held his little head in my hands.

"May I stay here with you?" he asked me.

"Until you get well, you may do whatever you like," I answered. "I have put a heater in your room," I said, "and a new radio, and a sheepskin rug."

He seemed on the verge of crying. "I mean I want to stay in this room with you, always," he said.

"Go to sleep," I said. In my darkroom I processed a series of Haller's wife. My little patient's request went through my head again and again. But I was afraid. I felt a strong desire to find his parents and send him to them. His parents. What had he ever said about his parents? Nothing. The story went on and on about the Count, the dancers, a defunct prince, and so many others. But no parents. I suppose that I had been content to believe he was born out of the sea foam.

"Where are your parents?" I asked him the next day. He was able at this point to come to the table.

"My parents. My parents." He laughed, but it was not the usual fun laugh. "I think my father is somewhere, where there is money, probably. My mother, somewhere too, I guess, only not with my father. My mother will do absolutely anything to keep from being bored. Anything. Did you finish those pictures of Larry Haller's wife; I would love to see them. Believe it or not, I think she is pretty."

I was on the verge of another question when I looked up and saw the eyes almost desperate across the table, the thin film of tears glistening in the candlelight. "Well," he smiled quickly, "did you finish the photographs?"

I promised to bring them to him later. I urged him to go back to bed.

"May I still stay in your bed?" he asked. I rose from the table and went into the hallway. "I'll give you my answer later," I said, looking over my shoulder. He rose trembling still and walked before me down the hall as though it were full of perils.

I could find nothing to do then in the studio except return to him, so I did and sat down on the side of the bed.

"Why did you take me from the Bat Cage, Nicholas?" he asked. "I think I would have died there. This time."

"Why did you go there, Jean?"

"I don't know," he shrugged. "Nicholas, if you would let me stay here with you, I mean really with you . . ." He closed his eyes.

I leaned over him until I could feel his uneven breath on my face. "If you would love me, Jean, I would let you stay here forever, but it must be me only; no dancers, no counts, no coming and going, unexplained . . ." It sounded so desperate that I could scarcely believe it, but he rose just the fraction of an inch that was between our lips. My hand perhaps pressed the bones of his shoulders too tightly; my fingers tried perhaps to bend or crush the beautiful shape.

PART TWO

Literary Critiques

Introduction

The contributors in this section offer a wide range of readings. I was pleased to find a practicing dominatrix with an experienced perspective on Rice's erotic fantasies as well as writers who could dig into the novels via archetypes, historical milieus, sociological issues, and sophisticated theory.

Anne Rice has written seventeen novels to date. Most of them are either mentioned or discussed at length in the following essays.

Gail Zimmerman offers a valuable summary of vampire literature, both before and after Anne Rice came on the scene, while Bette Roberts provides a strong overview of the gothic novel and its context for Rice's work. Then Richard Noll zeroes in on the vampire Lestat's relationship to the nineteenth-century concept of genius.

The movie of *Interview with the Vampire* gets a provocative analysis by noted Jungian film interpreter John Beebe after I provide a thorough history of how it got made.

Louisiana resident Robin Miller researched the places that are relevant to the community of the Free People of Color described in *The Feast of All Saints,* Rice's second novel.

Michelle Spedding spotted a theme in *Cry to Heaven* that highlights its relevance to modern culture: together, she and I compare the pressures of the eighteenth-century world of opera with today's abuses of elite female athletes. Then Mistress Claudia Varrin evaluates Elliott Slater and the sensual incubus Lasher as love slaves. Her knowledgeable account takes us from fantasy to reality and back. Following her, S. K. Walker describes how the religious imagery in *Belinda* heightens the experience of eroticism and creative expression. This conceptual trio has special meaning for Rice.

Leonard George is a specialist in alternative realities. He uses the context of dreams and visions in Rice's Mayfair series to educate us about various approaches throughout history to interpreting the imagination.

Gary Hoppenstand presents a thorough account of *The Mummy* when he compares it to a nineteenth-century story by Arthur Conan Doyle that bears clear similarities. Then his colleague in American Studies, Kay Kinsella Rout, takes us into the Mayfair-Taltos association with an eye to discussing race relations.

I end this section with an article I have wanted to write since my work with Anne Rice began. I have long noticed how the theme of forced consent threads throughout her writing, and I am happy finally to have the opportunity to work out my initial impressions in a formal context.

To learn more about the people behind the articles, see "About the Contributors" at the end of the book.

The World of the Vampire

RICE'S CONTRIBUTION

Gail Abbott Zimmerman

Before The Vampire Chronicles were published, many of us with a passion for vampire fiction were reluctant to admit it—and with good reason. Most of it was trashy, simplistic pulp fiction and juvenile horror stories. It was rarely intellectually satisfying. Since Anne Rice popularized the genre and raised it to the level of literature, we vampire aficionados no longer have to scrounge around dusty bookshelves seeking those rare tales that offer brief insight into the immortals' world. Vampire fiction—and vampires—have been forever transformed. Now, undying characters are likely to be well developed and charismatic. Their stories are often compelling, plentiful, and prominently displayed. Rice has made our dubious passion (somewhat) respectable.

THE TRADITION

From the time they left their moldering graves of folklore and entered the fanciful domain of literature, vampires have had great potential. "The most shallow treatments of the vampire will have some echo or resonance that you do not necessarily find with the other horror material," says Rice.[1] Vampires exist somewhere between life and death; they once were human but no longer are. They live among us, embrace us, and drain our blood to survive. Spared from mortality, they have an eternity to ponder their preeminent place on the food chain, but they are confined to the night. What would human history look like from such a lofty perspective? What would religion be without mortality? What would remain unknown? How would these creatures reconcile themselves with their uncontrollable lust for human blood?

It is no easy task for a mere mortal to address these issues. Before Rice, few had tried. John Polidori is said to have endowed the villainous Lord Ruthven (*The Vampyre*, 1819) with the aristocratic attributes of his companion, Lord Byron. There was the sensuous, seductive *Carmilla* (1871) and the remorseful—albeit tedious and shallow—*Varney the Vampire* (1847). *Dracula* (1897), of course, became nearly synonymous with *vampire*. Most undead creatures have since lived in its shadow, conforming forever to the grand rules of vampirism defined by Bram Stoker: Vampires shun sunlight, rest in coffins, cringe before holy objects, change into animals or mist at will, show no reflection in mirrors, and, most important, are evil incarnate.

Despite the concerns of parents and other moral guardians, most imitation Dracula stories are morality plays, in which a heavy dose of unwavering faith helps Good men protect their women by conquering Evil. The typical plot is something like this: Meet these virtuous people. Whoa! Something strange is happening to the fair maiden! It can't be—It is! It's a vampire! (Vampire makes a brief, snarling appearance.) Let's hunt it down! Remember our faith! We win! Goodness triumphs! End of story. How disappointing it is.

EARLY DEVIATIONS

While most authors adhered to this formula, a few ventured into new territory. Richard Matheson's *I Am Legend* unleashes a plague that turns all the people on earth—except one man—into vampires. (In the film, the exception is, ironically, Vincent Price.) Ray Bradbury's short story "Homecoming" features a forlorn mortal boy who somehow winds up in a family of vampires. Despite the family's ruthless attitude toward humans, they obviously care deeply for this "handicapped" child. "We love you," assures his mother, solemnly promising to look after his grave "when and if" he dies.[2] The tone is light, but there is a genuine compassion there, which Rice later develops more fully.

Another humorous but touching story, "Softly While You're Sleeping," by Evelyn E. Smith, deals with seduction, companionship, and choice—all themes that Rice would later explore. A thoroughly modern working woman is gently wooed in the wee hours with grace, poetry, and song by an old-world vampire. Although he is much more engaging than her cloddish human suitors, ultimately she rejects him. "My parents didn't come from the old country and work like slaves . . . so I should wind up spending my days in a coffin and my nights going out sucking people's blood!"[3] she explains to him before barring his entrance with an air conditioner. The sixties were upon us and the vampire's quaint ways were painfully outdated.

One vampire who did (sort of) reflect the emerging social consciousness was Barnabas Collins, resident vampire of *Dark Shadows*, an aberrant soap opera that ran from 1966 to 1971 and has become a cult classic. Barnabas did all those nasty things vampires do, only it seemed to bother him a bit. Viewers were touched by his pained look and hesitant manner (although cynics say the actor was struggling to read the TelePrompTer). Despite the sometimes campy, almost always confusing plots, the show broke new ground with a morally ambiguous hero at odds with his nature. If not as introspective and sensual as Rice's vampires would be, he at least had a sense of right and wrong, felt compassion, and was as intelligent as anyone else in that town. His popularity proved we were ready to hear the vampire's side of the story.

Shortly after, there were a few other attempts at "reluctant" vampires in story and film (*Blacula*, for example), but the vampire as evil incarnate soon returned with a vengeance. Stephen King's wildly popular *'Salem's Lot* (published in 1975, one year before *Interview*) is an acknowledged homage to Dracula, with the familiar elements intact: a mostly offstage evil vampire wreaking havoc, a heroic band of vampire hunters, and the satisfying catharsis of the vampire's demise. The twist is that the Victorian setting and milky-white throats of virginal maidens have been replaced by contemporary small-town America and its flawed residents. There are moments of great tension and genuine creepiness, but for those of us hoping for the insight of an intelligent immortal, King's Barlow falls woefully short. "I am crafty. I am not the serpent, but the father of serpents," he writes in a childishly spiteful note to his enemies.[4]

That same year, Fred Saberhagen also revamped *Dracula*, this time from the vampire's point of view. *The Dracula Tapes* deconstructs Stoker's plot point by point as the count wryly explains what *really* happened and how the tragic events were actually caused by a grossly incompetent and self-righteous Van Helsing. The count's dietary habits are pretty harmless—

he subsists on animal blood supplemented by nips of passion bestowed upon very consenting women—so there is no real ethical dilemma. The story was never meant to be anything but the very fun read that it is, but there are some compelling aspects that foreshadow Rice's work. We are definitely rooting for Dracula. He is not repulsed by religious items, and he claims to know something about God. He attempts restraint in an amorous affair, lest he turn an impassioned but ignorant lover into a vampire—a transformation, he ponders, that could be a "clear and present danger—or opportunity, depending upon one's point of view."[5]

There was now more opportunity than ever. Always alluring and seductive, the vampire now stood poised on the threshold of modern society, waiting to be invited into our contemporary consciousness. Surely we were ready to embrace him if he would confide in us, open a door of perception, and let us in on his secrets of survival. Anne Rice was up to that challenge.

INTERVIEW WITH THE VAMPIRE

Interview was the first vampire book I passed on to friends without apology. It won critical praise for its lyrical prose and stunning imagery. While *Interview* and the four other Vampire Chronicles have provided plenty of substance for scholarly and philosophical analysis, they are nevertheless popular stories—spellbinding, engrossing, and strangely plausible.

Even in the glut of vampire fiction that exists today, it is rare to find a story as relentlessly told from the vampire's perspective as *Interview*. Within the first few paragraphs all skepticism is dismissed. Make no mistake: These are vampires, not someone's nightmarish fantasy; nor "psychic" vampires who drain your energy; nor "metaphorical" vampires who drain your will. They are vampires who drain your blood, and, yes, they are the only major players in the story. Humans not destined for immortality are inconsequential.

Rice's immortals have shed many vampire stereotypes, especially those that indicate that they are "cursed" or that their souls are absent or corrupted. They freely enter churches and are unaffected by religious artifacts. ("I rather like looking on crucifixes," Louis remarks.[6]) When they look into mirrors, they cast reflections—very attractive ones, at that. The essential traits of vampiric conflict remain intact: They must drink blood (we later learn about extraordinary exceptions), they kill, and they are destroyed by fire and sunlight. They are denied the everyday human pleasures of sex and food but are more than compensated with heightened sensuality and enhanced perception. These have now become the common characteristics of the vampire in contemporary literature.

THE INTERNAL VAMPIRE

Unlike traditional vampires, who were ruled by instinct, Rice's characters are endowed with the ability to reason. "I saw them as angels going in the other direction," says Rice. They love even more deeply than humans but remain acutely vulnerable to sorrow and despair. They have distinct personalities: Louis, the tortured soul who tells the initial tale; Lestat, the arrogant mentor/tormentor (as we first know him); Armand, the detached, eternal adolescent; Claudia, the immortal child who never had the chance to develop her humanity and is arguably the most tragic and chilling character in vampire literature.

In changing the focus from victim to vampire, Rice transforms the visceral horror of the monster sneaking up on us in the dark into the psychological horror of the monster within. Rice says her vampires are "a metaphor for human existence" in that they chose to thrive despite what that means for others. They must learn to reconcile their deadly passions with their sense of morality. With the extraordinary insight of an immortal, Louis understands both suffering and the beauty of life; that is the real horror.

Louis vividly describes the world around him, but his journey is mostly an internal one. He mourns the loss of his mortal self and seeks some sort of spiritual redemption. He bitterly resents Lestat for being a selfish instructor who teaches only the practical matters of existence, the lessons "not so difficult to figure out for oneself."[7] His questions about God, the Devil, and the vampire's place in the scheme of things remain unanswered (we later learn that Lestat was holding back a bit).

That the brooding meditation of a painfully introspective vampire would have mainstream appeal is not so far-fetched in light of the times. Louis may be alienated from his society, but he is well suited to ours. In the idealistic sixties, we fought for social change; in the seventies, we were living it. People who had lived on the fringe, notably gays, were becoming more visible. Rebellious teens were now firmly entrenched in adulthood. Many rejected the religious absolutes and nuclear families of their youth and struck out on their own. Seeking more personal ways to find meaning, some people turned to ancient religions, brand-new religions, cults, and drugs. Others looked inward, hoping that reflection and self-examination would lead to a heightened state of awareness and truth—a state not unlike that experienced by Rice's vampires.

We were ready to embrace the moral relativism of Rice's vampires. Like them, we faced the awful task of defining for ourselves what is evil. When Armand suggests that if there is no God, no sin matters, Louis argues otherwise: "If God doesn't exist we are the creatures of highest consciousness in the universe. We alone understand the passage of time and the value of every minute of human life. And what constitutes evil, real evil, is the taking of a single human life."[8]

Rice's vampires pose the same questions we ask. Why are we here? How do we overcome our weaknesses? How do we resolve our needs with the needs of others? How do we fit into the community? The novels make us look deeply into ourselves and examine the choices we make in a world full of ambiguities. In Rice's domain, concepts that were once clear opposites no longer are; the lines between life and death, good and evil, are blurred. For us, too, there is no black and white; we must choose our shade of gray.

THE SEXUAL VAMPIRE

Rice's rendition of vampirism is not exclusively a cerebral experience; there are corporal pleasures as well. Her overt eroticism broke new ground. Certainly there had been a long tradition of implied sexuality as vampires lurked in bedrooms and victims succumbed in hypnotized swoons, although many "bite scenes" were pure visceral violence. In Rice's world, human sex is a pale memory compared to the ecstasy of taking a victim. "You get the other person's life, fantasies, dreams, all coming through the blood," Rice explains. "It would be great." For the victim, there is sensual rapture plus the promise of immortality. In the old tradition, all who were bitten usually became vampires themselves. In Rice's novels, the act of making a new vampire is an act of love, in which both parties give and take. This, too, is now standard in contemporary vampire fiction.

Prior to Rice, vampires clearly had strong sexual preferences. Although they rarely engaged in carnal sex, the vast majority were decidedly heterosexual. If they bit a victim in bed, that victim was almost always of the opposite sex. Rice's characters have the ability to transcend gender, which makes gender and sexual orientation irrelevant. Freed from traditional constraints, the vampire act becomes an abstraction of human sexuality. There are homoerotic overtones but no graphic descriptions of genitalia that might turn off some readers, as when Louis describes sharing a coffin with Lestat: "I lay face down on him, utterly confused by my absence of dread and filled with a distaste for being so close to him, handsome and intriguing as he was."[9] Since Rice, overtly homosexual vampirism—genitalia and all—has become a thriving and creative subgenre. (For example, Jeffrey N. McMahan's "Cruising with Andrew" and Jewelle Gomez's *The Gilda Stories*.)

Homosexuals have also found gay allegory in the "outsider" theme that is so central to The Vampire Chronicles. By nature, Rice's vampires are unable to conform to social norms. Louis and Claudia search the world for a community that will accept them as they are, a yearning that all outsiders can easily understand. Yet outsiders also represent the lure of exploring unknown territory. They are intriguing strangers who symbolize the seductive power of new possibilities.

INTERVIEW'S AFTERMATH

After *Interview*, Rice temporarily left vampires and moved on to equally strange literary territory, but her influence in the genre remained strong. *Interview* endured beyond the seventies—it has never been out of print—because it reflected more than the social and cultural currents of its time. Within a few years, other authors broke from the Drac Pack and offered their own refreshing tales. Whether or not Rice directly inspired them, she paved the way for alternative views of vampirism.

Center-stage vampires were becoming more common. *Hotel Transylvania*, by Chelsea Quinn Yarbro, introduces the wise and kind Saint Germain, a truly heroic vampire with mild hemophagic proclivities. "I need no more than could be put into a wineglass," he assures an eager young woman about to embark on the greatest sexual escapade of her life.[10] Like Rice's vampires, Saint Germain feels the loneliness of longevity, but he is too preoccupied with righting the wrongs of cruel humans to indulge in prolonged self-examination.

Professor Weyland, protagonist of Suzy McKee Charnas's distinguished novel *The Vampire Tapestry*, is more at odds with humanity (although he, too, is better than average in bed). Weyland is a solitary "parallel species" vampire, who, despite his best efforts to remain an aloof predator, grows fond of some of his human associates. He unwittingly succumbs to therapy, and, like Rice's vampires, is forced to confront his nature. Unlike them, he has no human memories and no opportunity to transform other people.

Many stories mimicked Rice more directly, but to mix meditation and gore is a challenging task and most of them are forgettable. Still, vampires continued to be creatively thrust into new settings and situations. In George R. R. Martin's colorful *Fevre Dream*, Abner Marsh seeks a way to make peace between his people and "the people of the day." Tanith Lee's vampires inhabit imaginative fantasy realms (the fairy-tale setting of "Red as Blood" and the science fiction landscape of *Sabella*). Whitley Strieber's *The Hunger* is about the alluring, intelligent, but chilling Miriam Blaylock, whose lovers really do face a fate worse than death. Rice had prepared us for all of these concepts by freeing us from the old clichés of vampirism.

LESTAT

Rice's second venture in the genre, *The Vampire Lestat*, came nearly a decade after *Interview*. She had since been influenced by mythological accounts by authors such as Sir James Frazer and Joseph Campbell, and her vampires were becoming more powerful and godlike.[11] *Lestat*—and the three subsequent Vampire Chronicles—are not formulaic sequels that imitate the first plot. Characters recur, but each novel is distinctive in character, style, and theme. Each enriched and expanded the immortals' universe.

The Vampire Lestat is a well-developed mythology that chronicles the history of vampirism with stories within stories that go back to the genesis of vampirism in ancient Egypt. But its greatest achievement is the redemption of the title character, who was so reviled by Louis. We last knew Lestat as a degraded demigod living off rats, a shadow of his former sadistic self. Now he is a rock star. And he is fun. Once again, vampirism was redefined.

Lestat, it turns out, has a different take on Louis's story, although he graciously forgives his sullen companion for his "romantic illusions" and "excess of imagination." We are drawn into Lestat's sphere; it is Lestat who thrusts the rest of The Vampire Chronicles into unexplored territory as Louis slips quietly into the background. Rice says that Lestat is the vampire she knows best: "He's the male I would like to be. My dream self." He is also the best-known vampire created in the twentieth century (admittedly with some help from Tom Cruise). As blasphemous to traditionalists as this might sound, Lestat is destined to rival Dracula's immortality.

Lestat is optimistic and witty, endowed with an irrepressible joie de vivre. He craves adventure as much as blood. Contrary to what Louis had told us, Lestat is also a spiritual explorer, only he confronts his predicament head-on. "He was made a vampire against his will and has made the best of it," Rice explains. "He is determined to be good at being bad if that's what's required of him."

Once again, Rice tapped into the sensibilities of the times. Who could be more "eighties" than Lestat? He is decadent, excessive, greedy, impulsive, and rebellious, a take-charge guy who is thoroughly committed to taking responsibility for his actions. Like his fellow rock stars, he is rewarded for his bad behavior. A vampire without apology, he breaks every rule of human and vampire society, sometimes, it seems, just for the fun of stirring things up.

Although he yields to every cruel impulse, Lestat is probably the most charismatic literary vampire ever. How can a monster be so appealing? Undoubtedly, his gorgeous appearance and exuberant personality account for part of it. But Lestat, like Louis, represents something more profound than today's cultural fashion.

Perhaps in Lestat we recognize something deep in ourselves. In *Danse Macabre*, Stephen King discusses how good horror stories touch our "phobic pressure points," primitive parts of ourselves deeply buried beneath the "civilized furniture of our lives."[12] Katherine Ramsland suggests in "The Monster in the Mirror" that it is beneficial to acknowledge our dark impulses, as they may "hide riches that belie their frightening appearances."[13]

Rice's increasing popularity is propelled by her desire to venture into new territory and fly in the face of old taboos. In one of the most harrowing bite sequences in all vampire literature, Lestat bestows the "Dark Gift" on his dying mother, Gabrielle. Their embrace is highly charged: "she was flesh and blood and mother and lover and all things beneath the cruel pressure of my fingers and my lips, everything I had ever desired. I drove my teeth into her. . . . "[14] Later, as she loses consciousness to the dawn, he drips blood from his tongue onto her lips. "The blood flowed into her opening mouth and slowly she lifted her head to meet my kiss. My tongue passed into her. Her lips were cold. My lips were cold. But the blood was hot and it flowed between us."[15] "When you have an eternity," Rice contends in her biography, *Prism of the Night*, "you can work out anything, even an Oedipal complex."[16]

THE VAMPIRE CHRONICLES CONTINUE

The third in the vampire series, *The Queen of the Damned*, is the novel that truly catapulted Rice to superstardom. It is vampire mythology of epic proportion—from the internecine conflicts of ancient vampires to Akasha's stab at a grand scheme of social engineering. "[Akasha's] mind and values were fixed in 4000 B.C.," notes Rice. "[She] . . . thinks in absolute terms and she is very dangerous." No matter how outrageous the plot, we never doubt that it could happen.

Woven into *QD*'s far-reaching plot are several personal tales, including the story of a prolonged relationship between a vampire (Armand) and a mortal (Daniel, the reporter who interviewed Louis). Such relationships have become common in vampire lore but are inherently difficult. Even if the vampire manages great restraint, there are always the issues of unequal power and unequal life expectancy. Armand does control his lust and even allows his lover Daniel little sips of his magical fluid, which makes the mortal "high" and even more obsessed. He protects Daniel from other immortals but is possessive ("You'll sleep when the sun rises, if you wish, but the nights are mine").[17] Ultimately, however, it may be Daniel who has the real power. Armand has vowed never to make another vampire, but Daniel begs him to do it, as he once begged Louis, and as other mortals have since begged their vampire companions. This is the essential conflict at the root of all "mixed" relationships: Vampires, according to Rice, are often no more comfortable playing God than we are.

Lestat, who refers to his kind as "dark gods," is faced with a similar dilemma in *The Tale of the Body Thief*, the fourth of The Vampire Chronicles. Lestat senses the vulnerability and failing health of his beloved mortal friend David Talbot. David has repeatedly refused the offer that Lestat had always asserted would be unrefusable as death became more imminent. David's obstinacy makes him even more enticing to Lestat, who agonizes over the burden of deciding David's fate on his own.

Despite his boasting that the "Dark Gift" is irresistible to humans, Lestat has always maintained that given the choice, he would not have become a vampire. In *Body Thief* he tests that conviction by switching bodies with a crafty mortal. By now Lestat has grown very comfortable with his being a vampire and so have we. Through vampire eyes we have seen the beauty of humans. Now, actually *in* one of those bodies, we see how awkward and clumsy they truly are. "[A] weak, flopping sloshy repulsive collection of nerves and ganglia," Lestat declares.[18] Through him, being human is a truly alien experience. His vision is blurred, his mind dulled, and he is horribly vulnerable to microbes. But he also finds pleasure in simple things, like orange juice, " . . . thick like blood, but full of sweetness and strangely like devouring light itself."[19]

In *Memnoch the Devil*, the fifth—and Rice says last—of The Vampire Chronicles, Lestat is escorted through a tour of Heaven and Hell. "It doesn't matter here that I'm a vampire," he says, but it does matter that he is Lestat.[20] Memnoch finds Lestat as compelling as we do, and specifically selects the vampire to help him battle a cruel and unjust god. As in all of the novels in the series, the issues of good and evil are examined, but there are no simple answers. More than ever, what is good and what is evil seems confusing and sometimes even reversed. Even after meeting God and the Devil in person, Lestat still does not have the answers he has always sought. "These are beings who play at a game only they can understand," he says bitterly.[21] The experience has overwhelmed him and he asks that he be allowed to pass "from fiction into legend."[22]

THE ALTERED GENRE

Lestat is already legendary. Rice has fundamentally altered our expectations of vampire fiction. We now expect immortals to be tragically doomed, but not stupid. They should be endowed with sensory gifts, like enhanced vision, ultrasensitive hearing, and a deep appreciation of music (this trait is now nearly universal in the genre). They should have distinct personalities. They should be wildly attractive and have strong erotic appeal, and should not shy away from conversation—either with immortals or with humans. They should cry and shed blood tears. Most important, we expect the stories to tell us what it is like to *be* a vampire rather than its victim.

Rice's vampire novels have gained the rare status of being "required reading" in Greg Cox's *The Transylvanian Library*,[23] a meticulously detailed review of vampire fiction since Polidori's tale. Horror writer and editor Martin H. Greenberg claims that Rice's books have "almost singlehandedly reinvented the vampire for the modern era."[24] "After absorbing those engrossing stories, I knew I wanted to write about such dramatic creatures," vampire-novel author Linda Lael Miller enthuses.[25] Publishers and critics often make comparisons to Rice in blurbs and reviews. "Move over, Anne Rice!" some optimistically exclaim. A book about highly artistic characters promises vampires "of the breed Anne Rice fans will love—graceful, sexy, sophisticated."[26] A *Publishers Weekly* review criticizes an author who "covers no ground that hasn't been explored in the historical vampire sagas of Anne Rice . . ."[27]

RESISTANCE TO RICE

Despite widespread acclaim for Rice's contributions, there is considerable resistance to what she has done to the genre. Intelligence, sensitivity, compelling beauty, and artistry are not traits that all readers want in their vampires. For those who yearn for the scary (uncomplicated and less talkative) monster in the dark, there is a backlash of vampires who are more violent and evil than ever. No longer just doing whatever it takes to get a meal, they are out to conquer metropolises (*They Thirst*, by Robert McCammon), nations (*Anno*

Dracula, by Kim Newman), and the world (*Under the Fang*, edited by McCammon).

"The vampire is the lowest form of creatures—a parasite," explains F. Paul Wilson, author of *The Keep*, in an interview. "I can't buy trying to romanticize that type of creature."[28] He laments that the vampire has lost its powerful image because it has been trivialized. Nancy Collins, creator of a world of subculture vampires, including the popular character Sonja Blue, claims that "while the vampire may look and try to pass itself off as human, it is basically everything that is bad with humanity."[29] Many young authors seem to agree—their vampires are often nihilistic and excessively brutal.

Although stories with less than sympathetic vampires are inclined to be grisly, perhaps their popularity represents more than a thirst for visceral horror. For people who hold strong moral absolutes, there may be something deeply disturbing about the very concept of sympathetic protagonist vampires. A stake through the heart is a confirmation of our cultural values. Good is good; evil is evil; good will triumph. Perhaps people who call for a return to simple, strict fundamental concepts of right and wrong want their monsters to be simple as well.

While evil-incarnate vampires are still in high demand, they have not entirely escaped Rice's influence. Even recent interpretations of Bram Stoker's novel (such as Francis Ford Coppola's 1992 film) seem at least partially inspired by Rice. In the concluding tale of McCammon's short-story collection *Under the Fang*, malevolent bloodsuckers are betrayed by a vampire who is unable to reconcile his existence with his human memories. While Nancy Collins's vampires are generally devoid of compassion, protagonist Sonja Blue, she explains, is an exception. "She refuses to surrender her humanity."[30]

CONTEMPORARY VAMPIRES

When vampire fiction does follow Rice's lead, it often has inherently melancholy overtones. We certainly do not want to see these vampires shrivel in the sun but we know they are doomed. Despite the clear benefits of vampirism (are we really surprised that the reporter begs Louis to grant him that alternative life?), we realize there is no easy solution to the ethical dilemma. In lighter fare, authors tend to "de-fang" their vampires by greatly reducing their desire for blood. They simultaneously engage in dinner and "lovemaking" with no detrimental effects on their human companions. Vampires know that when their thirst is kept strong, they cause suffering—no matter how they rationalize their choice of victims. In contemporary literature, vampires die as often from suicide as from stakes through the heart.

Rice's most lasting impact on the genre is undoubtedly the sheer volume of it that exists today. It seems publishers will print any story that features a vampire (especially a vampire from New Orleans). There are lots of self-loathing vampires who moan and groan their way through eternity and brave vampires who endanger themselves only to be saved by mortal friends who heroically offer their own blood. Some vampires are so amazingly stupid it seems they will never learn anything no matter how long they live. Others are pretentious—Mozart shows up a lot in vampiric form. Authors who do create viable vampires, including Saberhagen and Yarbro, often continue their adventures in series.

Traditionally all vampire stories were classified as "horror," and while many still are that, immortals have adapted well to other forms of fiction. There are a slew of mystery/detective vampires, including P. N. Elrod's popular, amusing *Vampire Files* series. Vampirism is fertile ground for science fiction writers, who find "scientific" explanations for the altered condition. Dark, mysterious strangers in romance novels are more likely to be toothsome these days (" 'I want you with me . . . Always. *Always.*' "[31]). There are generation-X vampires and an excess of X-rated vampires (the stories in Amarantha Knight's anthology *Love Bites* are an extremely explicit example). There is also an abundance of nonfiction that purports to analyze just what it is we like so much about vampire fiction—some of that is *really* scary.

A flourishing subgenre is children's stories. Once upon a time, such stories ended with the reassuring message that there are no such things as vampires. No more. Now, as in adult stories, we take their existence for granted, and they are often protagonists. Angela Sommer-Bodenburg's series chronicles the adventures of Tony, a human child, and his vampire child friend Rudolph. Tony knows Rudolph is feeding *somewhere*; in fact, the vampire is very frank about his habits. Still, Tony accepts him as he is—even though it means lying to his parents. There is also prepubescent sexual tension between Tony and Rudolph's coming-of-age-with-fangs-growing-in sister.

Rice's dominance is also strongly felt in the visual media. Today's vampire films are less likely to be adolescent camp than big-budget sophisticated fare. The Sundance Film Festival alone has produced three vampire films in two years. Once again there is a television series with a vampire hero: the moody, stylish *Forever Knight*. In one episode, the title vampire cop is protecting a very popular writer of vampire fiction whose stories take place in New Orleans (her name is Weiss). "She's got this sixth sense about us," Knight concedes, "it's extraordinary." "Her work is just a bit too accurate for comfort," complains his sexy immortal friend.[32]

Reading and viewing all the vampire material available today would take an eternity. Vampires are everywhere, adapting to every social change we ourselves experience. Finally, we can be selective. Having endured two decades of bad vampire puns ("a story with bite"), Rice has been crucial in giving the genre the respect and recognition it deserves. Her vampires are not the oldest, most powerful, or goriest, and maybe not even the most metaphysical. They are just the most likely to achieve true immortality. Whether or not Rice ever writes another word about vampires, she has rejuvenated a moribund genre. Too much of a good thing? Never! In the immortal words of Claudia, I want some more.

NOTES

1. Rosemary Ellen Guiley, *The Complete Vampire Companion* (New York: Prentice Hall Macmillan, 1994), 93.
2. Ray Bradbury, "Homecoming" (1946), in *October Stories* (New York: Ballantine, 1956), 262.
3. Evelyn E. Smith, "Softly While You're Sleeping" (1961), in M. L. Carter, ed., *The Curse of the Undead* (Greenwich: Fawcett, 1961), 192.
4. Stephen King, *'Salem's Lot* (Garden City, New York: Doubleday, 1975), 334.
5. Fred Saberhagen, *The Dracula Tapes* (New York: Warner, 1975), 103.
6. Anne Rice, *Interview with the Vampire* (New York: Ballantine, 1977), 23.
7. Ibid., 35.
8. Ibid., 237.
9. Ibid., 25.
10. Chelsea Quinn Yarbro, *Hotel Transylvania* (New York: St. Martin's Press, 1978), 68.
11. Katherine Ramsland, *Prism of the Night* (New York: Plume, 1992), 257.
12. Stephen King, *Danse Macabre* (New York: Everest House, 1981), 4.
13. Katherine Ramsland, "The Monster in the Mirror," *Magical Blend*, January 1991, 51.
14. Anne Rice, *The Vampire Lestat* (New York: Knopf, 1985), 138.
15. Ibid., 153.
16. Ramsland, *Prism of the Night*, 253.
17. Anne Rice, *The Queen of the Damned* (New York: Knopf, 1988), 86.
18. ———, *The Tale of the Body Thief* (New York: Knopf, 1992), 285.
19. Ibid., 223.
20. ———, *Memnoch the Devil* (New York: Knopf, 1995), 4.
21. Ibid., 337.
22. Ibid., 359.
23. Greg Cox, *The Transylvanian Library* (San Bernardino: Borgo Press, 1993), 135.
24. Martin H. Greenberg, ed., *A Taste for Blood* (New York: Barnes and Noble, 1992), xiii.
25. Linda Lael Miller, *Forever and the Night* (New York: Berkley, 1993), foreword.
26. Elaine Bergstrom, *Blood Alone* (New York: Jove, 1990), cover.
27. *Publishers Weekly*, 4 September 1995, 52.
28. Guiley, *The Complete Vampire Companion*, 98.

29. Ibid., 101.
30. Ibid.
31. Nancy Gideon, *Midnight Temptation* (New York: Pinnacle, 1994), i.
32. Phil Bedard and Larry Lalonde, *Forever Knight*, episode 203 (Toronto: Paragon, 1995).

FURTHER READING

Bergstrom, Elaine. *Blood Alone.* New York: Jove, 1990. (part of series)
Bradbury, Ray. "Homecoming" (1946). In Bradbury, Ray. *October Stories.* New York: Ballantine, 1956.
Brite, Poppy Z. *Lost Souls.* New York: Delacorte, 1992. (part of series)
Bunson, Matthew. *The Vampire Encyclopedia.* New York: Crown, 1993.
Carter, M. L., ed. *The Curse of the Undead.* Greenwich: Fawcett, 1970.
Charnas, Suzy McKee. *The Vampire Tapestry.* New York: Simon and Schuster, 1980.
Collins, Nancy. *Sunglasses After Dark.* New York: Onyx, 1989. (part of series)
Cook, John Peyton. *Out for Blood.* New York: Avon, 1991.
Cox, Greg. *The Transylvanian Library.* San Bernardino: Borgo Press, 1993.
Dalby, Richard, ed. *Dracula's Blood.* New York: Dorset, 1991.
Daniels, Les. *The Black Castle.* New York: Ace, 1979.
Elrod, P. N. *Bloodlist.* New York: Ace, 1990. (part of series)
Ferraro, Susan. "Novels You Can Sink Your Teeth Into." *New York Times Magazine*, 14 October 1990.
Gates, David. "Queen of the Spellbinders." *Newsweek*, 5 November 1990.
Gelder, Ken. *Reading the Vampire.* London: Routledge, 1994.
Gideon, Nancy. *Midnight Temptation.* New York: Pinnacle, 1994.
Gomez, Jewelle. *The Gilda Stories.* Ithaca: Firebrand, 1991.
Greenberg, Martin H., ed. *A Taste for Blood.* New York: Barnes and Noble, 1992.
Guiley, Rosemary Ellen. *The Complete Vampire Companion.* New York: Prentice Hall Macmillan, 1994.
Hambly, Barbara. *Those Who Hunt the Night.* New York: Ballantine, 1988.
Huff, Tanya. *Blood Price.* New York: DAW, 1991. (part of series)
Kilpatrick, Nancy, ed. *Love Bites.* New York: Pocket Books, 1994.
King, Stephen. *Danse Macabre.* New York: Everest House, 1981.
———. *'Salem's Lot.* Garden City, New York: Doubleday, 1975.
Knight, Amarantha, ed. *Love Bites.* New York: Masquerade Books, 1995.
Lichtenberg, Jacqueline. *Those of My Blood.* New York: St. Martin's Press, 1988.

Lee, Tanith. *Sabella.* New York: DAW, 1980.
Lumley, Brian. *Necroscope.* New York: TOR, 1988. (part of series)
Martin, George R. R. *Fevre Dream.* New York: Pocket Books, 1982.
Mattheson, Richard. *I Am Legend.* New York: Fawcett, 1954.
McCammon, Robert R. *They Thirst.* New York: Avon, 1981.
———, ed. *Under the Fang.* New York: Pocket Books, 1981.
McMahan, Jeffrey N. *Somewhere in the Night.* Boston: Alyson, 1988.
Miller, Linda Lael. *Forever and the Night.* New York: Berkley, 1993.
Newman, Kim. *Anno Dracula.* London: Simon and Schuster, 1992.
Polidori, John. *The Vampyre.* 1918.
Preiss, Byron, ed. *The Ultimate Dracula.* New York: Dell, 1991.
Ramsland, Katherine. "The Monster in the Mirror." *Magical Blend*, January 1991.
———. *Prism of the Night: A Biography of Anne Rice.* New York: Plume, 1992.
———. *The Vampire Companion.* New York: Ballantine, 1993.
Ricapito, Maria. "Creeping Back into Vogue." *New York Times*, 13 August 1995, section 2:11.
Rice, Anne. *Interview with the Vampire.* New York: Knopf, 1976. (Ballantine printing, 1977)
———. *Memnoch the Devil.* New York: Knopf, 1995.
———. *The Queen of the Damned.* New York: Knopf, 1988.
———. *The Tale of the Body Thief.* New York: Knopf, 1992.
———. *The Vampire Lestat.* New York: Knopf, 1985.
Romkey, Michael. *I, Vampire.* New York: Fawcett, 1990.
Ryan, Alan, ed. *Vampires: Two Centuries of Great Vampire Stories.* New York: Doubleday, 1987.
Saberhagen, Fred. *The Dracula Tapes.* New York: Warner, 1975. (part of series)
Smith, Evelyn E. "Softly While You're Sleeping" (1961). In Carter, M. L. *The Curse of the Undead.* Greenwich: Fawcett, 1961.
Sommer-Bodenburg, Angela. *My Friend, the Vampire.* New York: Mistrel Books, 1985. (part of series)
Somtow, S. P. *Vampire Junction.* New York: Berkley, 1984.
Stoker, Bram. *Dracula.* Westminster, U.K.: Constable, 1897.
Streiber, Whitley. *The Hunger.* New York: Morrow, 1981.
Sturgeon, Theodore. *Some of Your Blood.* New York: Ballantine, 1961.
Tilton, Lois. *Vampire Winter.* New York: Pinnacle, 1990.
Varney the Vampyre. London: E. Lloyd, 1847.
Wilson, F. Paul. *The Keep.* New York: Morrow, 1981.
Yarbro, Chelsea Quinn. *Hotel Transylvania.* New York: St. Martin's Press, 1978. (part of series)

Anne Rice and the Gothic Tradition

Bette Roberts

In 1990, Anne Rice told Susan Ferraro that she was annoyed by a reviewer's dismissing her as strictly a popular writer.[1] Two years later, in a television interview, she again expressed her eagerness to earn an academic audience, but she no longer felt the same frustration with her lack of serious critical attention; she had come to appreciate the enthusiastic response from a wide popular audience and enjoy a special relationship with her readers. With several full-length books and scholarly articles on her work published since 1993, along with two collections of critical essays forthcoming, Rice has now achieved what few writers can claim to have done: captured both a large popular readership and the attention of an academic audience. Her unique success has not only revitalized the genre of gothic fiction, which began in 1764 with Horace Walpole's *The Castle of Otranto*, but restored its literary richness and helped to establish it as a literary form worthy of critical exploration. Her original adaptations of vampiric fiction are particularly notable for their combination of the philosophical and psychological depth of romantic myths with issues that appeal to the fears and anxieties of readers confronting the realities of the late twentieth century.

In Rice's discussions of critical prejudice against gothic novels, she defends her choice of fictional materials and calls attention to the problems the genre has had in being taken seriously by literary scholars. Acknowledging the contribution of her Catholic upbringing to the kind of novels she wants to write, she explains in an interview in *Playboy* that many critics tend to believe that "to be profound a book has to be about the middle class and about some specific domestic problem of the middle class,"[2] a stance that she effectively argues reflects the triumph of a Protestant vision over the Catholic. Portrayals of the real, interior lives of people working out small problems and achieving moments of awareness is, according to Rice, "the essence of what Protestantism came to be in America," a faith in "the less magical, more practical, more down-to-earth," and for Rice, "the more sterile."[3] Like her forerunner Horace Walpole, she prefers the unreal and the marvelous, the grand lives of supernatural characters, and sees her choices as the result of her being "nourished on" the miraculous stories of Catholic saints that provided vivid memories for the creation of her vampires.

A brief history of gothic criticism shows that Rice's need to defend her romantic approach to novel writing is justified. Almost nothing was written about the genre before the 1970s. In part, the sparsity of early gothic studies was caused by Ian Watt's immensely influential *The Rise of the Novel* (1957), which established realism as the criteria for novel assessment, the "Protestant" standard to which Rice refers in the *Playboy* interview. Supernatural characters, medieval ruins, and horrific events acceptable as powerful metaphors in romantic poetry were deemed unworthy of serious textual analysis when they moved over from poetry to fiction. Before the mid-1970s, few doctoral candidates wrote dissertations on romantic novels. However, nearly every scholar of the gothic today acknowledges the pioneering Edith Birkhead, Montague Summers, and Devendra Varma, whose critical tasks in the 1920s through the 1950s included the sheer identification and recovery of gothic texts as well as attempts to define and legitimize the genre.

Between these early efforts and the real development of criticism in the late 1970s were several important contributors who took the gothic seriously: in 1932, J. M. S. Tompkins's *The Popular Novel in England: 1770–1800*, a cultural exploration of the relationships between popular readers' fantasies and the gothic, among other genres; Leslie Fiedler's psychosocial commentary on gothic and American literature in his 1960 *Love and Death in the American Novel*; Paul Frankl's comprehensive historical study *The Gothic: Literary Sources and Interpretations through Eight Centuries*, also in 1960; and Irving Malin's 1962 *New American Gothic*, a discussion of symbolic functions of gothic devices in contemporary literature not usually regarded as gothic.

It is perhaps no coincidence that while serious criticism of the gothic began belatedly in the 1970s, it virtually exploded during the late 1970s and 1980s, at exactly the time Rice was writing her gothic novels. Indeed, these new approaches to textual analysis helped to provide the literary climate in which the genre flourished. Extremely useful surveys of gothic fiction were published during this time that provided new reasons for interest in the genre: for example, Elizabeth MacAndrew's *The Gothic Tradition in Fiction* (1979) and David Punter's psychological-cultural *The Literature of Terror: A History of Gothic Fictions from 1765 to the Present Day* (1980). Shortly after Coral Ann Howells analyzed sensibility and the gothic heroine in *Love, Mystery, and Misery: Feeling in Gothic Fiction* (1978), Stephen King wrote his informal psychosocial study of the genre in *Danse Macabre* in 1979. While William Patrick Day traced the gothic as a subversion of the romantic in his book *In the Circles of Fear and Desire* in 1985, and Eve Kosofsky Sedgwick explored underlying gender issues in *The Coherence of Gothic Conventions* (1986), Kate Ferguson Ellis saw the gothic as a fantasized protest against values of the hearth in *The Contested Castle: Gothic Novels and the Subversion of Domestic Ideology* in 1989. In the same year, Joseph Grixti explored relationships between gothic fiction and popular audience in *Terrors of Uncertainties: The Cultural Contexts of Horror Fiction*. These and many other dissertations and articles on the gothic provide researchers today with excellent resources. In addition, there are at least two comprehensive bibliographies of primary and secondary materials: Frederick Frank's *Gothic Fiction: A Master List of Twentieth-Century Criticism and Research* (1987) and Benjamin Fisher's *The Gothic's Gothic: Study Aids to the Tradition of the Tale of Terror* (1988).

It is difficult to keep up with the current profusion of scholarship on the gothic, as new critical theories—psychoanalytic, feminist, reader-response, new historicist, culturalism—provide fresh interpretations. These new approaches are especially appropriate for a genre that, as Punter explains, relies on the fictional truth of the imagination rather than the truth of real experience[4] and shared cultural, as well as psychological, fears. That Rice's work attracts serious new scholarship, such as Barbara Waxman's postexistential analysis of *Interview with the Vampire* and Doane and Hodges's study of postfeminism in The Vampire Chronicles, attests to her role in dignifying the tradition and promoting critical interest that benefits the whole genre.

The psychological power and potential of gothic fiction to address compelling fears and engage in philosophical debates is part of the tradition and inherent to the mixture of real and unreal elements that began in Horace Walpole's *The Castle of Otranto*, which was clearly a reaction against the dominant vogue of fictional realism. Stating that the reader's fancy had been "dammed up" in the realist novel, Walpole planned to move away from the "strict adherence to common life"[5] to arouse the reader's imagination. The means he chose—the supernatural, the dreary castle, the prevailing atmosphere of fear and menace—inspired many other eighteenth-century novelists, such as Clara Reeve, and influenced the genre's two best-known forerunners, Ann Radcliffe and Matthew Lewis.

Ann Radcliffe and Matthew Lewis are the Samuel Richardson and Henry Fielding of the gothic. Just as Richardson and Fielding originated two major traditions in the history of realistic novel writing (the psychological, interior focus of Richardson's *Pamela* and the more exterior, panoramic scope of Fielding's *Tom Jones*), Radcliffe and Lewis established two different mainstreams of gothic fiction with identifiable characteristics still labeled as female and male. Despite the exceptions of newly recovered texts by women writers, and the obvious variations and mixtures of these characteristics over the history of the genre that have now made the typing of early gothic novels by gender a controversial issue in gothic studies, these gender distinctions still hold for the majority of early gothics and account for certain popular variations of the genre today.

Women writers following the Radcliffean tradition focused on the prolonged pursuit of the pure and passive heroine by the aggressive male villain in a dark, labyrinthine setting that intensified anxiety and fear throughout the novel. Usually, all ended well as the threats of the villain, whose powers appeared to be supernatural, were seldom realized, and the virtuous heroine, like Emily St. Aubert in Radcliffe's *The Mys-*

teries of Udolpho (1794), emerged triumphant over her oppressor. This restoration of moral order was accompanied by a return to the rational as well, since the seemingly supernatural elements were reduced to the natural by an elaborate, contrived explanation at the end of the action.

This moral rationalism was not the case with gothic novels written by men, in the tradition established by Matthew Lewis in *The Monk* (1796) and continued most powerfully in Charles Robert Maturin's *Melmoth the Wanderer* (1820). Though the persecution of the virtuous heroine still drove the plot, the male writer shifted the focus of interest from the heroine threatened by male villainy to the villain-hero, whose evil nature could indeed be aggrandized by his supernatural nature, such as vampirism. The innocent young woman did not stand a chance against this power; unlike her Radcliffean counterparts, she could actually be murdered, or worse, seduced or raped. Lengthy atmospheric descriptions conventional in the women novelists' works were discarded in favor of erotic and violent sensationalism, as the tormented villain indulged appetites only imagined in most women's gothics: hence the distinction between the atmosphere of psychological terror in the female gothic novels and that of physical horror in those written by men. The reader was asked to suspend disbelief in the actual and experience the reality of supernatural evil before the blackguard was destroyed.

Unlike male writers, who exposed the horrors of evil within, female writers depicted terrors caused by evil without, a distinction that reflected the social conservatism of their readers. Since the innocence of the heroine was never violated, she upheld and perpetuated the idealized virtues assigned to women in a patriarchal social structure—delicacy, fortitude, and chastity—by means of passive resistance. At the same time, she revealed the anxieties of women in a subordinate social position, particularly those who had to endure oppression and persecution by men. As many recent feminist critics have pointed out, the nature of evil was equated with male tyranny, with the villain remaining an unsympathetic character whose powers were finally removed and moral order was restored. The tremendous popularity of this genre with women writers and readers in late-eighteenth-century England shows that it addressed particularly female concerns. Women who were dominated by men related to fantasies of victory and freedom that did not require overstepping ideal codes of behavior. Commenting on the impact of women writers on the late-eighteenth-century novel, Tompkins writes that "in their hands the novel was not so much a reflection of life as a counterpoise to it, within the covers of which they looked for compensation, for ideal pleasures and ideal revenge."[6] The extent to which these early gothics gratified female readers accounted for the popularity of this relatively new genre.

In the gothic novels written by men, the focus on the villain-hero allowed the reader to identify with the source of evil, as the torment, rebellion, and power of this larger-than-life figure called up all forbidden desires: the beast within, the id, the subconscious. Convincingly identified by psychoanalytic critics of the gothic as a major, if not *the* major, source of the genre's appeal, the evil deeds and escapades of the gothic protagonist provided a vicarious experience of sensational pleasures taboo in actual life, where these desires were repressed. As Stephen King puts it, the horror scene is "an invitation to indulge in deviant, antisocial behavior by proxy—to commit gratuitous acts of violence, indulge our puerile dreams of power, to give in to our most craven fears."[7]

This subversion of conservative, middle-class values of restraint and respectability was simply too great a leap for most women writers to make; their more genteel gothicism, while revealing discomfort with the status quo, certainly was not openly rebellious. Women protagonists ultimately found their happiness in marriage and the social community. While the villains of the early gothic novels written by men exhibited a psychological power comparable with the Promethean figures of romantic poetry, evil played a secondary role to the portrayal of exemplary virtue in early women's gothics, and extensive didacticism justified the sensational action. Emily's learning to control her excessive sensibility was more important than Montoni's death in Radcliffe's *Udolpho*; Ambrosio's grisly destruction by Satan in Lewis's *The Monk* was paramount. Despite these different emphases, however, both traditions have depended on well-defined roles of male aggression and female passivity.

Surveying the scene of gothic fiction today, we see that the original distinctions are blurred and less meaningful. Clearly identifiable traits of the gothic—ghosts, monsters, hauntings, and other supernatural threats to humans—have merged with elements of other genres to form gothic science fiction, gothic detective fiction, gothic erotica, and other hybrids. Vestiges of the gender distinctions are evident in the contemporary pulp extremes of both types: the purely violent gothics that wallow in grisly gore and the equally shallow formulaic gothic romances now sold widely. With few exceptions, Radcliffean gothicism still dominates the popular gothic novels written by female writers for female readers. As Janice Radway explains, "Romance reading and writing might be seen therefore as a collectively elaborated female ritual through which women explore the consequences of their common social condition as the appendages of men and attempt to imagine a more perfect state where all the needs they so intensely feel and accept as given would be adequately addressed."[8] Despite modernizations of the female protagonists, the Radcliffean model continues, in that the plot hinges on the prolonged terror caused by male oppression of female, with the struggle ending in a fortunate male-female union. In today's more liberated gothics, writers may describe actual sexual violence, and acceptable choices of lovers may include rakish Lovelace types capable of reformation. Still, the predominant gothic novel sold over hundreds of bookstore counters to women readers remains conservative, nongraphically erotic, and Radcliffean.

In stark contrast, Anne Rice's gothics are non-Radcliffean. Just as Mary Shelley's *Frankenstein* transcended the boundaries of women gothic writers in 1818 and eradicated lines between male and female traditions, Rice's androgynous, philosophical, and erotic gothicism eludes gender distinctions. She immerses her readers in a supernatural world where physical violence is enacted primarily by romantic villain-heroes (such as Louis, Lestat, and Lasher) reminiscent of Melmoth, Victor Frankenstein, and Dr. Jekyll, burdened with inescapable physical conditions (vampirism, supernatural powers) that exaggerate their separateness from humanity. Rather than conform to the stereotype of male villains persecuting females, her sympathetic and self-divided protagonists stand for humans confronting the existential realities of the late twentieth century and timeless ontological issues. Their bizarre, violent experiences create dilemmas that call into question the purpose of their lives. As Susan Ferraro describes Rice's vampires, "They are lonely, prisoners of circumstance, compulsive sinners, full of self-loathing and doubt. They are, in short, Everyman Eternal."[9] Like their Byronic ancestors, they journey toward violence, suffering, awareness, and renewal. The imprisonment from which they are liberated is not the oppression of men over women but that resulting from Blakean mind-forged manacles, their own delusions concerning social institutions and religious myths.

While Rice has written four nonvampiric gothic novels (*The Mummy, The Witching Hour, Lasher*, and *Taltos)*, analysis of The Vampire Chronicles most effectively demonstrates her place in the gothic tradition because the conventions of vampire fiction are so well established. Her adaptations of vampirism expand the possibilities of a genre increasingly narrowed by stereotypical conventions and popular trivialization over the years. This artistic freedom is apparent in the wide-open space and global travel back and forth through centuries in her gothics, as compared with the claustrophobic interiors of many contemporary female gothics, and in the abandonment of traditional gender roles in the action. Eroticism becomes part of a liberating psychological process instead of a forbidden pleasure associated with male-female pursuits in conventional gothic romances. Endings concern vampires' struggles and personal triumphs instead of humans' moral victories over villains.

Other than the Frankenstein myth, whereby the unlawful creation unleashed on us can assume many different shapes depending on the current technology that we fear, perhaps no other gothic image is as persistent, powerful, and therefore appropriate for "cultural self-analysis" as that of the vampire. Joseph Grixti explains that "the figure of the vampire is one whose history is interestingly intertwined with the public and private concerns of the epochs which popularized and endorsed it as an objectification of uncertainly understood and disturbing phenomena."[10] Commenting on the longevity of the vampire myth, Ken Gelder points out that "it can be made to appeal to or generate fundamental urges located somehow 'beyond' culture (desire, anxiety, fear), while simultaneously it can stand for a range of meanings and positions *in* culture."[11] Since the actual supernaturalism of the vampire's existence and the eroticism of its attacks were considered improper subject matter for women writers, the vampire was the province of male writers since the early nineteenth century, culminating with Bram Stoker's great prototype, *Dracula*, in 1897.

Critical explorations of Stoker's novel have established the richness and potential power of the myth, where the villains' human appetites and transgressions are both feared and envied by Victorian readers. David Punter sees the Count's appeal to a Victorian audience as based on repression, loss of religious faith, empiric decline, and evolutionary theory; he argues that the novel illustrates the "continuous oscillation between reassurance and threat" that is the "central dialectic of Gothic fiction."[12]

Though there are too many variations of the vampire myth today to include here, Stephen King's *'Salem's Lot* (1975) and Whitley Strieber's *The Hunger* (1981) are notable, since both represent extremely successful combinations of traditional elements of vampirism and original adaptations that illustrate contemporary vampire fiction. King's frighteningly credible Mr. Barlow poses with the British Straker as a reputable antique dealer and turns a small town in southern Maine into a community of horrors. Though Ben Mears and Mark Petrie seem finally to destroy Barlow in the traditional way, with a stake through his heart, Barlow's teeth remain alive. Also,

Barlow's progeny, made up of familiar townspeople, live on, as is evident from the number of bizarre deaths reported in the local newspaper. As Ben and Mark leave the town permanently, they realize that the fire they set will dislodge but not destroy all of the undead.

Whitley Strieber's Miriam is a highly intelligent female vampire who allows herself to be examined by her major adversary, Sarah, a doctor researching potential links between genetics and aging. In this feminist confrontation (men are clearly the weaker characters in *The Hunger*), the best human resources prove ineffective, as it is Sarah, not Miriam, who is destroyed. Sarah ends up locked inside one of Miriam's trunks, in total darkness, listening to the "little rustlings and sighs" that "filled the air around her, coming from other chests" that have lain there in the attic for centuries.[13]

Both King's and Strieber's vampires demonstrate Leonard Wolf's description of the power of Dracula: "The vampire of greatest interest is, of course, the man or woman of overwhelming ego and energy whose will for an evil life is so great that he will not die or who, when surprised by death, has reacted with a burst of rage against the inevitable and refuses to lie still."[14] They are also ruthless and indestructible. As in many contemporary gothics that reflect a loss of belief in the establishment forces to overpower evil, their threat to the human race persists.

Rice's vampires live on as well, though not because humans are powerless to defeat them. Her vampires have an entirely different agenda. Instead of evil forces that threaten human survival, they serve as metaphors for humans who, having lost their connection to humanity, try to recover truths to live by. Unlike Count Dracula, Louis and Lestat become sympathetic and indestructible characters who illustrate Brian Frost's observation that in "contemporary horror novels the prevailing trend is to portray vampires as highly intellectual beings living a separate but not entirely incompatible existence alongside the human race, with the pursuance of knowledge (rather than nubile maidens) as their main recreation."[15] Louis resembles the world-weary Tithonus, who, in Tennyson's poem of that name, sees himself as a "grey shadow, once a man," in his alienation from mortality; Lestat, despite his bravado and Promethean rebellion against insignificance, searches for meaning through different quests in each novel.

The most radical variation in Rice's vampiric gothics is her shifting the narrative perspective from humans to vampires and developing interrelations among vampires rather than between vampires and humans, an adaptation that entails other major departures from the tradition. In *Interview*, she updates the discovered-manuscript device, often used in gothics to allow for the first person and to distance the supernatural, with the interview format, as the vampire Louis tells his story to a young man. Unlike the human recorders struggling to defeat Dracula, Louis's voice is appropriate for Rice's focus on his anguish as a vampire and his search for meaning. The device also frames the action in the same way as Robert Walton's letters contribute to the theme of unnatural ambition in *Frankenstein*: since the interviewer asks to be made a vampire at the end of Louis's narration, he confirms the decadence of late-twentieth-century mortals, who see only the power and pleasure of vampirism and not the pain. The voice creates suspense as well, since the reader knows that Louis's compassion for humans is greatly diminished, that the interview takes place at night, and that the two men are alone. Though Louis tries to put the interviewer at ease, he also tells him that he would be "very foolish" not to fear him.

Achieving an effective concentration on Louis with this single voice, Rice experiments with more complicated narrative perspectives when she shifts to Lestat as the protagonist. In the next two Vampire Chronicles, *The Vampire Lestat* and *The Queen of the Damned*, she interrupts the present-tense narration with other characters' stories that recount events deep in the past, and she uses multiple narrators to develop simultaneous actions and converging plots. As in *Dracula*, the experiences of different narrators create delicious ironies and suspense when the reader knows more than the characters do; however, in *Dracula* we fear that the humans may not be fast and clever enough against the Count. In Rice's novels, the menace arises from within the community of vampires—from Lestat's incurring other vampires' wrath and from the most powerful Akasha's destroying any other vampire who gets in her way. In *Lestat* we follow separate groups of characters in their movements toward a huge confrontation at Lestat's San Francisco rock concert; in alternating stories in *The Queen of the Damned*, Akasha and Maharet prepare for the battle between their forces. In this novel Rice loses the intensity of effect of *Interview* yet achieves an equally creative, epiclike saga in linking vampirism with ancient mysteries, primitive rituals, and Jungian archetypal myths, which are appropriate for the two centuries of Lestat's rites of passage. He writes his autobiography in *Lestat* on a word processor in hopes that his story will reenergize vampires and liberate humans by showing them real evil.

Instead of the solitary attack that exemplifies the horror of *Dracula*, the majority of violence in the Chronicles arises from large orgiastic scenes that indicate more about human desire for sensation as an antidote to general malaise than about the evil of vampires: the Parisian performance in the Theatre of

Vampires in *Interview*, the rock concert that mirrors Druidic ceremonies of human sacrifice in *Lestat*, the pagan rituals and Akasha's massacre of males in *QD*. In these scenes of frenzy painted on a large canvas, the vampires echo unfulfilled, unaware human beings in their vulnerability to be exploited. The mindless thrills of the mob reveal the importance of independent thought in order to detect the false motives of social institutions and individuals who feed on human need and perpetrate violence for their own ends.

In *The Tale of the Body Thief* and *Memnoch the Devil*, Rice leaves behind the large casts of characters and narrative complexities caused by simultaneous multiple voices and returns to the concentrated impact of the first-person voice so effective in *Interview*. Continuing Lestat's process of searching for new experiences and discoveries that will lead to awareness and truth, Rice again demonstrates her ingenuity with vampiric conventions by linking Lestat's justification for his vampire nature with literary allusions to Blake's "The Tyger" and Goethe's *Faust* in *The Tale of the Body Thief* and to biblical and theological controversies, along with Hawthorne's story "Ethan Brand," in *Memnoch*. Identifying with the beautiful but deadly insects in the South American rain forest, Lestat realizes that he, like Blake's tiger, has a role in the "fearful symmetry" of nature. In *Memnoch*, he remains uncertain about the meaning of his cosmic journeys with the Devil into the secrets of Heaven and Hell, an experience foreshadowed by David Talbot's reference to Ethan Brand earlier in the novel. When Brand learned the knowledge denied to humans, he "'lost his hold of the magnetic chain of humanity'"[16] and became a fiend himself because his "'moral nature had ceased to keep the pace of improvement with his intellect.'"[17] Picking up this allusion not long after receiving a note from

Memnoch suggesting that Lestat was his pawn in a larger scheme, Lestat vows not to drink human blood again, to dry up and be thrown into a kiln.[18] Inverting Hawthorne's gothic tale, where Brand's turning into limestone when he leaps to his death in a kiln symbolizes the hardening of his heart, Rice has Lestat's heart "harden" because he stops drinking human blood—that is, because of his sympathy for humans' suffering.

The primary source of gothic anxiety in Rice's fiction arises not from humans' efforts to destroy the undead but from the different psychological journeys of her vampire protagonists. Catholicism and other religious systems prove to be empty institutions unworthy of faith, so the restoration of moral order through them is not even considered. Also, since the vampires themselves become metaphors for humans who must respond to a meaningless universe and find their own truths, they are not satanic creatures to be destroyed or exorcised by crucifixes or wafers. As Armand tells Louis in *Interview*, most vampires do not have the stamina for immortality. In " 'becoming immortal they want all the forms of their life to be fixed as they are and incorruptible . . . When, in fact, all things change except the vampire himself . . . Soon, with an inflexible mind, and often even with the most flexible mind, this immortality becomes a penitential sentence.' "[19] Vampires self-destruct through the sheer boredom, loneliness, and despair of their endless lives unless they can find intimate relationships with others, adapt to change, and achieve some philosophical perspective. Often, Rice's vampires form family-like, triangular groups within the larger community, such as Lestat, Louis, and Claudia in *Interview*; Lestat, Gabrielle, and Nicolas in *Lestat*; and Maharet, Mekare, and Miriam in *QD*. Seen by Ken Gelder as variations of Eve Sedgwick's "erotic triangle" in the gothic,[20] these family members provide a sense of belonging that vampires require and miss greatly if lost, as when Claudia is burned to death and when Lestat's mother, Gabrielle, simply wanders away from him.

Obstacles in their journeys toward self-realization are usually rooted in misconceptions and delusions. Certain that being a vampire must have some purpose, Louis tries to find others of his kind to discover what it is, even to the point of seeking out Satan. Lestat, learning from Marius that vampires "have never had a true purpose,"[21] refuses to remain insignificant and tries to make a difference by using his evil nature "to do good." Later, in *Body Thief*, he experiences a rebirth of pleasure in being a vampire as a natural creature rather than a higher being. As Barbara Waxman explains, the "moral energizing" of Rice's vampires makes us suspend our aversions to them; their characters lead us to "reject the traditional compartmentalizing of good and evil."[22] As metaphors for humans confronting existential realities and liberating themselves from the false beliefs of social institutions and values, Rice's protagonists come to appreciate the beauty and barbarism of the Savage Garden, her consistent metaphor for life. With traditional human, ethical, and social systems powerless and irrelevant, it is a world where "only aesthetic principles can be verified, and these things alone remain the same."[23] Even if God created life, as the possibility certainly arises in *Memnoch*, he is indifferent to human suffering; the savagery is part of his "vision of Perfection."[24] In the end, since the vampires are telling their own tales, the reader identifies with their adventures and wonders if they will survive. Questions such as whether Louis will endure his own despair are more important than whether he can defeat the Parisian vampires; whether Lestat can conquer his aimlessness and recover his characteristic rebellious spirit takes precedence over retrieving his body from Raglan James.

Obviously these journeys cannot be undertaken by characters who show up only at night and remain in a coffin all day while humans try to figure out where they are. Rice expands their fictional world so greatly that her vampires seem constantly on the move and extremely active, which creates a restless and fast-paced atmosphere in the mainstream of the action. Riding motorcycles, driving elegant cars, taking planes, booking passages on the *QEII*, or even flying on their own, they travel from the Arctic wastes where Marius tends to Akasha and Enkil, to the tropical rain forests where Lestat meets Gretchen, to beyond the globe in the cosmos of Heaven and Hell. Their narratives in the contemporary present include comparisons and accounts of their lives in earlier centuries, with major immersions into creative historical pasts as told by Marius, Maharet, and Memnoch. Ken Gelder notes that while early vampire fictions show some link to the travelogue,[25] "contemporary vampire fiction is 'panoramic' in both space and *time*. It visits as many moments in history as it does countries, and each moment is as freely interactive in terms of class and ethnicity as the next one."[26] Within a single novel, as in *The Queen of the Damned*, Rice's keen attention to details of place lend credibility to the contemporary California scene of Lestat's rock concert and the tribal village of Maharet and Mekare. With coffin time rarely mentioned, Rice's vampires prefer warm climates and luxurious surroundings full of artistic treasures and the latest technological gadgets, such as Marius's opulent Greek island retreat in *Lestat* and Maharet's compound in the Sonoma Mountains of California in *QD*. In all of the Chronicles, New Orleans is the favored residence that vampires come home to. They relish its combination of old and new worldliness, its rich tradition and damp wilderness, its sophistication and savagery. San Francisco, too, is old-fashioned enough to make centuries-old vampires feel comfortable yet trendy and free to satisfy their modern tastes.

In Rice's occasional references to vampires' sleeping in coffins, she adapts the conventional motif to develop character traits and feelings, as when the lonely Lestat hides his coffin inside cottages to be closer to humans in *Lestat* or when he throws himself into the dirt when he feels degraded: "The earth was holding me. Living things slithered through its thick and moist clods against my dried flesh."[27] On a lighter note, when he abruptly transforms Louis into a vampire, he forgets to create a place for him, so the two have to share a coffin. In *Interview*, Claudia gives up sleeping in the same casket with Louis, who loves her as a daughter, and asserts her independence by requesting her own resting place.

The poetic use of setting to reflect emotional states recurs throughout The Vampire Chronicles, the most dramatic being Louis's nightmare of rats on a rotting altar as his illusions crumble in *Interview*[28] and Lestat's rebirth in the dazzling hideousness of the rain forest in *Body Thief*.[29] Less dramatic examples include Louis's seeing only blackness as he passes aboard ship through the Straits of Gibraltar in *Interview*,[30] a vision that matches his growing despair, and Lestat's suffering from the cold wind and snow of Georgetown, which complements his alien and unnatural state in a human body in *Body Thief*, a daring adventure he chose in order to find himself as a vampire.

Rice humanizes her vampires further as a group by providing them with a racial genealogy, of sorts, and as individuals by characterizing them according to age. Unlike the shadowy history of vampires provided by Van Helsing in

Stoker's *Dracula*, Rice's vampires have an elaborate creation story that goes back to pre-Egyptian civilization. The first vampires were created by accident when the evil spirit Amel, who had tasted human blood and wanted a physical form, invaded the bodies of Enkil and Akasha. Unwilling to destroy their own bodies in order to end this evil, Akasha and Enkil make Khayman a vampire to serve and protect them. With Khayman's transformation of others, vampirism begins.

In the process of their psychological and philosophical journeys, Rice individualizes and modernizes her vampires by creating different personalities and human traits (age, appearance, gesture, language, and attire) that are unconventional to vampirism. Though they share with their traditional counterparts a need for blood, a nighttime existence, and a fear of daylight, they have come a long way from the fanged aristocrats who wear dark capes and transform themselves into mists and bats. Louis's unhappiness is matched by his understated slim elegance, black hair, and soft green eyes; Lestat's ebullience shows up in his blond hair and purple sunglasses, use of slang, and taste for flashy clothes. He is equally comfortable in Edwardian velvet or in the black outfit he wears on his Harley-Davidson.

Distinctive human features not only humanize Rice's vampires but often convey larger meanings. Maharet's and Mekare's red hair symbolizes their link with natural fertility; Claudia's blond curls remind us of her being a mature vampire frozen in time in a child's body. Her preference for pastels contrasts with the inferior Parisian vampires, who all dye their hair black and wear black clothes in their dull conformity (thereby resembling conventional vampires). In *Interview*, the auburn-haired Armand tells Louis that even the blood of the Parisian Undead is "different, vile. They increase as we do but without skill or care."[31] In *The Queen of the Damned*, however, the blood of the Ancients is yet more powerful than that of Armand, Louis, and Lestat, until Lestat drinks from the most powerful Akasha.

In analyzing the appeal of *Dracula*, David Punter points out that blood is at the heart of the novel (his pun), with Stoker "well aware of the rich possibilities for ambiguity and bitter humour in this central motif."[32] Explaining the blood associations that Victorian readers found both subversive yet attractive, Punter explores the vampire's need for blood as a complex symbol for religious values (in an inverted way, blood sustains vampiric life), for social class issues (Dracula as the doomed aristocrat exploiting the bourgeoisie for survival), and for eroticism (the penetrating teeth and blood sucking representing both heterosexual and homosexual pleasure), all of which addressed taboos for the repressed, late-Victorian reader responding to challenges to religious faith and shifts from aristocratic power to the middle class.[33] Blood is central in Rice's vampiric fiction as well, as she retains its symbolic role and builds upon the ambiguities and associations established by Stoker. Descriptions of blood drinking, such as those between Dracula and Lucy or Mina, provide the major source of eroticism, but Rice downplays vampires' attacks on humans and focuses instead on the blood exchanges between vampires that strengthen their familial bonds and power. When vampires drink human blood, the act is integrated with other character issues. In *Body Thief*, the reborn Lestat exults in being a vampire and savors the pleasure and pain when he takes the resistant David Talbot:

> Here it comes, my beloved. Here it comes, not in little droplets, but from the very river of my being. And this time

> when the mouth clamped down upon me, it was a pain that reached all the way down to the roots of my being, tangling my heart in its burning mesh. . . . On and on he pulled, and against the bright darkness of my closed eyes I saw the thousands upon thousands of tiny vessels emptied and contracting and sagging like the fine black filaments of a spider's wind-torn web.[34]

Unlike Stoker's Count, who takes his pleasure with the young women Lucy and Mina, the sensual ecstasies of Rice's blood drinkers are often between members of the same sex, so that vampiric pleasures transcend gender roles. As Rice's biographer mentions, the vampires' blurred sexual identities account for a major source of their appeal: "Becoming a vampire involved a merging of like minds in a way prohibited to people with fundamentally different perspectives. Female readers strongly identified with Louis, and later with Lestat, because Anne provided for them a means to experience male qualities that society prizes so highly without a loss of the female-oriented perspective."[35] Doane and Hodges, who see the vampire as "ultimately maternal and the experience of initiation a preoedipal one,"[36] argue that Rice's vampire-initiation stories represent efforts to be one with the mother, a reunion that can never be fulfilled: "The pleasures of Rice's text are thus sadomasochistic pleasures, fantasies of power and surrender, linked . . . to the desires and fears of infantile dependency. . . . Rice's books are not simply enjoyed by women readers hungering for female nurturance; men hunger for the mother too."[37] While descriptions of blood drinking support this postfeminist interpretation, particularly Lestat's drinking of Dora's restorative menstrual blood in *Memnoch*, and explain in part the erotic appeal, they also show that Rice's vampires are indeed androgynous; her women are not more repressed than men or less liberated. Her female vampires, including Akasha, Gabrielle, Maharet, and Jesse, are boldly sexual and enjoy their independence and power.

Blood not only establishes family bonds that satisfy physical vampiric needs but sustains the vampire's spirit, so that it takes on sacred value. Rice often links blood drinking with images of the Catholic Holy Communion. In *Lestat*, she describes it as an act wherein "the spiritual and the carnal" come together: "Holy Communion it seemed to him, the Blood of the Children of Christ serving only to bring the essence of life itself into his understanding for the split second in which death occurred."[38] When the dying Daniel (Louis's interviewer) becomes a vampire, he is depicted as a religious supplicant at the altar of immortality receiving the body of Armand: "'Drink, Daniel.' The priest said the Latin words as he poured the Holy Communion wine into his mouth."[39] In a replay of the crucifixion in *Memnoch*, Rice brings these associations climactically together in fictional reality, as God in the form of Christ offers Lestat his blood.[40] Unlike the believing Armand, who wants to taste Christ's blood from Lestat to confirm his belief, Lestat connects it with the larger schemes of God and/or the Devil, who have tricked him into returning the veil to humans as the miracle necessary, the "infusion of blood into the very religion that Memnoch loathed."[41]

Rice's linking the drinking of blood, the vampire's signature, with larger issues of psychological quests, family bonds, and religious ambiguities demonstrates the creativity and complexity that she brings to the tradition of vampiric fiction. An important part of the lively and current critical discussion of the gothic, her vampires revitalize a genre that had seemingly run its course and become popularized into satire and triviality. Like her forerunners—Walpole, Shelley, and Stoker—whose innovative combinations of realism and the supernatural created new literary possibilities for romantic novels and new gothic myths, Rice's blend of old and new places her firmly in the gothic tradition yet opens up new realms for the vampire. The universal significance of her vampires, like the mythic figures of Frankenstein's monster and Count Dracula, makes them romantic images to be explored on a symbolic, psychological level. Louis's counterpart is surely the Romantics' cast-out Cain and Lestat the modern Prometheus, yet the threats they overcome to survive clearly appeal to the anxieties of contemporary readers.

NOTES

1. Susan Ferraro, "Novels You Can Sink Your Teeth Into," *New York Times Book Review*, 14 October 1990, 28.
2. Digby Diehl, "An Interview with Anne Rice," *Playboy*, March 1993, 60.
3. Ibid.
4. David Punter, *The Literature of Terror: A History of Gothic Fictions from 1765 to the Present Day* (New York: Longman, 1980), 408.
5. Horace Walpole, *The Castle of Otranto* (New York: Macmillan, 1963).
6. J. M. S. Tompkins, *The Popular Novel in England, 1770–1800* (Lincoln, NE: University of Nebraska Press, [1932] 1961), 129.
7. Stephen King, *Danse Macabre* (New York: Berkley, 1982), 43.
8. Janice Radway, *Reading the Romance: Women, Matriarchy, and Popular Literature* (Chapel Hill, NC: University of North Carolina Press, 1984), 212.
9. Ferraro, "Novels," 67.
10. Joseph Grixti, *Terrors of Uncertainty: The Cultural Contexts of Horror Fiction* (New York: Routledge, 1989), 14.
11. Ken Gelder, *Reading the Vampire* (New York: Routledge, 1994), 141.
12. Punter, *Literature*, 423.
13. Whitley Strieber, *The Hunger* (New York: Pocket Books, 1982), 304.
14. Leonard Wolf, *A Dream of Dracula: In Search of the Living Dead* (New York: Popular Library, 1977), 130.
15. Brian Frost, *Monster with a Thousand Faces: Guises of the Vampire in Myth and Literature* (Bowling Green, OH: Bowling Green State University Press, 1989), 24.
16. Anne Rice, *Memnoch the Devil* (New York: Knopf, 1995), 107.
17. Ibid.
18. Ibid, 351.
19. Anne Rice, *Interview with the Vampire* (New York: Knopf, 1976), 308.
20. Gelder, *Reading*, 113.
21. Anne Rice, *The Vampire Lestat* (New York: Knopf, 1985), 405.
22. Barbara Frey Waxman, "Postexistentialism in the Neo-Gothic Mode: Anne Rice's *Interview with the Vampire*," *Mosaic* 25 (summer 1992): 92.
23. Rice, *Lestat*, 124.
24. ———, *Memnoch*, 301.
25. Gelder, *Reading*, 4.
26. Ibid., 111.
27. Rice, *Lestat*, 447.

28. ———, *Interview*, 157.
29. Anne Rice, *The Tale of the Body Thief* (New York: Knopf, 1992), 344.
30. Rice, *Interview*, 181.
31. Ibid., 36.
32. Punter, *Literature*, 256–57.
33. Ibid., 259–62.
34. Rice, *Body Thief*, 418.
35. Katherine Ramsland, *Prism of the Night: A Biography of Anne Rice* (New York: Dutton, 1991), 148–49.
36. Janice Doane and Devon Hodges, "Undoing Feminism: From the Preoedipal to the Postfeminism in Anne Rice's Vampire Chronicles," *American Literary History* 2 (fall 1990): 429.
37. Ibid., 436.
38. Rice, *Lestat*, 206.
39. Anne Rice, *The Queen of the Damned* (New York: Knopf, 1988), 105.
40. Rice, *Memnoch*, 283.
41. Ibid., 341.

Lestat

THE VAMPIRE AS DEGENERATE GENIUS

Richard Noll

"It was thirst that awakened me," the vampire Lestat explains to us, "and I knew at once where I was, and what I was, too."[1] Lestat is describing the first conscious moments following his rebirth as an immortal. In contrast to his original birth in eighteenth-century France as Lestat de Lioncourt, this time he is born immediately and fully aware of who and what he is: no stainless innocent, but a monstrous amalgam of adult corpse and thirsty infant vampire whose entire being is defined by its searing lust for regeneration. A thirst for life itself.

We all suffer the blind tug of that thirst. Animal heat draws us like no other magic. We know that the stone-cold foreheads of our dead do not invite a second kiss. We crave the heat and supple motility of life. Some of us—and in this respect we are like Anne Rice's vampires—would do anything to feel it, to transcend it, a paradox of transcendence through total submission to the senses. We differ only in the degree to which we are awakened to this thirst. But it is clear that human society has no place for those of us for whom this thirst is the central fact of our being. It eventually renders us alone, outside convention, beyond good and evil, and outside conviction, except conviction in the absolute rightness, the vital necessity, of the thirst.

In the nineteenth century, the beloved century of Lestat, "that perfect moment in history, the perfect balance between the monstrous and the human,"[2] a cursed imperfection was found in the body of human society. It was first described by some notable *alienistes* of Lestat's incubatorial Paris in the 1840s. Such discoveries were shared with the physicians and alienists of Vienna and Berlin and elsewhere in Europe, and the alarm spread to the New World—to Boston and New York and no doubt to the French netherworld of New Orleans.

The shocking discovery was that within human society were individuals driven by fate to act in abominably inhuman ways. They acted on their sexual impulses with slavish frenzy. They fornicated, incested, adultered, raped, sodomized, and seduced. Morals, laws, and commandments were mere taunts. They took lives as easily as they stole kisses. They drank and drugged themselves, sleeping all day, not really working or even trying to, living only at night. Then, they lived to prey on others. They were not the day people of the bourgeoisie, but the gypsies and bohemians of the night world, those who scavenged in that fluid realm of art, music, youth, ambition, addiction, ingenuity, and criminality. True, it was said, some even masturbated to the point of madness. Many of them were called lunatics because they heard voices whispering to them at night or saw beings that other humans could not hear or see. Some were women who lapsed into strange paroxysmal trances because, so the doctors thought, they were waiting for lovers who would never arrive. Others—both male and female—were just brutish idiots or morons. Most were "morally insane." The prisons and poorhouses and madhouses were full of these abominations.

What's more, they could pass on this curse, this Dark Gift, to their progeny. But it was a perverse gift that kept on giving. Anyone who had such a person in his or her extended family also bore the stigmata of Cain. No one could escape it. Not one could escape the thirst that drove them to slither across the membranous border of sanity and decency that separates Good and Evil. So the doctors told everyone, and so everyone believed.

Sometimes a person with this Dark Gift used the acute sensitivity it also bestowed to produce writings or music or paintings or sculpture of a frightfully superhuman quality. Immortal works, in fact. But this sort of person was a fluke, a freak of nature, and despite the wonderful intellectual and artistic gifts and the taut sensitivity, this was not a condition that the *alienistes* regarded as spiritually or morally healthy. Parents were instructed by the doctors that they should never want such children. Parents instructed their children never to marry such taint.

Anne Rice does not reveal to us if, during Lestat's wanderings through the nineteenth century, he ever crossed the consulting rooms of the *alienistes*, but whether great or small they all would have recognized him instantly as one of this breed of abominations. In the nineteenth century, this Dark Gift was known in medical theory as *degeneracy* or *degeneration*, and the degenerate fluke who could produce works of immortal significance was called a *genius*. The immortality of the genius makes her or him blood kin to the vampire. Like Bram Stoker's Dracula of a century ago, Anne Rice's Lestat is the epitome, the case-history exemplar, of a degenerate genius of *our* time.

Why is this so? And what does this mean for us? Let's reenter the nineteenth century of the *alienistes*, find the roots of Anne Rice's imaginal world of The Vampire Chronicles, and explore the cultural sources of our fascination with immortality in the guise of the degenerate genius as vampire.

TAINT

THE DEGENERATE'S PRAYER

Have pity on us, good Lord, because we do the things we ought not to do, and we do not the things we ought to do—and there is no health in us. But Thou, O Lord, knowest that we are the tainted offspring of forefathers beggared in their bodies by luxury and riotous living, and of fathers who sapped their manhood in vice. Pardon our murders, our brutalities, our thefts, our crimes of cunning and cruelty, which we daily commit. Put sorrow and penitence in our hearts. Forgive our fellow men, who have helped to cripple our childhood and who now torture and curse us—for they are blind. Teach them how to be just to us, for Thou, O Lord, knowest the heart of man. All our hope is in Thee for justice, and our trust for mercy.

—*Unfinished Man* [3]

"God kills, and so shall we."

—*Lestat*[4]

Due to the work of eminent French *alienistes* Benedict Augustin Morel and Valentin Magnan, theories of hereditary degeneration dominated medical education in the latter half of the nineteenth century. By the decadent fin de siècle, the Parisian social critic Max Nordau brought it to its exaltation in popular culture with his famous, apocalyptic book of 1892, *Entartung*. Translated into English, it appeared as *Degeneration* in 1895 and became one of the cultural flashpoints that everyone that year seemed to have an opinion about. It was precisely at this time that Bram Stoker was working on his famous vampire novel that would appear two years later, and the authority of Max Nordau is indeed invoked in *Dracula*, as we shall see.

Degeneracy was thought literally to be transmitted in the protoplasm of the sperm (the germ plasm) to a man's progeny, and the physical and mental stigmata of degeneration were thought to worsen with each new generation, leading to idiocy, further vegetation, and eventually death, until the family line died out. Although the progression of degeneracy within an individual and therefore within a family could be halted through "therapeutics" (e.g., halting substance abuse, moving away from cramped urban centers, etc.), the weakness was still passed on to the next generation. Without exception.

Thus, the theory of degeneration has been called, and rightly so, "the Christian notion of original sin embodied in the nervous system,"[5] and it obsessed persons at all levels of society at the turn of the century. "Tell me, my brothers: what do we consider bad and worst of all? Is it not *degeneration*?"[6] Nietzsche rhetorically asked the world in *Also Sprach Zarathustra* and the world agreed.

We associate vampires with the delicious decadence of the fin de siècle. It was of course the appearance of Count Dracula in 1897 who set the tone for us, but this image of nineteenth-century satanic opulence and urban chic continues throughout Anne Rice's The Vampire Chronicles and in movies such as Francis Ford Coppola's *Bram Stoker's Dracula*. In our imagination, fin de siècle Europe will always be the Age of Vampires. The same can be said to the defenders of bourgeois morality and Christian civilization of that age, for the scourge of degeneracy was sucking the life's blood out of the human race. Particularly powerful parasites had risen to the highest levels of art, music, literature, and philosophy, or so it appeared. The new artistic and intellectual trends of the 1890s were seen by many as symptoms of a fatal cultural anemia. But *their* vampires are now *our* heroes, their degenerates our geniuses.

Max Nordau tells us in *Degeneration* that the fashionable late-nineteenth-century phrase *fin de siècle* "is a name covering both what is characteristic of many modern phenomena, and also the underlying mood which in them finds expression."[7] The "modern phenomena" he had in mind could be found in late-nineteenth-century degenerate movements in art (e.g. Symbolism), literature (Tolstoism, Symbolism, Naturalism, Realism), music ("the Richard Wagner cult," as Nordau refers to it), and philosophy (Schopenhauer and Nietzsche). Nordau's *Degeneration* is a massive diagnostic assessment of fin de siècle culture. This is how "Mad Max" sees it:

> The proposition which I set myself to prove may now be taken as demonstrated. In the civilized world there obviously prevails a twilight mood which finds expression, amongst other ways, in all sorts of odd aesthetic fashions. All these new tendencies, realism or naturalism, "decadentism," neo-mysticism, and their subvarieties, are manifestations of degeneration and hysteria, and identical with the mental stigmata which the observations of the clinicists have unquestionably established as belonging to these. But both degeneration and hysteria are the consequences of the excessive organic wear and tear suffered by the nations through the immense demands on their activity, and through the rank growth of large towns.[8]

"Dr. Max Nordau has by his book, *Degeneration*, produced no small sensation throughout the world," admits an anonymous reviewer in the 1896 volume *Regeneration: A Reply to Max Nordau*. Nordau's assertion that hereditary degeneration had progressed to the point where it tainted persons at all levels of European culture offended many—especially those in the arts—but *terrified* many more. "It is no wonder that his work has become as it were a nightmare to millions of minds," observes this same critic.

Despite the fact that one of Nordau's earlier books was ordered burned by the emperor of Austria, his contacts with influential persons of his day were quite extensive. Among these was fellow Hungarian (Nordau was originally from Budapest) and noted scholar, ethnographer, and linguist Arminius Vambery (1832–1913). Bram Stoker met Vambery several times in England and refers to him in *Dracula* (1897). It is thought by some *Dracula* scholars that Stoker based the character of Professor Dr. Van Helsing on Vambery. Based on my research on Stoker's original foundation papers for *Dracula* in the archives of the Rosenbach Museum in Philadelphia, I would argue instead that Stoker based Van Helsing on the founder of the famous University of Vienna Medical School and *protomedicus* to Empress Maria Theresa of Austria, Gerard Van Swieten, who wrote a treatise in 1766 offering various "scientific" explanations for the epidemic of vampires in the Austrian Empire of the mid-eighteenth century.

In Lestat we find echoes of Dracula. Dracula himself is the consummate fin de siècle cultural horror: something living hundreds of years yet dead, something dead but undead, draining the vitality of the living, like the traditions of European civilization itself. Bram Stoker deliberately sets much of *Dracula* in a cauldron of degeneration—a private madhouse run by Dr. Seward—and he based his character of Count Dracula on the prevailing psychiatric image of the degenerate.

Stoker's reliance on psychiatric textbooks concerned with degeneration is explicit. In chapter 25 of Stoker's *Dracula*, Dr. Van Helsing uses descriptions from the eminent Italian alienist and criminologist Caesare Lombroso to describe Dracula's essence to Mina Harker, who then, while in a somnambulistic trance, repeats back to Van Helsing: "The Count is a criminal type. Nordau and Lombroso would so classify him, and *qua* criminal he is of imperfectly formed mind."[9]

Count Dracula is degeneracy personified to the late-nineteenth-century reader, and Lestat is no less for our fin de siècle. But while that era's publishing houses and newspapers and arbiters of public taste and protectors of public decency, let alone the still-timid public, could only feel satisfied by a novel in which degeneracy was put down—the climactic killing of Dracula—Lestat thrives in The Vampire Chronicles and becomes the icon of immortality for millions. Count Dracula only makes sense in a world of degeneration and decay in which Good must needs triumph over Evil, where souls are saved for a better life in eternity. Immortality is assured through good deeds and faith in God. Lestat only makes sense in a world that has evolved beyond Good and Evil, beyond God and the Deceiver, in a post-Darwinian world red in tooth and claw that no longer offers the possibility of a soul's eternal salvation or damnation. To many in the nineteenth century, moral "laws" were inherent in nature itself, and adherence to the social and legal codes of civilization that were thought to reflect these natural laws was unquestioned. Rice's vampires—and in particular Lestat, who demonstrates the falsehoods of the rigid social and moral codes of the Parisian coven of vampires in *The Vampire Lestat*—are a law unto themselves and, like so many today, twist and bend their boundaries of sanity and morality to adapt to raw life. To Anne Rice's readers—that is, to us—Lestat offers the amoral, polymorphously perverse, bond-breaking path of pure genius as the way of eternal life.

MAD GENIUS

In the nineteenth century, genius and degeneration were sometimes linked by "madness." This is reflected in Stoker's invocation of Nordau and Lombroso, two of the most famous alienists of the late nineteenth century. Count Dracula is not only morally insane, he is a "mad genius." Dracula's intellect is acknowledged by Van Helsing as a formidable one, and the King of the Vampires is an evil genius. A standard medical textbook of the era warns of such dangerous characters:

> A degenerate may be a scientist, an able lawyer, a great artist, a poet, a mathematician, a politician, a skilled administrator, and present from a moral standpoint profound defects, strange peculiarities and surprising lapses of conduct. As the moral element—the emotions and propensities—is the base of determination, it follows that these brilliant faculties are at the service of a bad cause, of the instincts and appetites which, thanks to defects of the will, lead to very extravagant or very dangerous acts.[10]

The nineteenth-century fantasy of the "mad genius" continues to live in the twentieth century, particularly in any movie or book that contains his or her modern incarnation in the form of the "mad scientist." However, although Van Helsing's rendering the King of the Undead as a degenerate genius made sense to the nineteenth-century reader of *Dracula*, modern readers have long since forgotten how to "read" Stoker's book in that way—that is, as a dual psychiatric "case history" of the degenerate relationship between an immortal vampire (Dracula) and a mortal one (Renfield).

When it comes to Anne Rice, the psychiatric filter is entirely absent from her vision of Lestat. That he and indeed all vampires engage in vile acts that we associate with the evil and the mad is certain: sadism, murder, the drinking of blood. By the standard of his beloved nineteenth century, Lestat is a degenerate par excellence. But Rice keenly reflects the age in which we live by stepping out of this trap and refusing to portray him as a reflection of society's worst possible fantasy of its ills, as Dracula had been for the Victorian age. Lestat, despite being degenerate, is not depicted as the epitome of Evil, in its old sense, but is a "new evil." Instead of being reviled, he is cheered on by the legions of Anne Rice devotees as Lestat the genius-hero who is beyond Good and Evil and personifies the ultimate in personal freedom. He is a degenerate genius, but, because he's in the twentieth century, he's not a "mad" one.

GENIUS IS ITS OWN REWARD

"Don't you see?" I said softly. "It is a new age. It requires a new evil. And I *am* that new evil. . . . I am the vampire for these times!"

—*Lestat*[11]

To understand Lestat, we must understand what a "genius" was in the late eighteenth century, during which he lived as a mortal in France, when the notion of genius was not so closely linked to madness as it had become by the end of the nineteenth century.

Since the late eighteenth century, the conventional wisdom was that a genius was an original, born and not made. Generations of young people in the nineteenth century imitated genius using the blueprint provided by the philosopher Arthur Schopenhauer in 1844, who was improving upon the Romantic notion of genius from the century prior: "Genius is its own reward; for the best that one is, one must necessarily be for oneself."[12] Direct perception of the realm of Platonic ideas operating in life is his gift, for, as Schopenhauer tells those aspiring to greatness, "always to see the universal in the particular is precisely the fundamental character of genius."[13]

The genius has unusual powers of perception and intuition that set him or her apart from other mortals. Such a person is hypersensitive to the sensory world and can see, feel, hear, and imagine beyond the range of others. Schopenhauer tells us:

> The achievement of *genius*, on the other hand, transcends not only others' capacity of achievement, but also their capacity of apprehension; therefore they do not become immediately aware of it. Talent is like the marksman who hits a target which others cannot reach; genius is like the marksman who hits a target, as far as which others cannot even see.[14]

Thus they have a sixth sense, can see around the corners of time, and are unusually absorptive. In this last respect they are spongelike, and can swallow everything, like the open-beak hearts of children. Schopenhauer tells us that the genius is "childlike"; indeed, "every genius [is] to a certain extent a child . . . Therefore every genius is already a big child, since he looks out into the world as into something strange and foreign, a drama, and thus with purely objective interest."[15] To be a genius as an adult one must see with the eyes of a child. Or feel reborn with the heart and eyes of one.

The creative life of a genius stands outside convention, often even outside human society, and like the Nietzschean *Übermensch* he obeys only his own inner law. He—using the eighteenth- and nineteenth-century gendered notions of genius, for until only very recently the prejudice was that only males were capable of genius—is misunderstood in his own time and therefore must live "essentially alone." His creations are of eternal value and created ex nihilo—that is, without leaving footprints on the shoulders of any giants.

Genius is godlikeness. Rather, it is making manifest the latent immortal god within. One becomes great, according to Schopenhauer, if one's works have a superhuman quality, "and accordingly, what he produces or creates is then ascribed to a *genius* different from him, which takes possession of him."[16] When one becomes immortal, one feels oneself becoming a stranger to oneself. One has new, strange thirsts.

In the world of Anne Rice's The Vampire Chronicles, where vampires are the new gods, this is very much how those reborn and reawakened as vampires describe the experience of receiving the Dark Gift. All vampires receive it, but most never realize the promise of its power. It is only in Lestat that we find the Dark Gift enabling true genius to explode.

THE VAMPIRE GENIUS TRIUMPHANT

If we carefully examine Lestat in just the first two novels, *Interview* and *Lestat*, we see that his biography bears the unmistakable imprint of the mythic tale of genius in its original prealienist, Romantic, and Schopenhauerian senses. It is no wonder that Anne Rice's Lestat has a public following like no other vampire in literary history. He is, in manifold senses, truly an original.

Every bestowal of the Dark Gift is a rebirth, a transition from a mortal identity to a new state of consciousness, an awakening as a newly conscious being. No matter what the chronological age of the mortal, all new vampires are in fact thirsty neonates who must learn to feed. They are wise children, however, and come with language and knowledge and memories and practical knowledge that quickens their transition to self-sufficiency, unlike the many years of dependency suffered in their mortal lives.

Lestat is a special case, however. He is born not only with his own memories, but with the three centuries of knowledge of his "creator," the master vampire and former alchemist Magnus,[17] who then mysteriously destroys himself. Lestat is referred to as a "child" by the old queen of the Parisian coven of vampires, who knows that Lestat is in reality the first among immortals. He is a wise child born with the accumulated wisdom of the ages. No other vampire is born with such wisdom.

Lestat is awakened by his thirst. This is not merely a thirst for blood, human or otherwise, but a thirst for the world and the knowledge it brings. For example, orphaned by Magnus, he seeks the origins of his vampire kin and is led to Marius, the Wise Old Man of the vampires, who tells Lestat the creation myth of the vampires. Lestat's first days within vampire society are spent flouting their social norms and superstitions, challenging and questioning every belief, every value, every law among the undead. He is a monstrous child, an aberration, and his curiosity quickly offends. Most of the other vampires in The Vampire Chronicles may be immortal, but other than special exceptions like Louis, they seem to be a remarkably uncurious lot. It is Lestat's quest for knowledge that continually leads him to the realization of how alone, indeed, he is, and how different he is and will always be from other vampires.

Rebirth as a vampire endows one with an extraordinary enhancement of human abilities that, in most instances, are the legendary traits of genius. In *The Vampire Companion: The Official Guide to Anne Rice's The Vampire Chronicles*, Katherine Ramsland lists the following seven powers of vampires that compare favorably to much of what Schopenhauer described as the special divine qualities of the genius:

1. Heightened perception—the ability to see the environment in a fine detail that escapes most humans and to hear sounds beyond the range of the human ear. Vampires feel pleasure and pain acutely, and are much more physically sensitive than they had been as humans.[18]
2. Hyperdimensional consciousness—transcending limitations in awareness and gaining clarification on natural processes and the cycle of life and death. Lestat calls this the ability to see as if from a god's point of view.[19]
3. Lightning speed.
4. Clairvoyance—the ability to read minds and intrude on the thought processes of others.[20]
5. Androgynous power—the state of transcending socially imposed gender role limitations. As such, vampires have access to greater energy resources made available through the broader range of experiences that accompany transgender activities.[21]

6. Unitive mind—the knowledge that something greater than the individual connects the species.[22] (This is what Schopenhauer meant by the ability of the genius to see the universal in the particular.)
7. Greater concentration—the full participation in the experience of a vampire.[23]

But what of the "immortal works" of literature, art, and music that can also mark the genius? Lestat not only bestows the Dark Gift of vampiric immortality on others, making Gabrielle and Louis his "immortal works," but after his self-resurrection in the twentieth century he becomes the master of all media, writing the lyrics and music of the most successful rock music in history, indeed creating a new art form in rock and roll. His autobiography becomes a blockbuster best-seller, and his videos dominate MTV. In this new incarnation of the vampire legend in the first pages of *The Vampire Lestat*, Anne Rice successfully resurrects the Romantic genius of the late eighteenth century as Prometheus and, at times, Dionysus, bringing the fire of the immortal gods to humanity and breaking all bounds of art and sensual experience. The vampire reborn as degenerate genius.

Perhaps it is true that each generation submits to the seductions of its own unique fantasies. In an age where direct contact with the blood of another is a terrifying prospect, a unique period in human history when blood is no longer seen as the wellspring of life but is instead a symbol of death, the new, more powerful taboo against taking in the blood of another excites the equal but opposite impulse to do so. Our atavistic vampirism, our own latent degeneracy, becomes all too conscious when told we *cannot*, rather than simply "may not," do the unthinkable. For Anne Rice to mix this curiosity about the forbiddenness of blood intimacy with our equally urgent fantasies of the unlimited wealth, power, and fame of a rock star can only result in an irresistible attraction to Lestat, who acts out these abominations and triumphs for us. Unlike us, who do not have the Dark Gift, Lestat doesn't consider the need to rush to get an HIV test every time he feasts on the life juices of mortals. His acts of savage intimacy are pure, direct, unhesitating, unbound. His artistry, sublime. Rather than pathologizing genius or shunning degeneracy—as the public did in Bram Stoker's nineteenth century—icons of degenerate genius have become all that we wish we could be free to be, if we, in fact, were gods. Paradoxically, in the late twentieth century Lestat comforts us by tasting of the forbidden fruit that courses in our veins, renewing life and his creative genius by doing what we dare not do—by doing evil. When the very blood in our veins has become a lethal, corrosive substance, and all blood is now "bad," our images of divinity—including genius—change accordingly. We crave a god made in our own degenerate image. He is Lestat.

NOTES

1. Anne Rice, *The Vampire Lestat* (New York: Knopf, 1985), 109.
2. Ibid., 500.
3. Albert Wilson, *Unfinished Man* (London: Greening and Co., 1910).
4. Rice, *The Vampire Lestat*, 89.
5. Friedrich Nietzsche, *Also Sprach Zarathustra*, in Walter Kaufman, ed., *The Portable Nietzsche* (New York: Penguin, 1986), 187.
6. Ibid.
7. Max Nordau, *Degeneration* (New York: D. Appleton, 1895), 1.
8. Ibid., 43.
9. Bram Stoker, *The Essential Dracula*, Leonard Wolf, ed. (New York: Plume, 1993), 403.
10. Eugene Talbot, *Degeneracy—Its Causes, Signs, and Results* (London: Walter Scott, 1898), 315.
11. Rice, *Lestat*, 228.
12. Arthur Schopenhauer, *The World as Will and Representation*, Vol. II (New York: Dover, 1958), 37.
13. Ibid., 379.
14. Ibid.
15. Ibid., 390.
16. Ibid., 393.
17. Rice, *Lestat*, 219.
18. Anne Rice, *Interview with the Vampire* (New York: Knopf, 1976), 20.
19. Ibid., 82.
20. Rice, *Lestat*, 284.
21. Ibid., 171.
22. Anne Rice, *The Queen of the Damned* (New York: Knopf, 1988), 110.
23. Katherine Ramsland, *The Vampire Companion: The Official Guide to Anne Rice's The Vampire Chronicles* (New York: Ballantine, 1993), 127.

Interview with the Vampire

HOW THE MOVIE FINALLY GOT MADE

Katherine Ramsland

THE FIRST TEN YEARS

In the beginning was the word. Or the novel, at least. Anne Rice wrote *Interview with the Vampire* late in 1973 and it was published in hardcover by Alfred A. Knopf in May 1976. But even before it was published it sold to Paramount. Production designer Richard Sylbert, who optioned it with Marty Elfand, told Anne that he liked the novel's "polymorphous perversity." Anne wrote a screenplay with the French actor Alain Delon in mind for Louis, although she had a difficult time making her passive protagonist into a cinematic moral hero.

Throughout the script, Anne drew out certain scenes, such as Lestat's seduction of Louis, and insisted that they should look more like scenes in a foreign film than a typical American vampire movie. She was aware that the homoerotic overtones in the book might be too aggressive for film, so she understated them. She also included a scene in which a beautiful dog has obviously been killed by a vampire, showing Louis's propensity for animals more graphically than she had in the novel.

Anne finished the script, but Paramount did not put the film into production. Sylbert left, and, according to him, no one else there had enthusiasm for it. Anne soon learned from Hollywood sources that its production was stalled because it featured two male vampires, with a female child, caught up in an erotic relationship. Such a concept was too controversial. She dutifully rewrote the story, presenting alternative versions, but Paramount still failed to get the movie into production.

Eventually the project was thrown into a deal with John Travolta, then was passed over when Paramount made a new version of *Dracula* in 1979 with Frank Langella. Finally, NBC-TV commissioned a script for Richard Chamberlain by a team of writers experienced in miniseries. By now it was late in 1985. *Interview*'s sequel, *The Vampire Lestat*, had been published and was selling well. And time was running out for Paramount.

Anne's contract included a reversion clause stating that if principal photography had not commenced within ten years, the film rights reverted to her. Paramount asked for a contract extension, but producer Julia Phillips, who wanted to be involved with making the *Interview* film, urged Anne not to give it to them. If Anne got back the rights, she could sell them to CBS Theatricals, which had acquired the rights to *The Vampire Lestat*.

Anne thought it over. Then she saw a copy of the script for the television movie and was shocked by the changes in character and plot. "They had removed everything I had done that was original," she recalls, "and replaced it with a stock device. It was slick and smooth and eviscerated." She refused to extend Paramount's deadline and regained the film rights.

FROM CBS TO GEFFEN

When CBS moved away from theatricals, another company, Taft Barish, picked up the option for both *Interview* and *Lestat*, with the idea of making *Interview* into a Broadway musical. However, they eventually gave up the option, and Lorimar purchased the rights, along with those for the third vampire novel, *The Queen of the Damned*, to be published in 1988. Lorimar hired Anne to write a treatment for the project, with an emphasis on *Lestat* and *QD*. However, a writers' strike in Hollywood delayed her. Anne started to joke that the movie was cursed.

When she finally began to work on the treatment, in an effort to fend off charges of pedophilia and to preserve Claudia in the story as a child, Anne decided to turn Louis into a woman who dresses and acts like a man. She wanted to model this new character on famous transvestites of the era. In this story, Lestat falls under the female Louis's spell when he recognizes similarities between her and his mother Gabrielle. Anne envisioned an actress like Cher or Meryl Streep for this androgynous role. Someone else suggested Anjelica Huston for Lestat.

Both Anne and Lorimar were pleased with her ideas. Anne wanted Ridley Scott to direct the film because she had loved his work on *Bladerunner*. She also wanted an actor from the same movie, Rutger Hauer, to play Lestat. To her mind, he perfectly captured the coldness and cruelty she had intended for her blond vampire.

While all this was under discussion, Elton John approached Anne about putting *Interview* on Broadway. She and Julia Phillips met with him and liked what he had in mind. However, Lorimar owned the stage rights, so the project was put on hold. Very soon, Warner Brothers bought Lorimar, and Anne's script was left in limbo, although she still had a contract with Phillips. Anne liked the way Phillips seemed attuned to her story and hoped that their partnership would remain intact. Then David Geffen came along. He had tried previously to acquire the rights to *Interview*, because he loved the story. "After I read it, I thought what a great movie it would make," he said.[1] When he discovered that no one at Warner had asked for the project, he stepped forward. Warner gave it to him, through special arrangement, for Geffen Pictures. Although he was initially willing to work with Phillips, her subsequent published attacks on Hollywood contributed to Geffen's decision to fire her.

He had read Anne's treatment, but he wanted the story of *Interview* itself to be emphasized, rather than that of the Egyptian vampires, so he hired Michael Cristofer to write a script, which he then sent to Anne for her comments. While she appreciated being consulted, she read the script with a sinking heart. It seemed to contain gross inaccuracies that changed her characters and plot and that would surely upset her readers. Feeling sad, she refused to endorse this version.

Geffen flew to New Orleans to meet with Anne. He wanted to make the movie and he wanted her support. He told her he was not afraid of the material—the homoeroticism, the men-to-child relationship, or the more esoteric philosophical elements. He loved the story. "The one thing I had said to Anne from the beginning," said Geffen, "was that I was going to make a high-quality film and I wouldn't allow it to be made as an exploitation film."[2]

Anne was finally convinced of his sincerity and enthusiasm. Geffen urged her to write a script based only on *Interview with the Vampire*. Early in 1992, she completed a draft that satisfied her. Most of the elements were true to the book, but she made Lestat a rogue rather than a villain so that her other books could be made into films that would be consistent with one another. She wrote exactly what she wanted to write, and she felt good about it.

Geffen assured Anne that he liked her script and set about searching for directors. The people Anne suggested, like Ridley Scott and David Cronenberg, turned him down. So did Steven Spielberg. Finally, Geffen approach Irish writer and Oscar-winning director Neil Jordan, who accepted the challenge with the provision that he be allowed to direct without interference.

Although Jordan had not read The Vampire Chronicles, he had loved supernatural tales in his childhood. "I liked the horrific ghost stories, like the ones about people who are playing cards and one picks up a card and sees a cloven hoof."[3] Rice's tales in particular intrigued him because he preferred those in which people experiencing impossible passion struggle to develop or maintain a moral position in the face of hollow or irrelevant conventions. He also liked directing unique pictures. "I want to see images and emotional moments that I have not seen before . . . and I'm interested in a story that can strike very deep in areas of human nature."[4]

Jordan found Anne's script too theatrical, but when he read the novel, he was able to envision a more effective way to bring it to the screen. He replaced many of the elements of the original story that Anne's script had left out and made it primarily Louis's story, not Lestat's, although overall he described it as the story of a deeply dysfunctional family.

Anne was pleased with the selection of Jordan. She knew his work from *The Company of Wolves* and *The Crying Game* and liked the way he boldly approached gender illusions and controversial sexuality. When he called Anne to tell her what he had in mind, she felt her script would be safe in his hands.

THE CONTROVERSY

As for actors, Rutger Hauer, then forty-nine, was clearly out of the question for the role of Lestat. Anne next suggested Jeremy Irons because she felt that his rich voice and European look made up for his age. However, after casting Brad Pitt as Louis (Jordan had liked his vulnerability), Geffen and Jordan approached Daniel Day-Lewis for the role of Lestat.

It took the Irish actor six months to decide to turn down the part. Other names came up, among them Mel Gibson, Ralph Fiennes, and William Baldwin. Then Jordan suggested—and Geffen agreed—that the next person to approach was thirty-one-year-old Tom Cruise. He was a focused, powerful actor, the best of his age group, and in previous roles he had shown a covert savagery that could be brought forth. If he was willing to go deeper into that part of himself, he would be perfect for what Jordan had in mind.

"Vampires have to be young, perfect, sexy, and put across an aura of youth," Jordan said. "Sometimes when you go the opposite way from what people expect, you get the best results."[5]

Geffen called Cruise while he was vacationing in Australia. He was delighted. "I couldn't resist the role," he later told *Esquire* magazine.[6] He had read and loved *The Vampire Lestat*, and as a kid he had always liked vampire movies. In addition, he was eager to take on a role so different from anything he had done before. For the first time in his career, he would play a villain. It was an opportunity to stretch his talents and gain more range, even if it meant changing his image a bit. "[Lestat] is an incredibly internalized character," Cruise observed, "and has a wonderful sense of wit."[7] He accepted the part and began to think through what he would need to do to become the character.

"Lestat for me was a great challenge," he said. "There are places you get to go with that character. With this role, the fun was playing the humor and exploring the depth and trying to make him come alive and be what I envisioned him to be. I am the type of person who, at the end of the day, wants to feel that I honestly gave . . . every moment my best. When all is said and done, I want to look back and know that I pushed myself as far as I could. Lestat was just a monster role."[8]

Anne heard about this new development not from Geffen but through the media. At first she thought that Cruise would play Louis and Pitt would take the role of Lestat. That seemed to her an interesting combination. Then, when she learned the truth, she was stunned.

What could Jordan and Geffen be thinking? It disturbed her that no one from Geffen's office had consulted her, and she felt that the vision for the movie had definitely changed. She thought that Cruise was talented and had liked what she'd seen of his films, but she insisted that he wasn't tall enough and lacked the appropriate look for a blond, aristocratic Frenchman. He was an all-American. And his voice wasn't right. "I don't think I've ever fallen under the spell of an actor when the voice wasn't a big component, and of course the very sad thing about Tom Cruise is he does not have that kind of distinct voice . . . How is he going to exert the power of Lestat?"[9]

When she called Neil Jordan to ask how this casting choice

had happened, he assured her that he had made a good decision. (He later recalled that she in fact affirmed it.)[10] She asked again about Jeremy Irons and even suggested other actors, including Alexander Godunov and John Malkovich, but was told that the decision was firm: Cruise had already signed on. Jordan believed that using him as Lestat would make the film unique in the vampire genre, and he was excited about that. In defending his casting choices, Jordan said, "I thought these roles should be played by stars. The definition of a star is someone who's eternally young, eternally handsome, and has made some strange contract with some power to stay that way forever."[11]

Anne expressed concern quietly to friends and family, but letters and phone calls from fans poured into her office. Her readers were outraged and some of them blamed her. Then Anne heard through media sources that Cruise was trying to clean up the homoerotic sensuality in the script to accommodate his clean image. It seemed to her that commercial interests would surely compromise the artistic integrity of her work, so when the *Los Angeles Times* called her in August 1993, she decided to speak out on behalf of her novel and her readers. She went public, voicing her doubts quite strongly.

"It's like casting Huck Finn and Tom Sawyer in the movie," she said. "I was particularly stunned by the casting of Cruise, who is no more my Vampire Lestat than Edward G. Robinson is Rhett Butler."[12]

David Geffen stepped in to defend Cruise. "To his credit, Tom wants to play a broad range of characters, just as Jack Nicholson, Paul Newman and Al Pacino did before him."[13] Geffen could not understand why Anne was upset. He thought that since she had approved his choice of director, she should now trust Jordan's judgment. Their relationship began to cool, then further eroded over a misunderstanding about money and rights. Anne felt helpless.

Late in September, when she went on a book tour for *Lasher*, she was confronted by fans lined up with picket signs and petitions urging her to do something to reverse this shocking decision. But the whole thing was out of her hands. Praying that it would turn out well, she decided to just sit back and see what happened.

Tom Cruise felt hurt by all the negative publicity. "When it first happened," he said, "it was very upsetting. It really hurt my feelings."[14] It amazed him that Anne and her readers felt such strong antagonism toward his involvement, but he was determined to play the part. It was not the first time in his career that he had been discouraged from playing a role, although it was the most vehement attack. Still, he knew he could do it—if they would give him the chance. As he learned more about Anne and what the novel meant to her, he understood better why she wanted the project to be done right. Yet he also felt that Anne, as an artist herself, ought to support what he was trying to do. He had hoped to discuss the character with her but realized that any such meeting would be impossible. "I would have asked her a lot of questions," he said. "I would have discussed what were for me the pivotal scenes, like the doll scene with Claudia. I would have asked how she felt about Lestat, or what she thought Lestat felt about Claudia. Why did she write that scene in that way? And I would have asked about her feelings in the scene where Lestat is holding Claudia's dress. I would have asked about certain character and story points. For example, Lestat's humor. How did Anne Rice feel about his humor?"[15]

Petitions came in to Warner Brothers begging and demanding that Cruise be replaced by a more appropriate actor.

People involved in the production were bemused, but Anne had severed relations with Geffen, and there was some concern that Rice's readers could do real damage. Geffen was angry because he had a lot invested in the $60 million picture, he believed in his vision, and he wanted his star to be given the benefit of any doubt there might be. He felt that Anne was being unprofessional and unfair. Why couldn't she just leave the filmmaking up to those who knew what they were doing?

The controversy put *Interview* back on best-seller lists that October, which led to speculation in the media that Anne's outburst was a publicity stunt, but she was sincere. She would hold her position.

PRODUCTION

Jordan moved forward, selecting the talented River Phoenix to play the boy reporter and accomplishing the near impossible: finding an actress who could portray Claudia as a woman/child. Eleven-year-old Kirsten Dunst fit the bill. (She was the first one tested out of thousands of girls who were up for the part.) Talent scouts had spotted her shopping with her mother in Beverly Hills and had suggested she try out. She had already played small parts in films such as *New York Stories* and *The Bonfire of the Vanities*, and when Cruise arrived at her screening, the two of them looked so good together that the decision seemed clear. Dunst seemed to possess an unusual understanding of the demands of the role and could move easily between childishness and maturity, although she confessed to the difficulty of this transition: "She was a sad character, but she was a challenging role for me. I liked that she was a little devious but still innocent. I had to understand the pain Claudia was going through because she could never grow up."[16]

Antonio Banderas signed on as Armand, Steven Rea as Santiago, and Domiziana Giordano as the tragic Madeleine.

All the major roles were filled and it was nearing time to go on location. Pitt arrived from filming *Legends of the Fall* in Montana with just enough time to peruse the script on the plane. He lost a little weight for the part and skimmed the novel, but it may have been primarily his fatigue that immersed him in Louis's depressed perspective.

Tom Cruise, too, lost weight, wanting to acquire a gaunt look. "I had to run every day between six and ten miles," he explained. "I hate dieting, but I lost nineteen pounds. We were in Australia partying, my wife and I, going to the pubs and eating fried fish and I'm thinking, I'm going to have to lose all this weight. This is going to hurt."

He spent considerable time studying his character. "I read the script and then I read *Interview* several times after that. I underlined certain lines that I really felt revealed Lestat and that I thought were important for the movie. There are three or four sentences in the novel that tell you about the depth of his isolation and compassion and love." What he found interesting about Lestat was his capacity to love despite his loneliness. "He's so bright and so suspicious that it's love that really brings him down. My viewpoint on Lestat is that of his frustration. There's a line where Lestat said, 'In the Old World, Louis, they called it the Dark Gift and I gave it to you.' Lestat feels this is a gift he has given. He has chosen Louis and he's frustrated with his miscalculation of people. Everyone understands giving someone a gift and not having it appreciated. And especially when you think you've given them the *ultimate* gift. And Lestat tested Louis. He said, 'Do you still want death or have you tasted it enough?' He queried him: 'Do you really want death?' So he was very frustrated."[17]

Cruise visited museums in Paris and Versailles to bone up on the eighteenth-century aristocratic lifestyle, and read Baudelaire. "I worked on my diction, my movement. I read out loud from classics so that the language became easy for me." He also watched films of predatory animals in action.

By October 18, 1993, production had begun. Then a tragedy happened. On October 31, River Phoenix collapsed outside a Hollywood nightclub from a drug overdose and died. Everyone was stunned. Was this film indeed cursed, as Anne had said all along?

Leonardo DiCaprio and Stephen Dorff read for the part, but it was Christian Slater who was hired to step in, despite his hectic schedule. He donated his $250,000 salary to Phoenix's favorite charities. His special contribution was to add humor to the role, with his sarcastic responses to some of Louis's claims. "If I was interviewing someone," he explained, "and they told me they were a vampire, I'd think they were insane."[18]

The Stan Winston Studio, with their Oscar-winning crew from *Jurassic Park*, got right to work on the makeup. They were eager to move in a direction quite different from the beasts and aliens that had been their staples. They conducted many tests to determine the look they felt was right.

First, they had to create the translucent vampire skin with the veins barely showing, like a newborn's. They tried mixing metallic powder into the face makeup, but that failed to work on film. Then they experimented with white makeup, which proved too garish and stereotyped. Their other ideas required too much time. Finally, they drew fine blue lines on the skin, following each actor's vein patterns, then covered it all with ordinary pancake makeup. (The actors were asked to lie upside down on a slant board to make their veins bulge.) In the end, they appeared vaguely normal, but not quite, if one got close enough to get a good look.

The crew came up with special contact lenses that heightened eye color and suggested predatory hunger. "When you look at them, you're looking at this character's eyes," said Winston, "not his teeth, not his skin, not all the other aspects of being a vampire . . . Rather than being pushed away or being put off, you're attracted to him."[19] The colors were different for different vampires, and during more intense scenes, contacts with larger irises were substituted to produce an animal-like appearance. Bloodshot eyes were created via computer graphics.

The fangs had to be just right, longer than real teeth but more subtle than in typical vampire films. The effects team made clay molds of each actor's teeth, enlarging the canines and the two teeth next to them to make a gradual change, but taking care not to make them so big as to interfere with speech. These teeth were meant to stay in. Each set was cast as a single veneer of acrylic that had to fit tightly. Several sets were made for each actor, with the leads having as many as fourteen sets each. They also had sets in which the canines were a bit longer, for snarling or biting.[20]

The costumes were mostly silk, with color schemes chosen to reflect characters. Louis was earthy, Lestat cold blue and silver, Claudia pastel. The illusion of Claudia's maturation was produced largely through her changing clothing styles.

Hair design and other aspects of makeup were the province of Oscar winner Michele Burke, who had worked on Francis Ford Coppola's *Bram Stoker's Dracula*. The Stan Winston Studio designed the effects on paper for Burke to execute on the set. One of the surprises in the film for fans was Armand's long black hair: In the novel, he had wavy auburn hair. "I felt we'd done too much of that," Burke said. "Antonio and I decided he should look completely different."[21] After talking it over with Banderas, Jordan agreed to go with this image. "I thought he should be a throwback to an earlier time," Burke added.

Cruise's makeup was a special challenge: He had to go from brown hair, olive skin, and hazel eyes to a pale-skinned blond with gray-blue eyes. There were many other changes in his appearance as he went from healthy vampire to near-corpse to emaciated recluse. Some days it took as long as four hours to apply the special prosthetics and wigs.

Although *Interview* was a character-driven film rather than one that featured dramatic special effects, some of the more extensive illusions involved Digital Domain's animatronic puppets and complicated hydraulics, such as the scene in which Claudia tries to kill Lestat. These effects took months to perfect, with the actors having to be choreographed precisely with the puppets. Cruise acted out the death scene first so that it could be videotaped for reference in building the puppet, which was designed from a skeletal sculpture based on Cruise's body size that could be operated from underneath to make it crawl. A deflatable airbag torso was fitted around the skeleton, while four sets of interchangeable hands and heads in various stages of degeneration provided the illusion that Lestat was slowly starving. The sequence begins with Cruise falling forward, wearing an appliance that slashed open his throat, and ends with the hydraulic puppet in its final death stage. The many elements that had to be coordinated into a finely tuned whole were then programmed into a computer for integration. This scene, Winston claimed, was "probably the most elaborate fifteen seconds ever put on film."[22]

Another difficult rendering was Claudia and Madeleine's death scene. Body sculptures were made and heated under lamps, then sprayed with water to create steam. Computer tracking of digitally painted burns on the actresses' skin were paired with live-action plates to give the appearance of their skin dissolving with the sun's approach.

Although the production crew went to New Orleans to build sets, they also relied on digital matte paintings, computer duplications, adjustments in printing density, split-screen technology, and models of objects such as ships and buildings. "We tried to stay true to each period," said Jordan, "but we also had to convey a specific and different visual world for the picture. . . . Everything is slightly too rich, slightly too baroque."[23]

They constructed sixty-five sets in all (only about half on the various locations), including their own French Quarter and waterfront areas south of New Orleans at Jackson Barracks. They shot on several locations around town and used the gardens and drawing room of Destrehan and Oak Alley plantations. New Orleans sets emphasized color, while old-world Europe was more monochromatic to capture the colder, more melancholic atmosphere.

Most of the scenes were shot at night, which was hard on everyone, but the look that Jordan wanted to achieve for the film required darkness and shadow. Rousselot used Chinese paper lanterns to produce soft lighting. Scenes in which buildings were burned had to be carefully crafted with special effects, fireboxes, and miniature models composited with live-action shots. Subtlety and realism became the guiding factors.

Initially, the team had planned a more elaborate way of creating Louis's transformation sequence, to show his heightened senses, but opted instead for a simpler approach, with a statue's eyes opening and moving that captured the eerie mood. Claudia's transformation, with her hair curling neatly, proved even more difficult. Digital computer artists spent months making it look believable, curl by curl.[24]

The sets, closed to all but those directly involved in the production, were shrouded in great secrecy. Anne wanted to call Brad Pitt and Neil Jordan to wish them well, but even she could not get through. In fact, at Pinewood Studios in London where they later shot interiors, Jordan had a canvas passage set up from the actors' trailers to the sets to protect the "vampires" from an overzealous British press. "We didn't want photographs out of context, we didn't want anyone copying us," Jordan explained.[25] Throughout production, extras and crew members had to sign statements that they would not reveal any details.

After New Orleans, the crew and actors went on to San Francisco to shoot on Market Street and the Golden Gate Bridge. Christian Slater joined them for six days before they left to finish outdoor shots in Paris. Locations there included the Rue St. Jacques, Rue Hirondelle, the Seine under the Pont Neuf, The Palais Royale, Père Lachaise Cemetery, and the Paris Opera.

After twenty weeks, they wrapped it up during the spring of 1994 by shooting on thirty-four interior sets (including the Theatre of the Vampires) built on seven stages in London's Pinewood Studios. The film was scheduled for summer release, then for October, with some talk that it might even be as late as December.

INTERVIEW WITH THE VAMPIRE: THE FILM

There were clear deviations from the book: For starters, Claudia was a few years older, the reporter was a bit more cynical, and Louis was grieving over a wife and daughter rather than a brother. There was no Freniere family, no Babette, and no scenes in Eastern Europe with Old-World vampires. Lestat had no companion vampire with whom he attacked Louis and Claudia, and he never showed up in Paris (although scenes were shot in which he did). The ending was also quite different, with Lestat returning triumphant and ready for a sequel.

The vampires in Jordan's vision were more brutal than Anne claims to have imagined them—not quite angels. A few scenes were bloody enough to earn an R rating, even though some of the more graphic ones had been cut. There were also comic moments original to the film, such as when Claudia killed her piano teacher and Louis went for the poodles over their decadent owner. Jordan elected to emphasize Louis's short-lived predilection for animal blood, which provided a trail of rat corpses and inspired some of Lestat's more acerbic remarks. Jordan also underplayed the vampire swoon. It was not as richly sensuous as Rice had depicted, but other types of sensuality abounded.

The vampires touched and flirted with one another in dances of seduction, and in one scene, Pitt and Banderas drew so close it seemed certain that they would actually kiss. Banderas later claimed that he and Pitt themselves had planned this unscripted scene: "It's just that we wanted to push a little bit the sexuality of these characters. Sex between vampires is not the same as with normal people. . . . I feel that art in general and acting in particular should make the audience a little uncomfortable."[26]

It was rumored that Cruise had resisted the homoerotic aspects, but he insisted that he had not. "That was no concern of mine," he said. "It wasn't a problem. [The movie] is *vampire*-erotic to me."[27] In fact, because he was so eager to be involved, he had consigned to Jordan his typical power of waiver over the script. "There is an eroticism," he admitted. "But I think if someone is a homosexual, it will be homoerotic. And if they're not homosexual, it will be hetero-erotic."[28]

David Geffen agreed: "Homoerotic is in the eyes of the beholder."[29]

After reiterating his acknowledged feat with gender and sexuality in *The Crying Game*, Jordan said he had less to be concerned about with *Interview*. "What's so great about this movie is that vampires don't have sex—the blood-sucking act itself is their orgasm. Therefore every possible facet of life becomes an erotic possibility. If you eliminate the act of two people mating, you can put eroticism into everything. That, more than anything, is the visual metaphor of the movie."[30]

The vampire performance in the Theatre of the Vampires turned out to be more brutish than Anne had intended. The vampires were supposed to be cruel but elegant and seductive, rather than aggressive. Nevertheless, Jordan captured the aura of vampires pretending to be humans pretending to be vampires and put force into their collectively inbred, malaise-infected personalities. He clearly brought his own vision to the production even as he remained faithful to the original story.

However, when Jordan tried to get credit as coauthor on

the script, arbitration by the Writers Guild of America assigned sole credit to Anne. To Jordan's surprise, he had to prove that he had contributed more than 50 percent original material, and many of his additions had been taken from Anne's novel. Thus, although Jordan added his own flourishes, he received no official acknowledgment.

THE FILM'S RECEPTION

In February 1994, Anne quickly wrote her fifth vampire novel, *Memnoch the Devil*. Anxious about how the film might affect her sense of Lestat, she wanted to finish before she heard anything more.

Anne received no communication from Geffen or Jordan or anyone on their team. What she heard came via rumors. Everyone was horrified by the sneak look at Tom Cruise in creepy vampire makeup (from the swamp scene) that showed up on one TV evening entertainment show, but the film remained cloaked in mystery. No one was talking, yet a sense of anticipation was building. This movie would either be great or a major flop. Predictions came from all sides. David Geffen prepared to go on ABC's *20/20* to discuss the project. To his mind, the movie was terrific. "It's not a Hollywood movie," he claimed. "I made *my* movie."[31]

There were several test screenings, and a few people who had seen the early version sent negative comments to companions on the computer networks. These reports eventually reached Anne. She was dismayed. Geffen later admitted that the initial version had been more brutal than the final cut and some toning down of the blood and gore had to be done.

That September, he decided to take a risk. He was so pleased with the way *Interview with the Vampire* had turned out, and particularly with Tom Cruise's performance, that he called Anne and told her he wanted to send her a videotape. "I sent her a tape of the finished film," he explained, "because I wanted her to stop knocking Tom Cruise. She had no idea how good he was in the movie, or how bad. She had not seen a frame of it and it was hurting his feelings. He had worked very hard on the film. I don't think Anne realized that you can't decide that a good actor can't rise to the occasion that he believes he can. It's the willingness to go for it that really dictates the ability to accomplish it. I had no doubt she would love the movie if she saw it. I thought it was a great movie. I never had a moment's doubt about it or about Cruise. I sent it to her without any concern. She could have hated it, but in my mind, if she did, so what? She'd be wrong. I had complete faith in it."[32]

Cruise thought sending it was a bad idea and was nervous, but Anne agreed at least to give it a shot. When the tape arrived, she felt great trepidation. What if she hated it? She would be sick over it, and there would be nothing she could do to stop it. Anxious, she slid the tape into her VCR and let it roll onto her large-screen, theater-style television.

To her astonishment, she liked it. She watched it several times in a row and *loved* it. "I was knocked out by it. I completely forgot that I had written it. I was swept up." She called Geffen to express her enthusiasm. He was both delighted and relieved. She wanted to send flowers to Kirsten Dunst. "I feel special love for her," she said, "because that role was so much beyond the imagination."

She also had praise for Tom Cruise: "He became Lestat; he did his own Lestat without stealing my character from me."[33]

"I was tremendously relieved," Cruise said when he heard of her positive response. "I quite honestly expected the opposite. I was disappointed in the beginning with her reaction in coming out so strongly, because I had read a quote about her being someone who artistically wanted to take chances. I get excited when I hear that other actors are taking chances or trying something totally different. But then I started reading more about her daughter and I realized this project means so much to her that she wants it to be right. So I understood really."[34]

Anne decided to call Tom Cruise to let him know of her deep appreciation. He was gratified, and they spoke together for a few minutes. "It was a very classy thing to do," he observed, "because she didn't have to do that."[35]

And she *had* changed her mind. In a big way. She prepared a two-page statement for publication and sent it to *Variety* and *The Advocate*. In it, she urged readers to give the movie a chance. She did not feel she was wrong about her earlier statements, because she had sincerely meant them, but she was ready to stand by her feelings just as boldly now. "I was honored and stunned to discover just how faithful this film was to the spirit, the content, and the ambience of the novel," she wrote. She went on to urge readers: "If I'm wrong, if you don't like the picture, let me know. Laugh in my face, write me letters. Call . . . I can take it."[36]

At the end of October, as the film was being screened in several major cities, Anne called New York columnist Liz Smith, who had predicted a Tom Cruise triumph all along, to say that she had learned something. "This has taught me a valuable lesson about jumping to conclusions and making negative public comments," Smith quoted her as saying. "When I didn't want Tom in the movie, that was hot news, but my reversal does not seem to be as newsworthy."[37] She went on to praise the movie effusively.

The film received a lot of early press, most notably Oprah Winfrey's lament that she had walked out of her private screening after ten minutes, unable to tolerate the movie's dark message: she could not stomach the scene in which the vampires drank from a rat. Others who joined her in the lobby reportedly formed a prayer group for those who remained inside. Winfrey scheduled Tom Cruise for an interview after her screening was over but assured him he would not have any uncomfortable questions. When audience members attacked him for taking the role and insisted that the movie was evil, he finally threw up his hands in gentle exasperation and said, "It's a vampire film!"

The actual world premiere was scheduled for November 18, 1994, in Los Angeles, then was moved up a week to November 11. Anne wanted it to come to New Orleans. David Geffen agreed to a private showing there for her friends and family, so she reserved seats for five hundred in a theater downtown and launched a gala event.

Anne and her husband sat in the back of the theater filled with well-wishers. Together they watched the camera pan to the room in San Francisco where the vampire was about to tell his story. Christian Slater and Brad Pitt got right into it, and the narrative swept Louis into a scene two hundred years earlier.

Scene after scene was filled with authentic detail from New Orleans, San Francisco, and Paris. The costumes were exquisite, but Anne's readers at once recognized that the makeup wasn't quite right: the vampires did not look angelic at times, and they failed to cry blood tears, as described in the novel. Many viewers felt that the long, black wig seemed wrong for Armand. And Jordan had clearly added some black-humor scenes that had not been in the book. Still, there was something magical here. By the time the film ended, many in the audience had done an about-face on their opinion of Tom Cruise. He seemed to have captured, against all odds, the roguish charm, humor, and brutality of Lestat. And Pitt had convincingly played out the gloom and passive despair of Louis de Pointe du Lac.

Anne watched every frame with high expectation. When it came to the scene in which Claudia and Madeleine die in the sun and disintegrate—a scene that she herself had been unable to describe fully in the book—she experienced a wave of emotion reminiscent of what she had felt twenty years earlier, after her daughter's death. All that grief came back to her as she watched the film. By the end, she was stunned. "I was shaking more violently than I ever had in my life," she recalls. "It was a hysterical reaction. My body just gave out."[38] Rather than remain to greet her guests and hear their reactions, she had to go home.

Anne now viewed Geffen as a hero for making the film in a way that preserved the poignancy of the story. "I think they did something larger with this film than they even know," she said. "They got the larger questions we all face. They really got the dilemma, that we don't know if there's a God. You have been hit with that giant question in this film. They got the fear, they got the despair, they got the anguish."[39]

The following week, at the film's premiere in Los Angeles, Anne signed thousands of small rubber rats to pass out to people in line. Geffen threw a huge party afterward. The next day, he reported to Anne that several members of the audience had fainted, which prompted theaters across the country to hire paramedics to wait in the lobby for such emergencies.

In New York, Anne went on several talk shows and then visited the Ziegfeld Theater, with its chandeliers and elegant red carpets, to ask people what they thought of the film. She was gratified by the positive responses.

By the end of the weekend, the news was good. The film had opened at number one and grossed over $36 million. It was the fourth-largest debut in motion-picture history, and the largest nonholiday opening. It would go on to make over $100 million in the United States, coming in as the tenth top-grossing film of the year, and do equally well internationally.

However, the reviews were decidedly mixed. Siskel and Ebert gave it two thumbs up, while Liz Smith found it repulsive and walked out with several of her friends. Some New York magazines were cool on it, while the *Los Angeles Times* felt it was uneven: "Whatever else it lacks, *Interview* does a gorgeous job of re-creating not only eighteenth-century New Orleans and nineteenth-century Paris but also the book's genuinely weird, disturbing, almost unimaginable world of those who can never die."[40]

Called hypnotic, perverted, sexy, erotic, haunting, elegant, revolting, boring, and brilliant, the film ran the gamut of praise and criticism. Several reviewers commented on the unrelenting darkness, and one observed that "it never really emerges from its twilight sleep." One of the hosts on *AM Philadelphia* commented that the greatest flaw was that there was never any mention of what vampires do for a living. Conversely, some critics raved about finally having a film that got into profound issues.

Jordan was praised for being faithful to the novel and slammed for the same reason. He was credited at least with courage, and one reviewer said that he directed the film with great power and involvement: "Jordan gives the forbidden its rightful allure."[41]

Many reviewers cited Tom Cruise's surprisingly competent, even "incandescent," performance, although a few dismissed him as still being wrong for the part. Brad Pitt was said to be either anemic or eloquent and exacting in his role as Louis. *Rolling Stone* called Claudia "the film's most unnerving character."[42]

Anne Rice took out an eight-page supplement in *Variety* to express her own views, unedited. She described what she liked about each actor and each aspect of the film, questioned some decisions, attacked shallow responses, and went on to say what she thought the story represented about humanity.

The actors made the rounds, commenting on their performances and their feelings about the film. When he won critical praise, Cruise graciously said, "I always wanted to be faithful to the book because I thought the characters were so well drawn." He viewed Lestat as the definitive vampire and had ideas for the next time around, should there be a sequel. "I think I would follow the same line as I did in *Interview*. Lestat is an adventurer. He was the only vampire in New Orleans. There were no other vampires in America when he arrived. That is an adventurous spirit. Here's a guy who goes out among people and goes to the opera and studies music. He's a fascinating character.

"I knew this was a great role for me. Sure, there were some tough moments. Acting is difficult. You're on the edge and you have to put yourself in some tough places emotionally. Sometimes you wake up in the morning and think, I don't want to go there. When I was doing the scene with the prostitutes, I was sick as a dog, but as an actor, I couldn't wait to play that scene."[43]

On *The Today Show*, Brad Pitt admitted that he had set out to find a difficult character, but decided that he had bitten off more than he could chew. He told Bryant Gumble that he hated doing Louis. "I loved this book going into it and loved Louis coming out, but he messed with me a bit, the character. You got a guy who's stuck in this situation. First of all, he's miserable from the beginning to the end. . . . Six months of that is not a happy time."

When Gumble mentioned that Rice viewed a vampire's killing as the ultimate orgasm, Pitt responded with a smile and said, "Well, it didn't work for me."

Although he had told an interviewer for *Sky Magazine* that he had actually preferred Louis over Lestat, Pitt later told *Rolling Stone*, "My character wants to kill himself for the whole movie. I've never thought of killing myself. It was a sick thing."[44] He affirmed again that he loved the book and was even proud of the movie, but had not anticipated what playing Louis would do to him. Questioned about animosity between himself and Cruise, he denied it, saying that there was some competition, but it was the kind that made him work harder to do a good job. Any resentment Pitt felt came from within their roles, and if he had carried it over, that was his own problem. He denied any overt homoeroticism in the scenes in which Cruise was biting his neck, saying, "You have to follow vampire logic—once you're a vampire, male and female doesn't matter."[45]

Cruise also denied the rumors of animosity. "I enjoyed working with the cast. And I had my family there, my wife and daughter, so I got to go home and get lots of hugs and kisses. Whereas Brad was a single guy going home to a darkened apartment. It's tough."[46]

Questions to Christian Slater concerned his feelings about stepping in for River Phoenix. "There was a darkness about it," he conceded, "the idea of taking over the role of someone who died." About the appeal of vampires, he said,

"It's a sexual thing. Someone floating into your bedroom and caressing your neck, and biting into it and so passionately sucking the life out of someone, is very exciting and erotic."[47]

Despite critics who insisted that a child should not have been cast in such a film, Kirsten Dunst was not the least bit disturbed by the role she played, with all the blood and rats and death. "It's just pretend," she insisted. "It was weird to see myself bite people. All I kept seeing was fake blood." She became quite famous for her repeated expression of "yuck" at her memory of kissing Brad Pitt, whom she viewed as being more like a brother. "I hated that!" She also disliked the corsets and the intense makeup sessions. Overall, however, she was proud of the film and was thrilled that there was talk that she might win an Academy Award nomination.[48] Anne had told her that her performance was brilliant and very much in tune with the character, which pleased her.

Antonio Banderas won a legion of new fans with his Latin interpretation of the four-hundred-year-old Armand. He viewed the film as a classic rather than a typical horror movie. "It's deeper than normal vampire movies," he insisted. He saw plenty of philosophical symbolism about people and about life. "The movie is more a reflection about immortality."[49]

Whether the film will cut a path for more stylish vampire films or even become a classic metaphor on the human condition remains to be seen. However, one thing is clear: Although it was a long, complicated road from the novel to the screen, *Interview with the Vampire* was a unique event in film history.

NOTES

1. Author interview with David Geffen.
2. Ibid.
3. "Interview with Neil Jordan," *Philadelphia Inquirer*, 13 November 1994.
4. Warner Brothers' Production Information, 2 February 1995, 3.
5. Jennet Conant, "Lestat, C'est Moi," *Esquire*, March 1994, 73.
6. Ibid., 74.
7. Ingrid Sischy, "Tom Cruise," *Interview*, November 1994, 104.
8. Author interview with Tom Cruise.
9. Martha Frankel, "Anne Rice," *Movieline*, January/February 1994, 97.
10. Alan Jones, "Interview with the Vampire," *Cinefantastique*, December 1994, 26.
11. Ibid.
12. *Los Angeles Times*, 23 August 1993.
13. Ibid.
14. Sischy, *Interview*, 104.
15. Author interview with Tom Cruise.
16. Author interview with Kirsten Dunst.
17. Author interview with Tom Cruise.
18. Rachel Abramowitz, "Young Blood," *Premiere*, November 1994, 72.
19. "The Lord of Illusions," *Empire* (February 1995): 69.
20. *Cinefex* 61 (March 1995): 45.
21. Steve Biodrowski, "Vampire Glamor (and Gore)," *Imagi-Movies*, winter 1994.
22. *Empire*, 69.
23. Production Information, 7.
24. *Cinefex*, 49.
25. "Interview with the Vampire," *Empire*, February 1995, 71.
26. Stephen Rebello, "The Real Don Juan," *Movieline*, August 1995, 39.
27. Abramowitz, *Premiere*, 68.
28. Sischy, *Interview*, 104.
29. Abramowitz, *Premiere*, 68.
30. Steve Biodrowski and Anthony P. Montesano, "Bonfire of the Vampires," *Imagi-Movies*, winter 1994, 20.
31. Abramowitz, *Premiere*, 68.
32. Author interview with David Geffen.
33. Frankel, *Movieline,* 60.
34. Author interview with Tom Cruise.
35. Sischy, *Interview*, 127.
36. Statement by Anne Rice sent to author and then published in *Variety*.

37. Quoted by Liz Smith in her syndicated column, October 1994.
38. Said to author in conversation.
39. Said to author in conversation.
40. Kenneth Turan, *Los Angeles Times*, 11 November 1994.
41. Ibid.
42. Peter Travers, "Interview with the Vampire," *Rolling Stone*, 15 December 1994.
43. Author interview with Tom Cruise.
44. Chris Mundy, "Brad Pitt," *Rolling Stone*, 1 December 1994, 94.
45. Ibid.
46. Author interview with Tom Cruise.
47. Christian Slater on MTV special, November 1994.
48. Author interview with Kirsten Dunst.
49. Rebello, *Movieline*, 39.

He Must Have Wept When He Made You

THE HOMOEROTIC *POTHOS* IN THE MOVIE VERSION OF *INTERVIEW WITH THE VAMPIRE*

John Beebe

The male homoeroticism in the film *Interview with the Vampire* scarcely needs commentary to bring it into daylight. What is interesting is how many viewers who would not be caught dead going to a gay film have succumbed to director Neil Jordan's rendering of Lestat's enduring love for Louis and Louis's ambivalent nostalgia for the strikingly elegant ménage they create, complete with adopted daughter. What does this symbolism (which Anne Rice insists is "not just about vampires, it's really about all of us"[1]) mean, and what is its hold on our imagination?

The film develops the imagery of the novel in cinematic ways, adding Hollywood overtones to the materials of the original story. Neil Jordan's emotional starting point is Brad Pitt's face, as seen by the far more ordinary-looking Christian Slater. As the haunted Louis, Pitt conveys the frozen beauty of an eternal, semidivine adolescent caught in revulsion for the kind of man he has become. Guarded and powdery, as if on the verge of crumbling, his is the face of a fallen innocent. He has the wistful look of a suburban boy who has ventured into the city on a Saturday night, palpably an outsider. It would not have surprised the interviewer who spotted him in an alley in San Francisco to learn that he had come up from a town on the Peninsula and that he still lived at home with his parents.

Not yet in possession of a real life himself, the wonky interviewer feeds vampirically on other people's stories, and he is drawn to the vampire's doomed grace, which for him portends a satisfying tale. Eventually we sense that the story the interviewer really wants to hear is that of Pitt's seduction by his fate. In the interviewer's imagination, that fate becomes an even more gorgeous figure of fantasy than the reserved Louis, who tends to disappoint him. Lestat, as played by Tom Cruise, is no disappointment; he is the unambiguous superstar of androgynous, fixated boyhood, boasting a fabled capacity for endless self-reinvention as well as the power to draw all others into his spell of eternal youth.

The interviewer, who personifies Anne Rice's enthralled audience, is gripped by the horror and thrill of Lestat's attempt to seduce Louis, which is visualized for us with unusual audacity as a handsome, established male star coming on to a slightly younger, attractive actor. Jordan dares this breach of popular taste because he knows that in Hollywood movies it is common for the archetypal figure in the background of a psychological situation to be depicted by a familiar, mythic movie star. For instance, in Howard Hawks's *Red River*, John Wayne is the established patriarchal hero severely overseeing newcomer Montgomery Clift's rite of passage into movie-western manhood. According to this visual logic, the image of Brad Pitt must temporarily give over to that of Tom Cruise. Lestat precisely personifies the unconscious archetype that is pressing for realization through Louis, and the tension of their encounter lies in Louis's inability to accept and value what Lestat would like to offer him. By opposing Cruise with Pitt, the film draws energy from the recurring generational rivalry among Hollywood stars. Just as Cruise rose to full stardom under the wings of Paul Newman in *The Color of Money* and was vetted by Jack Nicholson in *A Few Good Men*, Pitt now seems more than ready to hold his own against Cruise, languidly resisting Cruise's intensity. Yet Cruise is no more easily vanquished than Lestat, and Pitt, for all the power of his performance, is not quite initiated into superstardom in this film, while Cruise has done an undeniable star turn.

A first effect of this competitive casting is to dramatize the tension attending the total takeover of a young man's soul by the archetype of the *puer aeternus*. *Puer aeternus*, which means eternal, or endless, boy, refers to one of the most peculiar of the named archetypes of the Western psyche, a charming, perennial opponent to our culture's traditional emphasis on commitment, responsibility, and earned achievement. The *puer aeternus* was first identified in Jungian psychology as the archetypal aspect of the narcissistic neuroses of our time, in which men become caught in an adolescent identification with the godlike possibilities of eternal youth, to the detriment of their ability to commit themselves to any sort of real life.* This archetypal fixation is one that Jungian analysts have

*The Latin term *puer aeternus* may have been invented by Ovid to describe the child-god Iacchus, a Roman variant of Dionysus, the god of bisexual, loosening charm. This is a god who particularly stirs the eros of both men and women, but often leads them into maddening rejections. As Jung noted, Ovid addressed the "unending youth" ambivalently: "Thy face is virgin seeming if without horns it stands before us." [Ovid, *Metamorphoses*, quoted in C. G. Jung, *Symbols of Transformation*, *Collected Works*, vol 5, 2d ed. (Princeton: Princeton University Press, 1967), 340.] This passage is also cited on p. 22 of Joseph Henderson's *Thresholds of Initiation*.

found in men who cannot settle down to a stable love or working life and who seem like promissory notes that never come due. Such a man often flirts with homosexuality, though he usually cannot make a commitment to it, seeing this solution as an even greater threat to his identity, which remains, for the most part, ambiguously and seductively bisexual.

The most sustained discussions of this problem are to be found in *Thresholds of Initiation*, by Joseph Henderson; *Puer Papers*, edited by James Hillman; and *A Psychological Interpretation of the Golden Ass of Apuleius*, by Marie-Louise von Franz.[2]

The first Jungian analyst to look closely at the problem of someone who is too identified with the *puer aeternus* archetype was Marie-Louise von Franz:

> The man who is identified with the archetype of the *puer aeternus* remains too long in adolescent psychology; that is, all those characteristics that are normal in a youth of seventeen or eighteen are continued into later life . . . He lives in a continual sleepy daze, and that too is a typical adolescent characteristic: the sleepy, undisciplined, long-legged youth who merely hangs around . . .[2]

This description of the *puer*-identified man is a rather exact image of Brad Pitt's Louis, who, despite all his scripted involvement in the management of property and the memory of marriage, is very much the young man hanging around waiting to be picked up by some gust of life.

The man identified with the *puer aeternus*, however, is not the archetype itself—or he is only the human face of it, as Louis continues to be in this film even after his transformation into a vampire. (His being "made" immortal by Lestat indicates the beginning of his identification with the archetype and the loss of his former self.) Usually, the dark, demonic current estranging a man from the ability to make commitments and forcing him into the provisional life is invisible. No one can quite figure out what's wrong with him. Only by studying his effects on those who attempt to draw him into reliability, such as a woman or man who might fall seriously in love with him and want to establish a permanent relationship, does one get a glimpse of the cold ruthlessness, even viciousness, of the possessing archetype.

In *Interview*, this outrageous ruthlessness is visualized for us, embodied in Lestat. Lestat gives startling depth to the movie as he did to the novel because he takes us directly to the figure of the unconscious that is hiding in the shadow behind the *puer aeternus*—the trickster. In Rice's novel, Louis refers to Lestat as a "prankster," someone he dismisses as being unable to teach him anything, but whose force in his life he vastly underestimates. This is typical of the psychology of the *puer*-identified man—he fails to acknowledge the trickster shadow as a vital part of himself and an unconscious value in his life; indeed, this denial of his own capacity to do evil is what creates part of his unreality. Like Peter Pan, this kind of man finds it hard to stay connected to his shadow. Angel-seeming, he is always seeking to make connections with transcendent archetypal wisdom. Yet, in the structure of the unconscious, the trickster lurks as the insistent Faustian shadow of the ambition for access to divine secrets.

The trickster provides a bridge to the rest of the unconscious life of the *puer*-identified man, particularly to the capacity for love and suffering that his life notoriously lacks. Lestat brings Claudia into Louis's life and forces him to assume responsibility for her fate. It is Anne Rice's mediumistic gift to have visualized Claudia as the symbol of the bond that links the apparently opposed figures of Louis and Lestat. The figure of Claudia is especially well realized by the young actress Kirsten Dunst. Although Claudia complains that her hair, which Lestat forces her to keep in elaborate ringlets, makes her look like a doll, the cinematic image seems to have been taken from Velázquez's famous painting *The Infanta Margarita in a Pink Dress* (1653–54). Margarita was a child of a family bearing a congenital defect, and she has the strange aspect of a beautiful dwarf, her hair extending outward to suggest a growth totally lacking in vertical possibilities.

In the script, Claudia is called an "eternal child," and her face suggests that archetype in sharing both the angelic radiance of Louis and the demonic gleam of Lestat. The leading female figure in Louis's life, she represents, as a mirror image of his soul, the developmental level of his emotional life and makes it more evident that the pouting, flat-voiced Louis is stuck in the infantile psyche.

Together, Louis, Lestat, and Claudia constitute the very trinity that Jungian analyst Joseph Henderson identified as the typical figures of the counterculture youth who created the *puer* revolution of the late 1960s: the angel, the adept, and the orphan.[3] Through their interaction we get a rare insight into *puer* dynamics. The angelic Louis (Claudia refers to him as her "dark angel") is dependent on Lestat's adeptness at survival and his comfort with evil, which are the traditional prerogatives of the trickster. Lestat, in turn, needs the orphan Claudia to feel his own vulnerability. When Claudia seduces Lestat into believing that her gift of "sleeping" twin boys is a peace offering rather than a deadly trick, his initial gratitude betrays his longing for a family connection with her and Louis.

Claudia carries for both Lestat and Louis a reminder of their shared orphan status. Hers is the most emotional presence in the film. She is the image of a traumatized child forced into an unreal perfection at the expense of genuine maturation. She represents a fixation at the level of the infantile psyche that makes a mockery of the pretty possibilities usually associated with the figure of the divine child. Her inability to mature is as confining as the coffin Louis most fears getting stuck in, and her rage at the doomed pair who have conspired to give her such hollow immortality is the strongest emotional color the film projects.

Claudia's bond with Louis is especially strong. His own disaffection began with the death of his wife in childbirth, and Claudia symbolizes and replaces both wife and child. She, in turn, having lost her mother to the plague, later seeks to make another mother for herself out of Madeleine, a mortal woman who has lost her own child and is willing to become a vampire to have in Claudia "a child who cannot die." Through Claudia we are led to feel as well as see the core of the *puer*-identified man's suffering—the premature loss of the mother. The mother's absence, in various forms of physical or emotional abandonment, is often the deepest root of the son's disdain for close emotional attachments. Louis's mother is shown fleetingly, but unforgettably, as he burns her portrait; hers is a cold, disapproving visage, and it is not hard to see why a man with such a mother would feel so negative about his home. Beyond individual psychopathology, it is important to recognize that motherlessness is a symbolic problem of our time, in which we are all estranged from Mother as earth, community, and nature.[4] Just as the Mother Goddess is missing from the patriarchal Christian trinity, so she is absent from this trinity of vampires who live in Christianity's shadow. This is the deepest religious meaning conveyed by the symbolism of these characters—the extraordinary estrangement of the *puer* archetype from the Mother.

Louis imagines himself to be unconnected to any time, "at odds with everything." It takes the four-hundred-year-old Armand, the closest thing to a wise vampire that Louis is able to find, to give him a more historical view. He tells Louis that his personal alienation reflects "the very spirit of your age, the heart of it. Your fall from grace has been the fall of a century." Speaking in 1870, Armand is referring to the nineteenth century, whose present face he imagines Louis can illumine for him. We need this perspective to understand that our cultural vampire—the alienated, uncommitted, and ultimately perverted youth—that so drains our moral and emotional resources is not a feature of late-twentieth-century America only, but a problem that belongs to the entire modern period, as an expression of the mother-estranged *puer aeternus* archetype. We are only just starting to recognize and to "interview" the troubled archetype that shadows our civilization and to get an historical perspective on it.

Lestat makes Louis a vampire in 1791. Their names, their French origins, and the year convey the historical emergence of the *puer* problem as a shadow within the Enlightenment political attitude that came to the fore with the French Revolution. The year 1791 was a particularly important one for the development of Enlightenment consciousness, because it marked the end of the period of the Revolution's accommodation to the sovereign's authority, the true end of Louis XVI's ability to say, as Louis XIV, the Sun-King, had been able to do, *"L'état, c'est moi."* Lestat, as a name, is cognate with *l'état*, "the state," just as Louis bears the name of the kingship whose power declined precipitously in 1791, when Louis XVI and his family were prevented from escaping

France and it was clear that he no longer ruled by divine right but only at the fickle pleasure of the directors of the Revolution. *L'état* had overcome Louis.

This period, when the link to God through monarchy was broken, corresponds to the rise of liberalism as a new kind of Enlightenment religion in which the notion of self-invention—which we in America know as the right to life, liberty, and the pursuit of happiness—became the West's leading cultural ideal. It has taken the ironies of "progress" in the twentieth century to recognize the narcissism embedded in this set of secular suppositions, which imply an unreal psychological freedom from the sacred, as well as a destructive denial of our dependence on the earthly Mother from which we all must draw sustenance.[5] For the *puer*, independence is a transcendent, even stratospheric ideal. But this kind of limitless freedom is unsuited to human beings. It is finally an earth-endangering solar striving, as mythology teaches not only through the *puer* figure of the unwisely guided Icarus, whose wax wings melted when he flew too near the sun, but also through Phaëthon, who, in seizing the sun's chariot for himself, found that he could not control its horses and ended up scorching the earth, an eerie prefiguration of global warming. Damage to the maternal earth is the unintended consequence of *puer* progress.

It is particularly poignant that Madeleine and Claudia are scorched by the sun's rays at the bottom of the sewer in which they have been imprisoned by the company of the Theatre of the Vampires, who seem to represent the decadence of the ancien régime, which ushered in the terrible assurance of the Enlightenment. The destruction of the female pair is an image of the cultural disposal of the mother archetype in the pitiless, solar glare of rational, Enlightenment values, and it is significant that the desiccated bodies crumble to dust and the remaining form of the archetype itself disappears under Louis's despairing touch.

This moment is Louis's epiphany—a recognition of the religious problem of the modern period, in which the feminine vanishes as a sacred value even though her memory remains a source of vain regret. The fact that the mother archetype has vanished is the psychological secret Louis has been seeking and provides the key to his and Lestat's damnation. Louis cannot adequately convey to his interviewer the core of this mystery—the loss from his world of an archetype that could provide comfort, warmth, and meaning.

The psychoanalytic term for such an internal catastrophe is *object loss*, which produces a restricting of the possibilities of personality, so that an emotional flattening and deadening takes place. The film tells us less about the object that is lost than about the flatness that follows. As Mephistopheles grieves for Faust, so Louis despairs over the young interviewer who does not understand what Louis has lost and who is himself all too willing to enter the Faustian bargain of becoming a vampire for the sterile purpose of attaining immortal beauty and power.

For Louis, the collapse of the feminine occurs internally as well as externally. He has lost his soul, and with it the possibility of becoming the basis of any other character's renewal. Armand, whose idealization Louis rightly rejects, appears not to perceive this limitation in Louis, and therefore his love seems perverse. Here is another irony. The archetypes of youth—adolescent angel, hell-raising trickster, and divine child—would seem, even in the shadowy forms of Louis, Lestat, and Claudia, to portend some possibility of renewal, if only because youth itself is eternally self-renewing, despite its mistakes. But renewal, as Jung has shown, depends on the capacity to experience the unconscious as a sort of mother, a source of new life. In destroying the mother-child pair, the vampires, in addition to breaking Louis's heart, reveal to him that they can offer him only a gratuitous, narcissistic immortality that does not include any nurturing basis for growth and transformation.

And yet . . . we are reminded by Lestat at the end of the film that he has been listening to this version of the vampires' sad reality from Louis for centuries and that he's tired of it. Indeed, this style of *puer* self-pity is as old in our culture as Goethe's *The Sorrows of Young Werther* (1774), which Louis might well have read in his mortal years. The brooding over the loss of the mother archetype moves all too easily into the nostalgic, fashionable despair that James Hillman has called the *pothos* of the *puer aeternus*—the "longing toward the unattainable, the ungraspable, the incomprehensible, that idealization which is attendant upon all love and which is always beyond capture." According to Hillman:

> *Pothos* was not only a concept and a feeling; he was also a divine personification, an actual figure, for example sculpted by Skopas (395–350 B.C.), which has been described as a "youngly ripened boy's body." . . . According to Pliny, the main cult figures on Samothrace were Aphrodite and Pothos.[6]

The connection to the ripe image of Brad Pitt's Louis is inescapable. Like the god, he personifies "a specific erotic feeling of nostalgic desire." As Hillman tells us:

> Plato defines [pothos] in the *Cratylus* (420a) as a yearning desire for a distant object. Its associations in the Classical

corpus are with longings *for that which cannot be attained*: yearning for a lost child, or a beloved, . . . longing for sleep and for death.[7]

Part of modern man's sad story is his tiresome tale of estrangement from the feminine. It has become a cliché. Lestat will not let Louis get away with the notion of helplessness that is involved in this fantasy of alienation, which is, I think, why Anne Rice herself, who has said that Louis took root in her imagination after the death of her own child[8], states in her preface to the video version of the film that sometimes she sees Lestat as her conscience. He corrects for the passive, learned helplessness of Louis, perhaps the most insidious attitude in our culture, the assumption that we can do nothing about the alienation that plagues us all.

To overcome this depressive anxiety, a robust moral imagination is required.[9] Rice's imaginative effort in creating a visionary series rather than letting Louis have the last word is a bracing example of this robustness. Moral imagination is an energy that depends on a vital masculinity, in both men and women, as much as on the healthy feminine principle of sensitive relatedness that Jungian psychology has taught us to value. But to be able to imagine decisively, we have to get over our prejudice against the union of male counterparts, a prejudice that is emphatically, if ambivalently, addressed by Anne Rice and Neil Jordan in the strongly homoerotic male imagery of *Interview with the Vampire*.

Louis's refusal of Lestat, and the homophobia that informs it, is itself a sort of *puer* problem—the listless disavowal of the very masculine energy that could overcome the *puer* symptom of impotent, outraged vulnerability. Louis assumes that if he joins with the trickster Lestat, he will no longer be able to choose between good and evil, and it is as if he were saying through his sullen eyes and resistant lips, "If I were to succumb to this homosexual temptation, I would truly be trapped in my empty adolescence forever, unable to relocate myself in a productive human family. I need to despise that fate, even if it is too late to reverse it." Similarly, he spurns the seductive Armand, who wants him to give up his care of Claudia.

For most of the film, Jordan seems to count on the audience's siding with Louis and supporting his cool repudiation of the homosexual vampires' advances. Nevertheless, Lestat insists, at the end, on his right to share whatever is Louis's, and this forces the audience to reconsider its glib acceptance of Louis's homophobic attitude toward Lestat.

Homophobia, on the full evidence of *Interview*, seems the logical conclusion of the *puer* neurosis that emerged with the Enlightenment. From the limited perspective of Louis, our cultural fear of emotional commitments between men would seem a healthy taboo, a brake placed on our dangerous, modern capacity to construct identities that pay no heed to the feminine. For today's middle-class *puer aeternus*, represented through the gothic trappings of Louis, a real life, whatever one's leanings, has to involve mothers and daughters and wives: everything else is alienation and evil. But such well-rationalized rejection of the homoerotic, so easy to go along with in the name of helping the *puer*-identified man find a socially grounded life, is actually an impediment to Louis's solving his unconscious problem. Taken symbolically, his teasing disdain for homosexual involvement signifies the *puer*'s refusal to engage psychologically with the male initiative lurking within his own stance of noninvolvement. Lestat's masculine vitality, which Louis refuses to embrace, is disavowed to his, and our culture's, stagnation. Louis's is finally a despairing, negative attitude whose claim to higher moral ground is rightly mocked by the queerly wicked Lestat.

The ending, which gives Lestat another opportunity to initiate an undeveloped youth—the interviewer of the vampire, who stands for the audience itself, Anne Rice's "all of us"—leaves us with the thrill of a dangerous renewal in the teeth of the shadow. The excitement is qualified, however, by the threat of a new cycle of disappointment, the feeling that sterile fate is about to be repeated. Even though we are glad to have Cruise's character back in full force, we aren't sure of the point of the compulsive repetition of the vampire-making ritual. Is there, after all, some hope that this secret rite of passage will turn out differently this time? It is not the least of the ironies of the film that the question remains open, even as we cross a significant bridge to another chapter of the story.

NOTES

1. Anne Rice, spoken preface to the video version of *Interview with the Vampire* (Warner Home Video, 1995).
2. Marie-Louise von Franz, *Puer Aeternus* (New York: Spring Publications, 1970), 1–3.
3. Joseph Henderson, unpublished lecture, San Francisco, 1969.
4. Marie-Louise von Franz, "The Religious Background of the Puer Aeternus Problem," in *Psychotherapy* (Boston: Shambhala Publications, 1993), 306–23.
5. Christopher Lasch, *The True and Only Heaven* (New York: Norton, 1991), 120–26.
6. James Hillman, "*Pothos*: The Nostalgia of the *Puer Aeternus*," in *Loose Ends* (Dallas: Spring Publications, 1975), 49–62.
7. Ibid., 53.
8. Katherine Ramsland, *The Vampire Companion: The Official Guide to Anne Rice's The Vampire Chronicles*, rev. ed. (New York: Ballantine Books, 1995), 262.
9. Andrew Samuels, "Original Morality in a Depressed Culture," in *The Plural Psyche* (London and New York: Routledge, 1989), 194–215.

FURTHER READING

Henderson, Joseph. *Thresholds of Initiation.* Middletown, Connecticut: Wesleyan University Press, 1967.

Hillman, James. *Loose Ends.* Dallas: Spring Publications, 1975.

———,ed. *Puer Papers.* Dallas: Spring Publications, 1979.

Interview with the Vampire (film). Directed by Neil Jordan. Written by Anne Rice. Warner Home Video, 1995. (Includes a filmed preface spoken by Anne Rice.)

Jung, C.G. *Symbols of Transformation. Collected Works.* vol. 5. 2d ed. Princeton: Princeton University Press, 1967.

Lasch, Christopher. *The True and Only Heaven.* New York: Norton, 1991.

Ovid. *Metamorphoses*, trans. Frank Justus Miller. 2 vols. London and New York: Loeb Classical Library, 1916.

Ramsland, Katherine. *The Vampire Companion: The Official Guide to Anne Rice's The Vampire Chronicles,* rev. ed. New York: Ballantine, 1995.

Rice, Anne. *Interview with the Vampire.* New York: Ballantine, 1977 (paperback).

Samuels, Andrew. *The Plural Psyche.* London and New York: Routledge, 1989.
Von Franz, Marie-Louise. *A Psychological Interpretation of the Golden Ass of Apuleius.* New York: Spring Publications, 1970.
———. *Psychotherapy.* Boston: Shambhala, 1993.
———. *Puer Aeternus.* New York: Spring Publications, 1970.

The Real World of the Free People of Color in Anne Rice's The Feast of All Saints

Robin Miller

In her second novel, *The Feast of All Saints*, Anne Rice provides rich detail about the physical world inhabited by Louisiana's Free People of Color. Known before the Civil War as *les gens de couleur libre*, these people are of mixed black African and white European descent. Since their history derived from other races, and since many of them attempted to assimilate into white culture, they needed something purely their own to ground their identity. They chose to cultivate their community's sense of place. The *gens* centered themselves in three principal locations in Louisiana: New Orleans, Isle Brevelle, and Opelousas. As they established themselves, they grew in number and developed their own separate culture.

However, one of Rice's characters, Marcel Ste. Marie, fears that this community may one day dissolve. He believes that the identity of his people is based on "an illusion sustained day in and day out by a collective act of faith,"[1] and thus cannot possibly survive. Is his perception correct, or has this fragile culture stayed intact? Examining the world Anne Rice brought alive in *The Feast* can help answer this question.

The mixed-race Free People of Color emerged from unusual circumstances in the 1800s. White men in Louisiana took mistresses from among the blacks around them—sometimes slaves, sometimes Caribbean refugees—and, as allowed by law in that state, the children of such liaisons were often granted their freedom. The white men educated their sons and for their daughters made sexual matches among white men of prominence, further mixing the blood. Many of these boys learned prosperous trades. When they married, their families had much more social mobility than did their black cousins, who were slaves. Typically, these families could amass wealth and dress as elegantly as whites, yet they had fewer rights and were often reminded of their limited status. Their black blood, however diluted, prevented them from achieving the full rights of citizenship. They could not legally marry whites, vote, or participate in the more powerful social institutions. Many sought to escape the community of Free People of Color, particularly those who could pass for white, but others worked hard to create their own class.

In *The Feast*, Anne Rice dramatizes this dilemma. Each of the characters must decide whether to be part of this culture or to escape it. Marcel, a blue-eyed blond with coarse, kinky hair, is the son of French planter Philippe Ferronaire and his mulatto mistress, Cecile Ste. Marie. Being a bastard, he takes his mother's name. He has a sister, Marie, who looks white. Marie can make a good match, as mistress of a prominent white man, but Marcel will always be held back if he remains in New Orleans. He looks forward to going to Paris for his promised education, since his idol, Christophe Mercier, had experienced great success in Paris as a writer. However, to Marcel's surprise, Christophe returns home to become part of the *gens* community. Marcel fails to understand Christophe's attachment to his racial identity.

Unfortunately for Marcel, he never gets to Paris; thus, he must find his place in his hometown among his people.

Most of *The Feast* takes place in 1840s New Orleans, in the French Quarter. It was a time of prosperity for the European-like city just before the Civil War. English-speaking Americans were a minority to French-speaking Creoles, or people of French and Spanish descent. The origin of the word *Creole* can be traced to 1718, to the arrival of Louisiana's French founders. Spain took possession of the territory in 1768, which resulted in marriage and interbreeding among the Spanish and the French. The Spanish labeled people born in their new colony *Criollo*. When the French eventually adopted the name, they quickly changed it to *Creole* to accommodate their language.

Authors Lyle Saxon and Robert Tallant are emphatic in describing Creoles as people born only of white blood. "No true Creole ever had colored blood," they write. "This erroneous belief, still common among Americans in other sections of the country, is probably due to the Creoles' own habit of calling their slaves 'Creole slaves' and often simply 'Creoles.' "[2] M. H. Herrin's description of Creoles is much the same: "The word is never to be used to identify persons with both white and Negro blood."[3]

Still, these authors point out that as time passed, a different definition for Creoles evolved. From the white Creoles emerged another people born of Creole blood mixed with that of African slaves. This group had existed since the early days of the French in Louisiana. Saxon speculates that many mixed-blood children were born to African slave women at that time because there were few white women in the colony. Even after the arrival of white women, white men continued to couple with their slaves and other black women.

In many instances, white men set their Negro concubines and mulatto children free, so the ranks of freed slaves grew. With that growth, and the passing of time, came the change of their label, from *les gens de couleur libre* to "Creoles of color" and finally "Creoles." With this transformation of name, they took on the Creole identity, which in eighteenth- and nineteenth-century Louisiana had been given only to whites of European heritage.

But Mickey Moran, a modern-day Creole of color who considers himself an historian among his people, has another definition: "A Creole is a person whose heritage begins in French colonial Louisiana and whose origins are European—French and/or Spanish. This can be any native of these cultures as long as one side or the other is of European origin. This includes those people of European and African blood. 'Creole' isn't a racial word. It's who our ancestors are. It's who we are."[4]

Les gens de couleur libre lived within the realms of French culture, adopting the same values and traditions since they were, by all rights, part European. They married other people of color and raised their families in the Catholic faith. Alliances between white men and women of color were prevalent, and children born to these unions were privileged, yet still restricted. Labels were assigned to these children according to their percentage of white blood. For instance, mulattos were half Negro, half white. Quadroons were one-fourth Negro, three-fourths white. An octoroon had one-eighth Negro blood and seven-eighths white. Marcel's mother, Cecile, was mulatto, so Marcel was considered a quadroon.

Many of the women of color in that time were considered the most beautiful women in New Orleans, and their chastity was closely protected. While the ultimate goal for a white woman was marriage to a proper white gentleman with a respectable family name, preferably attached to wealth, women of color basically had two choices: either marry within *les gens de couleur libre*, or arrange an alliance with one of the white gentlemen whom the white women hoped to marry.

Many times these arrangements were made at what Herbert Asbury calls "the scene of the most magnificent of the *Bals du Cordon Bleu*, better known as the Quadroon Balls, the most celebrated of all the entertainments of early New Orleans and the most shushed by Louisiana historians."[5]

Chaste young women of color attended these balls with chaperons or older women who acted as their guardians. Some historians say the balls were held in the Orleans Ballroom on Orleans Street, directly behind the St. Louis Cathedral and just around the corner from St. Ann Street. Others dispute this, saying that ballroom was not built until long after the discontinuation of the infamous balls.

Nevertheless, the ballroom is still intact, trimmed in full elegance on the second floor of what is now the Bourbon Orleans Hotel. Asbury writes that the ballroom was constructed by John Davis some five years after he built the Théâtre d'Orléans in 1813. The ballroom was an addition to the theater and looked quite plain from the outside. Inside, however, the room was elaborately decorated with crystal chandeliers and costly paintings. Statuary lined the fine wood-paneled walls.

Asbury notes that a stairway led to the rear of the ballroom from a flagged courtyard where parties were conducted, and the building's ground floor was divided into private card and reception rooms of varying sizes.

"The principal feature of the building, however, was the ballroom itself—a long, gaudily ornamented chamber with a lofty ceiling, balconies which overlooked the gardens in the rear of the St. Louis Cathedral and a floor constructed of three thicknesses of cypress topped by a layer of quarter-sawed oak," Asbury adds.[6]

Walk into the Bourbon Orleans Hotel, and the scene becomes vivid. The bottom floor is no longer a series of private rooms but a large lobby trimmed in brass and decorated in shades of green. The wood in the now-carpeted stairway to the ballroom creaks beneath each footstep, as it probably sounded in the 1800s when suitors ascended to the second floor where their prospective lovers awaited. One can only imagine the anxiety felt by the women of color as they listened for the sound of this wood, waiting for the first of the masculine white faces to enter the doorway. *White* is the key word here, for only white men were admitted to the balls. Free men of color, along with free blacks, were banned.

Three doors now serve as entrances to the ballroom. Open the door, and crystal chandeliers immediately catch the eye. One large fixture dominates the room from the center, looking much like a crown of diamonds. Gone are the statuary and paintings, replaced by gold trim and wallpaper flourished in swirls of gold and black. The floor, like the stairs, is carpeted. The courtyard stairway has long disappeared, and balcony entrances are blocked by locked windows.

Asbury's description of the building remains accurate for the most part. The ballroom is long but not wide, and when looking at the Bourbon Orleans' plain facade, one would never guess that such a ballroom is housed just above. Deals were made in this ballroom between suitors and guardians, contracts signed. Women were given cottages, many on St.

Ann Street, where they set up households. Suitors supplied their mistresses with slaves, food, money, clothing, and all other needs.

St. Ann Street and other sections of the French Quarter along North Rampart Street were filled with such households. It was also on St. Ann where Philippe maintained a cottage for Cecile and her children. Leaving the ballroom on Orleans Street and turning the corner onto St. Ann, it is easy to conclude that Marcel's neighborhood has not seen much transformation, even with twentieth-century modernization.

Pavement now covers streets once surfaced in mud, and utility poles join houses with electrical wires. Bulky automobiles have replaced horse-drawn carriages, which better suited the narrow French Quarter streets. Just around the corner, a few blocks down, restaurants, bars, art galleries, antique stores, and tourist gift shops occupy centuries-old town houses. And the house that once served as residence to voodoo queen Marie Laveau, who, like Marcel, was a free person of color, has been torn down and replaced by a cottage duplex, the result of an address mix-up by New Orleans city workers on a demolition project.

But surviving the changing times are the lines of neat cottages, many the former quarters of colored mistresses and families of white planters. On the corner of St. Ann and Dauphine Streets is the perfect match to the residence of Christophe Mercier. The gray building is large enough to accommodate residential quarters on the second story, where Marcel spent many nights with Christophe's mother, Juliet, and classroom space on the bottom floor, where Christophe opened his school for boys of color.

West down St. Ann Street toward North Rampart sits a red-brick cottage with green trim, placed among wooden counterparts in white-trimmed pinks, yellows, and blues. This could be the Ste. Marie cottage, gleaming, as described in the novel, "with respectability beyond its short fence and dense banana trees, a sprawl of magnolia limbs over its pitched roof."[7] Absent are the banana trees and short fence, but the cottage appears large enough to house a small family in comfort. A peek through a locked gate barring a short driveway reveals a *garçonnière* on the bounds of a small courtyard, just as is described in the story. This was Marcel's world. This was where he grew from boyhood to manhood, surrounded by whites, blacks, and some eighteen thousand of his *gens de couleur libre*.

Marcel had heard about his background. His aunts had told him bits and pieces about the slave riots in Santo Domingo, where they took Cecile from her mother. He watched as his childhood friend Anna Bella Monroe passed into womanhood as the colored mistress of Philippe's brother-in-law Vincent Dazincourt, carrying on the tradition befallen his people. He witnessed as his friend Richard's father, Rudolphe Lermontant, went to trial for a confrontation with a white man.

He knew the rules of his world, and he lived by them. There were bars in which he was not admitted, not because of age but because of race. He was required to sit in the balcony in the St. Louis Cathedral when attending Mass, and in a separate box at the opera. He was allowed into all of these places, yet he could not mingle with whites.

Marcel's cramped, limited world and the places he visited daily make it easy to understand his confusion. He did not question anything because he knew he would one day leave for Paris, to be a man equal in status to all other races. Then he lost that prospect, and his thinking suddenly became clear: He was a person born into a race created, as he saw it, by mistake. And because he was born into that race, he had to abide by rules that he had no part in making.

However, Marcel had not experienced the true scope of the world of the Free People of Color until he was sent to Sans Souci, located in Isle Brevelle, an unmarked community that stretches about thirty miles north to south between the Louisiana municipalities of Natchitoches and Cloutierville. The area was named for its earliest French settler, Jean Baptiste Brevel, Jr., but the community's main residents were not French. Free People of Color dominated the area in the eighteenth and nineteenth centuries, and their descendants continue living there today.

When he arrived, Marcel realized that these people had isolated themselves from the outside world. The only faces he saw there were colored.

The origins of Isle Brevelle's colored population date from some one hundred years before the Civil War, long before Marcel's arrival there in the 1840s. The story begins with a woman named Marie Therese CoinCoin. She was born a slave in the household of Louis Juchereau de St. Denis, the French commandant who, in 1714, founded the first military post and settlement in the Louisiana Purchase territory, Fort St. Jean Baptiste des Natchitoches. Though there are no paintings or drawings of Marie Therese, many described her as beautiful.

Legend says that Marie Therese's outstanding loyalty as a slave eventually won her her freedom. This loyalty supposedly came into play when St. Denis's wife fell ill. Marie Therese had learned herbal medicine from her African parents and used it to cure Madame St. Denis. The St. Denis family was so grateful that they rewarded her not only with freedom but a grant of some of the most fertile land in the colony. She bought slaves and worked with them in her indigo fields. She named her spread Yucca, known today as Melrose.

That is legend. Gary Mills, in his book *The Forgotten People: Cane River's Creoles of Color*,[8] writes that Marie Therese was a slave when Madame St. Denis died in 1758 and remained so for twenty more years. Still, she did become matriarch of Yucca.

Mills also writes that Marie Therese was known to have four children while in slavery, and that after being set free she used her profits from the plantation to buy their freedom. Meanwhile, she met Frenchman Claude Pierre Thomas Metoyer, with whom she formed an alliance. The St. Denis family leased Marie Therese to Metoyer, who eventually bought her and set her free. Metoyer was staying at the Natchitoches post and was reputed to be the descendant of a noble family. The two fell in love, and she agreed to be his concubine, since the Code *Noir* forbade them to marry.

The couple had ten children, all baptized in the Catholic Church. Their oldest son, Augustin, later became known as the father of the colony because he was its true firstborn person of color. He established what is speculated to be the nation's oldest church built by Free People of Color—St. Augustine Catholic Church. The church continues to be the cornerstone for Isle Brevelle's people of color today, with many of their activities centering around it.

It is easy to see how this church shaped Marcel's perception of his people. When attending Mass there with his aunt Josette, he noticed, just as he had in the community, that the congregation was made up of colored faces, much different from *les gens de couleur libre* community in New Orleans, where other races also mingled. In Isle Brevelle, black slaves remained outside the church, and the priest was the only white person in attendance.

The scene is basically the same today. Take, for instance, the congregation's celebration of All Saints' Day. Blacks and whites attend services at the church now, but they are the minority, their faces standing out among those of the people of color. Descendants of *les gens de couleur libre* fill the church's simple wooden interior, the overflow filling balcony stairways. Plain, white wooden arches support the ceiling, and a painted portrait of Augustin Metoyer watches the activity from the back of the church.

The presence of so many people of color living in one place, making up this congregation, affirms their claim to being a separate race. Mickey Moran candidly admits that even today, people of color are still encouraged to marry within their race.

"But people aren't discouraged from marrying outside the race. At the time you're ready to marry, you find yourself a good Creole."[9]

This effort toward race preservation existed even in Marcel's time. He realized this when he saw the colored congregation inside the church, closing themselves off from the outside, their history spanning only one hundred years. Marcel concludes that his heritage is based on a collective act of faith: His people have banded together in a common belief that by isolating themselves from the outside world of white and black, they can preserve their race and maintain their societal status. Although Louisiana recognized the Free People of Color as a separate race at that time, after the Civil War, they were placed in the same category as blacks. Yet the faith identified by Marcel prevailed, especially in Isle Brevelle. The community survives.

Yet Marcel considered Isle Brevelle extreme in its isolation and decided to return to New Orleans. He concluded that his place in society could be affirmed only by daily contact with blacks and whites: By seeing them, he knew where he stood, which was somewhere in between.

He also concluded, above everything else, that he was a man. Not black. Not white. Not a person of color. A man.

Still, Marcel senses the apparent fragility of his racial existence. When his people separated themselves, they sought to preserve their race through faith and isolation. Marcel considered such a foundation too weak.

But in time, the people of color have proven Marcel wrong. Their faith has been strong enough to sustain their identity for more than two hundred years, and though they are no longer recognized by law as a separate race, they continue to work toward racial preservation, collaborating to establish a separate identity for their people as a whole. Simply put, they are survivors. There was never any illusion at all. *Les gens de couleur libre*'s culture, ideas, traditions—their world—was always real, from the time they came into existence. Grounding themselves in their own communities, they have created a secure identity.

NOTES

1. Anne Rice, *The Feast of All Saints* (New York: Simon and Schuster, 1979), 470.
2. Lyle Saxon and Robert Tallant, *Gumbo Ya Ya* (New York: Bonanza Books, 1955), 159.
3. M. H. Herrin, *Creole Aristocracy* (New York: Exposition Press, 1952), 28.
4. Author interview with Mickey Moran, July 1994.
5. Herbert Asbury, *The French Quarter* (New York: Garden City Publishing, 1938), 126.
6. Ibid.
7. Rice, *The Feast*, 14.
8. Gary Mills, *The Forgotten People: Cane River's Creoles of Color* (Baton Rouge: Louisiana State University Press, 1977).
9. Author interview with Mickey Moran, July 1994.

The Price of Perfection

CRY TO HEAVEN, ART, AND HUMAN SACRIFICE

Michelle Spedding and Katherine Ramsland

In her third novel, *Cry to Heaven*, Anne Rice explores sexual identity and artistic expression in the lives of the castrated opera singers of eighteenth-century Italy. She also forcefully illustrates the cruel demands that culture can make for the sake of aesthetics and status. But the historical context of the novel may deflect the full impact of that cruelty. If we closely examine the castrati's milieu, we can find within it surprising similarities to the pressure we put on today's performers. A specific example is the abuse we tolerate in the training programs for our elite female athletes. When it comes to power and perfection, human nature clearly transcends culture, and history can offer an enlightening perspective that we might not otherwise achieve.

Eighteenth-century Italian culture celebrated opera as the ultimate art form, with an emphasis on powerful arias, or solos. Audiences across Europe expected Italian singers to perform to the highest standards. The *bel-canto* style, in which beautiful singing predominated, demanded supreme vocal range and agility. Since the Catholic Church had banned women from the stage (based partly on St. Paul's biblical injunction against women speaking in church), the beautiful sopranos needed for the arias were sung by men who had been castrated before puberty to preserve their youthful voices.

As boys, they were taken from their homes (often sold by their parents) and sent to music conservatories to determine their potential for operatic excellence. Some had it, but many did not. "Hundreds were submitted to the knife each year for a handful of fine voices."[1] This cruel surgical disfigurement left them an enigma in society—seemingly not quite male, but not female either. Those whose voices changed in spite of castration or who could not live up to the demands of their art were often forced to make a life apart from normal society, with no hope of return. Unable to have families, they were also forbidden to participate in many other social institutions, such as entering the orders of the Church. If they were to experience community at all, they had to find it among others like themselves.

Cry to Heaven shows the cruelty and despair inherent in such an existence. Both of the principal characters, Tonio Treschi and Guido Maffeo, certainly know firsthand the suffering involved. Sold by his parents to the conservatory, Guido is castrated when he is only six years old. And, though he shows great promise as a singer, he loses his voice just before his debut at the age of eighteen. Fortunately for him, he can turn to a life of composing music and teaching other castrati, but he endures quiet despair over his divestiture and more than once tries to end his life.

Tonio's story is even more tragic. Growing up in an aristocratic Venetian family, he has a promising political future. However, his brother, Carlo, wants to remove him and any of his future progeny from the family legacy, so he has him forcibly castrated at the age of fourteen, just on the brink of manhood. Tonio awakens to the horror of what he is to become: To him, the castrati are monsters, "these *things* that were not and would never be men."[2] He studies Guido, his new mentor, and notes his abnormally long limbs and lack of muscularity. In addition, Guido informs Tonio that his voice will remain shrill and his bones elastic, which will allow his lungs to expand for great vocal range and endurance.

These discoveries shock Tonio. Aware of the scorn he will endure, he can hardly bear to be in his own body: "that less than man that arouses the contempt of every whole man who looks upon it."[3] To them, he is disturbing, pathetic, the butt of jokes, an artifice of culture. He is an outcast. Even in the sheltered world of the conservatory, Tonio notes the self-loathing of the neutered boys who recognize their degraded state, and he is mortified to be one of them.

Nevertheless, he comes to realize that he does have a magnificent voice, potentially "a human instrument so powerfully and perfectly tuned that it rendered all else feeble in comparison."[4] With practice, there is hope of triumph. As the maestro points out, with Tonio's talent, he can dwarf ordinary men by soaring toward accomplishments they could never achieve.

There were, in fact, castrati such as Caffarelli and Farinelli who used their singular status to launch themselves into a sort of superstardom. The equivalent of contemporary rock stars, they sang with authority and dignity, becoming larger than life and reaping the benefits in wealth and fame. "It was the soprano singer whom the world worshipped. It was for him that kings vied and audiences held their breath; it was the singer who brought to life the very essence of the opera."[5]

Still, such luminaries were rare, and most castrati failed to make it to the stage. More often, they were relegated to lesser roles such as singing in church choirs. They had no way to ensure their personal immortality or sense of masculine identity by having children or providing for a family. Some of Rice's fictional characters eventually learn to distinguish their masculinity from their physical endowments, but they do so only through arduous psychological transformation. It is likely that many of the real castrati struggled with issues of identity and manhood most of their lives.

As a result, an underlying theme of *Cry to Heaven* is the tyranny of fashion in the form of "children mutilated to make a choir of seraphim, their song a cry to heaven that heaven did not hear."[6] With women banned from the stage, patrons still craved the aesthetic experience of the angelic soprano voice. The audience for this vogue of forcing boys and men into roles that violated them was insatiable. The civilized world looked to Italy for a continual supply of singers who could outperform preceding stars, so more boys were "cut" toward the goal of absolute perfection. Such was the price of maintaining cultural dominance in Europe. "It was taste that kept such a shape as [Tonio's] fashionable . . . when all he ever saw in the mirror was the ghastly ruin of God's work."[7]

Eventually, even the most successful performers in the Italian opera became passé. By the 1820s, with the change in the political and cultural fashions of Europe, their great popularity began to decline.[8] Then, with the accession in 1878 of Pope Leo XIII, the practice of castration for the opera ended. In the afterword to *Cry to Heaven*, Rice describes a recording of Alessandro Moreshi, the last castrato ever to sing in the Sistine Chapel. With his death, the clear high sound of an adult male soprano also died.

Yet we must ask, was their country's artistic achievement worth the price these men paid? Was their culture immeasurably improved by having required so much, or should there have been limits to what human beings could subject others to for the sake of art?

True, the custom of castration for preserving vocal purity has ceased. Although young boys continue to train and sing, nature is allowed to take its course, and in retrospect we view such castration as a cruel way to feed the cultural appetite. But are we less cruel today? The general practice of sacrificing children to the image of excellence continues—it just occurs in a new arena. In our culture we find demanding routines for youngsters similar to those involved two centuries ago in preparing boys for the opera. In fact, these practices lead to some of the most popular events in the world—gymnastics, dancing, and figure skating.

In elite athletics such as these, girls as young as five and six are taken from their normal routines and subjected to long hours of stringent training. Worse, they endure discipline, drugs (sometimes), and unhealthy regimens that aim to defy their development and maintain their bodies in childlike shapes. Self-esteem suffers as puberty sets in and these girls are directed to do everything possible to thwart the effects of encroaching womanhood. The female child's body is light and flexible—like a young boy's voice—and can perform feats that the heavier, more rounded body of a budding young woman cannot achieve. Thus, the child becomes the ideal in many of these sports—the image of physical and aesthetic superiority.

Unfortunately, when menstruation is delayed through extreme measures of weight control, girls fail to produce estrogen (parallel to young boys not producing testosterone), and their bones become brittle. Several studies have found that young female athletes have the bone densities of post-menopausal women and risk premature osteoporosis. And highly correlated with the need for perfection are the well-known eating disorders, anorexia nervosa and bulimia. "Anorexia is a metaphor," says psychologist Mary Pipher. "It is a young woman's statement that she will become what the culture asks of its women."[9] Thirty-eight percent of dancers, for example, show anorexic behavior, and the average dancer is thinner than ninety-five percent of the female population.[10]

Figure skaters have similar problems. They need light, flexible bodies to perform impressive leaps and turns. Many of these girls suffer from eating disorders, and they willingly compete with fractured or broken bones on their way to stardom. This sport encourages its women to be thin and childlike at any cost. Olympic skater Nancy Kerrigan's coach, Evy Scotvold, purportedly told the young athlete that success must be achieved before her body acquired a womanly shape. When Kerrigan explained that, at the age of twenty-three, her body was naturally changing, her coach reprimanded her, telling her that "rigorous self-discipline can beat back nature."[11]

Perhaps the worst practices occur among the elite female gymnasts, and we can speculate that what has been documented of their experience may parallel what the struggling castrati suffered. In 1972, a young Russian, Olga Korbut, captured the hearts of the entire world with her stunning gymnastics performance in the Olympics. Four years later, our fascination with gymnastics was sealed by the perfection of Nadia Comaneci. Her tiny, light body performed feats that no one had ever seen before. The judges awarded her a 10, the first perfect score in the history of the sport. Not yet fifteen years old, Comaneci had been practicing rigorously for that moment since she was six. In the years following her victory, women's gymnastics has steadily evolved toward training younger girls whose flexible, waiflike bodies are capable of performing the many, more difficult moves. A small body has become the ideal and is imperative for achieving international presence. The sport now belongs to the child.

In the last fifteen years, the average age of American female gymnasts has dropped from seventeen and a half to sixteen. The average height has gone from 5 feet 3½ inches to 4 feet 9 inches. Perhaps the most telling statistic is that the average weight, once 106 pounds, is down to 83.[12] A national champion and one of the newest Olympic hopefuls, Dominique Moceanu, weighs in at 70 pounds. Dedicated, hardworking, fearless, talented . . . all these adjectives describe the female gymnasts. Yet, in order to achieve the small, thin body required for success, there is a price to pay that borders on that inflicted on the castrati.

The road to athletic achievement is littered with those whose quest for perfection cost them their lives or their health. Dr. Pipher, who specializes in the treatment of adolescents, tells the story of "Heidi," a sixteen-year-old girl who had trained rigorously in gymnastics since the age of six. She had taught herself to vomit as a means of weight control and soon was practicing it daily: "I blame my training for my eating disorder. . . . Our coach has weekly weigh-ins where we count each other's ribs. If they are hard to count, we're in trouble."[13]

Joan Ryan, an award-winning *San Francisco Chronicle* sports journalist, took a good hard look at this sport. Her book, *Little Girls in Pretty Boxes*, documents the unbelievable pressures endured by girls whose natural hormonal changes were treated as tantamount to a crime. She points out that while gymnastics and skating are among the world's most watched sports events, little is known of what goes on behind the scenes. There are more health problems and burnouts than most people realize. A number of young gymnasts practice and compete with sprains, broken bones, and torn muscles because the race against nature allows them little time to heal. Too, many parents get so caught up in the drive to succeed that they become accustomed to their daughters' injuries and cries of pain.

"I found a girl," Ryan claims, "who scraped her arms and legs with razors to dull her emotional pain and who needed a two-hour pass from a psychiatric hospital to attend her high school graduation. Girls who broke their necks and backs. One who so desperately sought the perfect, weightless gymnastics body that she starved herself to death."[14] Ryan discovered sexual and emotional abuse, shaming techniques that seriously eroded self-esteem, and startling personal and familial sacrifices, all in the name of achievement. Like the cultural environment in Italy that condoned random castration to gain a few stars, "the American obsession with winning has produced a training environment wherein results are bought at any cost."[15] To aspire to the highest honors—a gold medal in the Olympics, which also brings big money from endorsements—a young woman must reject what makes her female. Often she learns to hate her own body. Yet, out of hundreds of aspirants, only seven girls every four years reach the Olympics, and once there, winning the gold is a long shot.

Who is to blame for this trend? It's difficult to determine, but there seem to be several colluding factors. Some of the best Olympic performers have been trained by coaches who use verbally abusive tactics to motivate them. Bela Karolyi, who coached Nadia Comaneci and Mary Lou Retton into becoming all-around gold medal winners, demands that his girls remain thin at all costs and purportedly calls them degrading names like "stuffed turkey" and "imbecile" when they gain weight. Yet parents who bring their girls to him do nothing to stop it. Amy Jackson's mother admitted on the television show *60 Minutes*, "We weren't worried about what was happening to these children's minds. It was, 'How many rotations do they get . . . ? How many minutes do they get with the coach?' It wasn't, you know, 'Is this good for our child? Does she want to do this?' "[16] Kathy Scanlon, president of USA Gymnastics, insists that the federation should play no role in regulating alleged abuse. Some of the girls are even resolved to it. Despite Olympic hopeful Kristie Phillips's awareness that developing into a woman was considered "the sin of all sins," she shrugged off the potentially negative effects of Karolyi's techniques. When correspondent Leslie Stahl asked her if she might have accomplished her best without being humiliated and demeaned, Phillips said, "I don't think I would have because . . . that wouldn't have given me the motivation to keep going to prove him wrong."[17] Such attitudes may arise from society as a whole, from our intense focus on achievement, excellence, and victory. However, as with the castrati, there are victims.

Julissa Gomez was ten when she began intensive training for the Olympics. Suffering from stress fractures in her ankles, shinsplints, and sprained knees, she learned to ignore her pain. Pushed by her parents and coaches to be well rounded and to achieve a faultless performance, she moved toward more and more difficult routines. "Keep going, her coaches always told her, because she could hurt herself worse by balking."[18] When she was sixteen, she attempted a vault for which she lacked sufficient strength and broke her neck. Totally paralyzed, she died three years later. A gymnast who had watched Julissa practice commented that it was not a safe vault for her to have attempted: "Someone along the way should have stopped her."[19]

Christy Henrich had begun gymnastics before kindergarten and was practicing four to five hours a day by the time she was seven. A perfectionist by nature, she developed anorexia to keep her weight correct for competition. In 1991, she retired from gymnastics due to declining strength and health. Despite years of medical treatment, she died in 1994, at the age of twenty-two. Other gymnasts such as Cathy Rigby, Erica Stokes, and Kristie Phillips suffered from bulimia. Cathy made it to the Olympics, although she was hospitalized twice during her twelve-year battle with her condition. Erica and Kristie both retired, their self-esteem crushed and their health in shambles, without ever seeing the Olympic floor.

When Kristie Phillips's weight climbed during puberty from 88 pounds to 98, she feared she was growing fat and that her larger body "prevented her from performing some of the spectacular moves that she could once do so well."[20] In a last attempt to make the Olympic trials, Kristie took laxatives and diuretics. Although she lost twenty pounds, she also lost the strength necessary to perform the difficult moves. After years of intensive training and personal sacrifice, she failed to make the team and her career was finished.

It may be that social encouragement to starve and to delay puberty for the sake of enhanced performance and perfect image is a bit less cruel than the surgical castration that young men like Tonio and Guido suffered. For most of these girls, certainly there is hope of eventual physical recovery. Yet what is similar is the willingness of society to submit children at an early age to stringent and demanding conditions for the sake of an art form, for entertainment, for an ideal. The personal cost is all too often of secondary concern. This is not to say that children should not train or practice in order to excel at a given task. But we must be careful not to treat them as pawns in a game of prestige. Art can then become an instrument of harm rather than a means of enrichment.

The insatiable appetite for the ultimate aesthetic experience that once encouraged the mutilation of boys may also cause today's society to overlook abuse in girls' athletics. While perfection in the service of art involves certain, limited sacrifices, lines must be drawn to protect individuals. If not, they may become victims, used by others as a means to an end, and perhaps forfeiting their health or their lives. "It was the horror of this world," Rice writes, "that a thousand evils were visited on those who were blameless."[21] Although she points to injuries of the past, this statement should as effectively prod awareness in our own culture. By examining the parallels, perhaps we can arouse in ourselves the same alarm over what *we* allow in the name of excellence as we may feel over what Europe once promoted. The similarities should at least make us examine our practices. Whether Rice intended it or not, in *Cry to Heaven* she has provided us with a valuable social mirror.

NOTES

1. Anne Rice, *Cry to Heaven* (New York: Knopf, 1982), 5.
2. Ibid., 160.
3. Ibid., 182.
4. Ibid., 76.
5. Ibid., 4.
6. Ibid., 477.
7. Ibid., 300.
8. Camille Paglia, *Sexual Personae: Art and Decadence from Nefertiti to Emily Dickinson* (New Haven, CT: Yale University Press, 1990), 394.
9. Mary Pipher, *Reviving Ophelia: Saving the Selves of Adolescent Girls* (New York: Ballantine, 1994), 175.
10. Naomi Wolf, *The Beauty Myth: How Images of Beauty Are Used Against Women* (New York: Doubleday, 1991), 185.
11. Joan Ryan, *Little Girls in Pretty Boxes* (New York: Doubleday, 1995), 97.
12. Ibid., 65.
13. Pipher, *Reviving Ophelia*, 166.
14. Ryan, *Little Girls*, 4.
15. Ibid., 5.
16. "The Stars on the Parallel Bars," *60 Minutes*, 8 October 1995.
17. Ibid.
18. Ryan, *Little Girls*, 49.
19. Ibid., 25.
20. Ibid., 114.
21. Rice, *Cry*, 477.

FURTHER READING

Bordo, Susan. *Unbearable Weight: Feminism, Western Culture, and the Body.* Berkeley: University of California Press, 1993.

Brennan, Christine. *Inside Edge: A Revealing Journey into the Secret World of Figure Skating.* New York: Scribner, 1996.

Foster, Patricia, ed. *Minding the Body: Women Writers on Body and Soul.* New York: Doubleday, 1995.

Orenstein, Peggy. *School Girls: Young Women, Self-Esteem, and the Confidence Gap.* New York: Doubleday, 1994.

Thomas, Helen, ed. *Dance, Gender and Culture.* New York: St. Martin's Press, 1993.

How Do They Rate?

ELLIOTT SLATER AND LASHER AS LOVE SLAVES

Claudia Varrin

Most people I know would curl up on the sofa with a blanket and a cup of tea for a night's reading with a good book like *Exit to Eden*. When I read it, I got in "the mood" by lacing myself into my corset and slipping on my favorite spike heels. Please allow me to introduce myself. My name is Claudia Varrin, Mistress Claudia, Goddess Claudia to my slaves. I excel in the art of sensuous female domination. I am delighted to share with you my views on *Exit to Eden*'s Elliott Slater and *The Witching Hour*'s Lasher because the subject of dominance and submission is so close to my heart.

Before comparing the dominant and submissive sides of both Elliott and Lasher, I would like to explain why I prefer to call this lifestyle "Dominance and Submission" (D&S) rather than "sado-masochism" (S&M). Using the terms "S&M" and "D&S" interchangeably is misleading as well as inaccurate. Dominance and Submission implies, and embraces, a much broader spectrum of sexual behavior than plain old S&M. *Webster's* accurately describes a sadist as one who derives pleasure from hurting another, with or without that person's consent, and a masochist as one who derives pleasure from the pain inflicted on him or her by another.

By contrast, a Dominant can be well versed in role-playing, bondage and discipline, verbal humiliation, sensual teasing, feminine transformation, foot/body/leather/latex worship, and a variety of fetishes, as well as the psychology behind some of the fetishes and scenarios the Dominant creates for the slave. The Submissives can look forward to having their deepest, most secret sexual fantasies fulfilled by a Dominant who is concerned about their needs and desires, who is a good communicator, and who shares the same sexual interests as the slave. Unlike a "straight" date, both parties know of, and appreciate, each other's "dark side" explorations and do not sit in judgment of the fantasies. Surprisingly, some Submissives do not like pain but accept it from their mistresses or masters to please them and to demonstrate their devotion and obedience.

For those not familiar with Dominance and Submission as a lovestyle, I think an explanation of its appeal would be helpful. Speaking with switchable or submissive colleagues, and drawing on my personal experiences, we agree that from the Submissive's perspective (whether male or female), being a sexual slave is provocative, alluring, and enticing. The slave, flesh or phantom, exists to fulfill the wishes of the mistress (or master). The slave surrenders control to the strong, dominant partner. As in Elliott's case, consensual submission is a powerful aphrodisiac for him.

The slave's consent is also a heady dose of power for the dominant. I have felt this with my own slaves many times as I enacted their fantasies. When playing the slave in a monogamous, ongoing relationship, or with a steady, professional mistress, the slave literally lives his or her days and nights in a state of constant, anticipatory sexual arousal. From the first moment that the games begin, both Dominant and Slave become sexually aroused and often stay that way for days (yes, days) afterward.

Anne Rice demonstrates a fine understanding of the sexual

slave's excitement in *Exit to Eden*. Elliott, a photo-journalist, has become a slave at The Club, an opulent resort devoted to exotic sex. He relates to his master a fantasy of slavery and servitude in the ancient world. This particular fantasy involves "an old, sacrosanct arrangement" in which youths in a great Greek city were sent, "like in the Theseus myth," to another city to "serve as sexual slaves." Elliott says, "There has to be consent and coercion for it to be a really good fantasy. . . . [I]t has to be a humiliation, with a struggle inside between the part of you that wants it and the part that doesn't; and the ultimate degradation is that you consent and grow to like it."[1] The fantasy is laid out so as not only to remove guilt, since the sacrifice is for religious reasons and therefore "good," but to give the fantasizer permission to enjoy his sexual slavery.

Elliott's Theseus-myth fantasy exemplifies one of the most exciting things about being a slave: It allows one to fulfill his or her fantasies without guilt. In Elliott's case, since he has no choice but to obey, he is no longer responsible for his rampant sexuality; he has given the reins of control over to someone else. That person knows his deepest desires and turn-ons and dominates him in his or her own style, but still in accordance with the slave's fantasies, making the session a tremendously stimulating sexual adventure for both of them.

The dominant takes the reins of control offered by the slave. Together, dominant and submissive open up to each other by communicating their sexual needs and desires, establishing trust and enacting the scenarios they have created. The D&S pair often develop an intimacy that is almost spiritual. Many couples, or long-term partners, claim that since they have added acts of dominance and submission to their love lives, they have gained a new understanding of themselves and of their mates. D&S has not only added spice and romance to the relationship but has made it stronger, more fulfilling for both of them. In a loving relationship, D&S play is considered "foreplay," followed by sexual gratification for one or both partners.

It is important here to point out a subtle fact about Dominant and Submissive relationships that the uninitiated may not realize. Healthy D&S relationships are safe and consensual; the partners are not hurt any more than they want to be, nor are they bound or beaten against their will. In truth, the Submissive is the one who controls the severity of the D&S activities.

For example, the slave will have a prearranged "safe word" or, if he is unable to speak, a "safe signal." This is the word the slave will say if the session seems to be pushing or passing his or her limits. As soon as the slave utters that word, the dominant immediately stops and discusses the problem. Additionally, until the couple gets to know each other's fantasies and limits, each scene is fully discussed before its enactment. After time, generally only new additions to their repertoire will be discussed. A mistress, for example, with a male slave has only the *illusion* of control, because she and her slave have laid down rules by which she must abide. The mistress strives to test the slave's limits, to push him and probe him, but the slave knows that he will not be marred, scarred, or seriously harmed in any way. All D&S play is safe, sane, and consensual.

From many experiences as a professional dominatrix, I can tell you of the seductiveness and empowerment of having a human slave. The love and deep sensuality of the permanent mistress/master–slave relationship is largely overlooked by many who see only the beatings and the weird paraphernalia and clothing. This type of play often gives both partners "permission" to have fantasies, thus removing guilt and helping them to become more fully developed sexual beings.

I believe that the sessions I conduct with my clients often have a therapeutic value. They come to me, nervous and shy, and hesitantly "confess" their most secret sexual scenarios, usually in soft tones. Then we discuss the specifics of the fantasy: Some people have a word or phrase that triggers their response, like "beating" or "you are my slave." Others react to a garment or to a body part. After the session, many of my clients have expressed gratitude for my acceptance and enactment of a fantasy that they were afraid to share with their mate. My acceptance of their fantasies grants them permission to act them out. It also validates their sexuality and lets them know that they are not alone, that others have similar fantasies of exotic sex.

In a professional setting, the turn-on for the slave is not sex as we usually know it, but instead *consent* to slavery, submission, and servitude to the Dominant. Even the slave's orgasm is controlled by the Dominant. Usually, at the end of a professional session, the Dominant will allow the slave to gain release as a reward for good behavior. Or, sometimes, the Dominant may not grant such permission, depending on his or her mood and the quality of the service received.

To have a slave, whether phantom or flesh, is alluring enough without the elaborate trappings and rituals of *Exit to Eden*'s setting, The Club. But when the experience is accompanied by guilt-free, luxurious sensuality and opulence, it becomes intoxicatingly seductive. At The Club, people can surrender to their erotic nature without fear of harm or guilt, give in to impulses otherwise squelched, abandon themselves to the bacchanalia of their sexual fantasies. Elliott's thoughts on the subject are: "It's paradise, all right, and we're pleasure slaves in it, just like something out of the ancient Egyptian tomb painting, where all the slaves are naked and the lords and ladies exquisitely dressed. We were here to be used and enjoyed like the food being eaten, the wine being poured."[2]

In *Exit to Eden*, Rice has captured much of the ambience, sexual tension and arousal, and attitude of those who prefer exotic sex. The humiliations, subtle and overt; the punishments, sublime and worldly; the concept of The Club itself, an intoxicating world where sexual fantasies come to life—all are faithful reflections of the world of D&S. The siren call of that world can be very alluring, and it is easy to get lost there. Elliott wanted to drown in that world, to immerse himself in living out his fantasies and then conjure up more. Even Lisa, Elliott's mistress and lover, was more at home in her fantasy world than in the world inhabited by most of society.

Rice has also captured, in Elliott, the type of man who seeks release as a slave. Having confronted whatever fears he had about his courage in his career as a war photographer, he now wants to confront his deepest sexual fears. He considers himself testy and somewhat macho, a nuisance as a student, not given to obeying the rules. He doesn't think he is the type of guy who would like sexual submissiveness. But he is exactly the type who often enters into an S&M lifestyle.

The mistresses I have spoken to about the professions of their clientele all tell the same tale. Among their clients, as well as mine, are doctors, attorneys, judges, CEOs, CFOs, business owners, accountants, stockbrokers, advertising executives, retired military officers, etc., with the occasional arms trader or art and antiquities dealer tossed in for good measure. They are all in positions of great power, responsibility, stress, and occasionally, like Elliott, some sort of danger. All of them are exploring their sexuality.

Becoming a slave, for an hour or a day or a year, has an undeniable allure to this type of man. For the first time in his life, he is not the one in control. A chance to turn himself inside out, to surrender, abandon himself with someone who is sympathetic and well versed in the art of sensual female domination, is a powerful aphrodisiac for those who have decided to explore this "dark" side of their lives. Many male slaves refer to their mistresses as goddesses.

In Elliott's case, he wants to pass behind the veil, to have his limits tested, and to be confronted with what he fears most. The idea of being treated as a "body," an object for the amusement of his masters and mistresses, a mindless sex toy, consenting yet coerced, is provocative for a man whose responsibilities weigh heavily upon his shoulders. Wanting to be a "toy" is not uncommon among males or females who fantasize about D&S sex. Many of the games at The Club are aimed at making the slaves toys or part of a boardwalk game of chance for this very reason.

Imagine yourself as the one who takes Elliott to this limit, disciplining him, using him as a sex object. Think of him serving you, bringing you refreshments or dinner, giving you a pedicure or a bath, brushing your hair, all at your command. Now imagine him cooperating, actively assisting you as you tie him up or down, positioning himself as you demand so that you may humiliate him. Imagine the rise and fall of the lash as you beat him for an infraction of your rules, or just because you like to beat him. The slave's striving to please is part of his pleasure, and silent, devoted service to the dominant master or mistress is a slave's highest aspiration.

* * *

As I explained earlier, the life of a sex slave is spent in a state of constant sexual excitement and anticipation. To be deprived of sight, either by total darkness or by blindfold, to be handled, teased into sexual arousal, to be touched by someone unknown and unseen is deeply erotic, highly stimulating. If you allowed yourself to be put in bondage and deprived of sight, you would experience a tremendous heightening of your other, unfettered senses. Perhaps the scent of your mistress's perfume would invade your nostrils, signifying her approach. The fall of her foot, even on the carpet, would boom as loud as thunder in your ears. Your skin would become ultrasensitive, tingling with anticipation and desire, quivering at your mistress's touch.

In *The Witching Hour*, Lasher, the spirit conjured by the first witch of the Mayfair family, seems submissive to the current heir to the Mayfair fortune. Lasher as an incubus, a spirit come in the night to gratify sexual passion, to grant your every wish, becomes as erotic as a human slave. Beautiful to look at, wanting only to please and gratify, Lasher as a submissive, is, on the surface, the manifestation of every woman's dream lover. But his servitude is a veneer that covers a more complex, even malevolent form of domination than Rice explored in Elliott's character.

The spirit Lasher was conjured up at Donnelaith, Scotland, by the village "cunning" woman Suzanne. From the moment of his conjuring, Lasher attached himself to the Mayfair family as their familiar spirit.[3] Like Zeus assuming the form of a swan to seduce the mortal Spartan woman Leda, Lasher assumed a shape and manner of dress to please his witch. Suzanne's vision of Lasher was that of a young man with long, dark hair and the leather jerkin and hose of her own time.

It was Suzanne's inability to control Lasher that led to her being burned at the stake as a "witch." Her daughter Deborah witnessed her death and inherited Lasher. Her escape with Petyr van Abel to the Talamasca in Amsterdam, and her subsequent sexual relations with him, founded the Mayfair line. The Mayfairs were a matriarchal dynasty, so Lasher himself, as well as the wealth he helped the family amass, was passed on to female children, girls who possessed the ability to "see" him, for thirteen generations.

Lasher showers attention and affection on each successive witch, like a good slave, and acts as if he is totally devoted to her, wanting only to please, to be allowed to touch her, to be submissive to her. But Lasher is not the benign, loving spirit he appears to be. He certainly has his own agenda and has taken on the witches to further his own ends. He hungers to become flesh, yearns for it, and sees his hunger someday being sated through the Mayfair witches. But in the meantime, he is dependent on them for his very existence in the world.

Both the witch and the mistress deal in the exercise of power—and, as we all know, real power is exercised in the mind, just like sex or magic. Additionally, witches and dominants cloak their practices in ritual and employ many implements in the execution of their art. There are many ritualized questions that dominants ask of their slaves, who respond with the proper, formulaic answers. Lasher was first summoned by Suzanne's chant in the circle of stones. Centuries later, the witch family still used a formula to call their spirit to them whenever he was needed. The witch Katherine ignored him completely and still he came to her immediately the one time she said the magic words, "Come now, my Lasher."[4]

Many slaves and mistresses share a love relationship, and Lasher's association with his witches is no different. Many of his witches loved him, and he, in his own way and for his own reasons, loved them. He showered them with riches, protected them from physical and financial misfortune, and positively doted on whatever girl-child was to become the next heir. What a lovely tribute it was to the dying witch to have Lasher's anguish at her passing manifest itself in a rainstorm.

As a human slave is used as a toy by his mistress—or, as Elliott was used at The Club, as part of a game—Lasher was used by his witches to amuse themselves. He was an invisible playmate for them when they were young girls. He would fill their famous purse with coins, or make flowers float through the air in the schoolyard for the amusement of the young witch and her friends. Lasher delighted in keeping his witch "company" and was elated when two of his witches were together.

Part of the power the Dominant wields is the ability to give permission to the slave *to be* the slave. In the case of the witch, she allows Lasher to show himself in order to please her, to service her, and to do her bidding. She gives him permission to manifest himself to her and sometimes even to others. The Mayfair witches used much the same methods to control Lasher the spirit as earthly mistresses use to control their human slaves. Although the purpose of the witch differs from that of the dominant female, both consciously use their power to bend their slaves to their will. The witch and the mistress promise rewards for good behavior—in Lasher's case, intimacy with the witch, or possession of a human body for a short time, among others; in Elliott's case, an opportunity to show his devotion to his mistress, to pleasure the mistress as all slaves aspire to.

Slaves, both human like Elliott and spirit like Lasher, occasionally exhibit a willfulness and independence that needs to be dealt with by the dominant. Both Elliott and Lasher show their rebellious sides in their first encounters with their dominants. Elliott's parade down the runway at The Club earned him the title "Proud Slave" and three days of scrubbing the lavatories. Lasher caused Deborah's husband to fall from his horse, sustaining injuries of which he ultimately died, because he "thought" it was what Deborah wanted. The witch's preferred method of punishment was to ignore the spirit, making him rattle around, and fade out, begging her to let him be seen. The occasional witch even knew how to use music to make him docile, to enthrall him. While a band played merrily in the background, the witch Marie Claudette told Julien of the secret power the music held over the spirit. Lasher became hypnotized by the music, powerless against its rhythmic beat. But the earlier witches, like Suzanne, Deborah, and even Charlotte, had little or no idea of what Lasher was capable of, and, with the exception of Charlotte, his independent thinking cost them their lives.

The witch and the mistress often choose to demonstrate power over their slaves simply because they can. Deborah disdainfully called upon Lasher in the Amsterdam Motherhouse of the Talamasca to demonstrate her power over him. At her command, her spirit gleefully destroyed every clock in the room. She took an angry pride (but still pride) in showing off her "slave spirit's" abilities to the shocked scholars in the room.[5]

Of course, the dangers to the witch are much greater than the dangers to the mistress. Human slaves do not threaten hapless scholars on deserted roads as spirit slaves seem to do, or endanger people with their supernatural abilities. Personally, I love a good scare once in a while, and there would be something so deliciously, frighteningly seductive about having my own personal Lasher that I might forget that he was a dangerous elemental thing, capable of great, uncontrollable violence. The human slave is so much more manageable.

Not all the Mayfair witches were adept at controlling Lasher, but some were especially strong mistresses. Among the earlier ones, the plantation owners from Saint-Domingue, Charlotte, Jeanne Louise, Angelique, and Marie Claudette, emerge as powerful sorceresses. Mary Beth, the ninth heir, was the last great nineteenth-century Mayfair witch and one of the most adept at controlling Lasher, as well as the vast Mayfair fortune. But at her death, her frivolous and beautiful daughter Stella inherited the legacy and became the first of a series of weak witches. Stella could certainly see and summon "the man," but she died young. After her death, each designated witch "reigned" for a shorter and shorter period of time until Rowan Mayfair came into possession of the spirit.

Rowan was indubitably the most powerful Mayfair witch even though she was raised away from the family fold in New Orleans. Her first contact with Lasher was when he appeared at her home in California when her mother, Deirdre, died in New Orleans. When Lasher approached Rowan on the plane to New Orleans on her way to her mother's funeral, Rowan thought his caress was part of a dream. Later on, when she knew who he was, Rowan used her power over Lasher to deny him "access" to becoming visible, to pleasing her, to serving her. This made him strive to please her and kept him in a state of constant arousal, just like any slave at The Club when confronted with a stern mistress.

Lasher is the phantom lover, come in the night to make

love to mortal women. There is no doubt that Lasher was able to sexually gratify every witch who allowed him the opportunity. Rowan admitted that his caresses were perfect, although distasteful, since no human was involved. Lasher as an incubus is as compelling a figure to a dominant as Elliott is as a slave.

But Lasher's sexual power did not just please the witches—it also enslaved them. Once the Mayfair women allowed Lasher to pleasure them, they became their slave's submissives. The sexual gratification the witch allowed Lasher to give her changed the very nature of their relationship. The witch was left thinking she was still in control, all the while hungering for the touch of her phantom lover. And it appears that Lasher was so capable of sexually satisfying his witches that, in later years, many of them no longer bothered with the pretense of having a husband.

The figure of a Dominant and/or a "switch" appears in many of Rice's works. A "switch" is the D&S term meaning a person who can be either dominant or submissive. When I read both *Exit to Eden* and *The Witching Hour*, I was struck by the pose of submissiveness adopted by such dominant males as Elliott and Lasher. One flesh, one phantom, both infinitely stronger than the women who dominate them; yet both willing to surrender to the wishes of their mistresses.

By incorporating both the dominant and submissive sides into each of her leading males, Elliott and Lasher, Rice has captured the exciting duality of the switch. But while Elliott became the dream lover, emotionally balanced and happy with his newly found role in life, Lasher became a terrifying Dominant. Using his witches as his harem, he expected the witch to give her life for him: the highest expression of love a sadist can hope to inspire in a slave.

Rice's work on "switchable" lovers demonstrates, in fiction, what is reality for each of us, whether we play in the scene or not. Each partner in every relationship assumes either the "top"/dominant role or the "bottom"/submissive role at one time or another. Although a great amount of time is spent interacting as equals, life is a series of compromises, and compromise often means switching roles from time to time. This enables the couple to achieve a balance in their lives—the balance that Elliott sought and found; and the balance that Lasher was unable or unwilling to grasp, losing his one chance at life as a result.

NOTES

1. Anne Rice, *Exit to Eden* (New York: Arbor House, 1985), 23–24.
2. Ibid., 49.
3. Anne Rice, *The Witching Hour* (New York: Knopf, 1990), 292–94.
4. ———, *Lasher* (New York: Knopf, 1993), 302.
5. ———, *The Witching Hour*, 284–85.

Erotic Art and the Birth of Self in Belinda

S. K. Walker

The second of Anne Rice's two novels under the Rampling pseudonym returns to a theme she developed in *Cry to Heaven*—the merging of sexuality with art as a generative force for shaping a character's identity. Rice depicts this convergence as a way to liberate the creative self from the false spirit of conformity, security, and timidity. Such freedom demands that limitation transform itself into possibility, so wherever art and sex significantly come together in *Belinda*, Rice includes imagery from religious ceremonies that honor spiritual transformation. Thus, she strengthens the impression of transcendence. Associating sexuality with the most intense religious experiences not only adds dimension to the narrative but makes possible—*within* the story—a new level of artistic achievement for Rice's protagonist.

Jeremy Walker is a forty-four-year-old author of books for little girls, which he illustrates himself. His stories have won him wealth and fame, but he has learned a disadvantage of public demand: giving his audience what it wants has numbed his artistic spirit. He continues to write about such characters as Angelica and Bettina, but he feels his writing has become fraudulent. This artistic duplicity mirrors his secret authorship of a popular mainstream novel published under his mother's name, Cynthia Walker. Before her death, Cynthia asked him to continue her work—to become merely an extension of herself—and he had complied. Similarly as a children's author, he yields to his conservative public, and for both acts of self-nullification, he suffers. Privately, he paints dark images of pest-infested mansions that resemble his childhood home in New Orleans. "It feels like driving my car at a hundred miles an hour to paint them," he says.[1] He only vaguely senses that these paintings signify suppressed confusion, blocked yet beckoning.

Jeremy exemplifies the dilemma that Swiss analyst Alice Miller describes in her book *The Drama of the Gifted Child*: "An adult can be fully aware of his feelings only if he had caring parents or caregivers. People who were abused or neglected in childhood are missing this capacity and are therefore never overtaken by unexpected emotions. They will admit only those emotions that are accepted and approved. . . . Depression and a sense of inner emptiness are the price they must pay for this control. The true self cannot communicate because it has remained unconscious, and therefore undeveloped." Only after the true self is liberated, she points out, can it express itself in genuine creativity.[2] Yet such emancipation involves facing one's demons and taking control of one's life.

Caught in the "golden handcuffs" of public acclaim, economic security, and duty to his image, Jeremy evades the message conveyed by his private paintings. Yet he keeps hoping for something to occur that will shatter his artistic malaise—"I wish something violent would happen, something unplanned and crazy"[3]—and finally it does, in the form of a voluptuous sixteen-year-old girl named Belinda.

She first appears to him dressed as a Catholic schoolgirl, but her intentions are less than innocent. Precocious and daring, she plans to seduce him. Belinda knows Jeremy's work and needing respite from her own abusive family, she seeks him out. At the point of contact, their lives synchronistically converge toward an eroticism that could provide what they both desire: a powerful sense of self. Jeremy seeks courage, while Belinda wants to be loved for the woman she is rather than the child her family sees, for this will give her identity—"I wouldn't be nobody."[4] Neither knows what will result from their encounter, but instinct propels them into it nonetheless. They approach life from nearly opposite perspectives, each complementing the other's search, each bringing light to the other's darkness.

Although Belinda's youth guarantees that a scandal will come from any sexual connection, Jeremy makes love to her. Despite his guilt, he feels alive to something that eludes him; he senses the threshold of possibility. Belinda moves into his house in San Francisco and he begins to paint provocative pictures of her in various seductive positions: nude on a carousel horse, kneeling naked beside a dollhouse, and partially clothed in a riding outfit (the boots and whip, anyway). Casting aside his paintings of rats and the drawings of elusive little girls in his books, he works feverishly on his new vision. His paintings have an "hallucinatory vibrancy," as if coming from some oddly lighted dream. They feel "dangerous" to his little-girl characters.[5]

Belinda fully supports him, posing in whatever manner he wishes, but when he insists that he cannot show the paintings for fear of offending his public, she reacts with anger. Attaching no such stigma to her sexuality, she feels that hiding the paintings deprives her of substance and makes their love shameful. Nevertheless, Jeremy cannot redeem his talent or provide for its rebirth without first experiencing the burden of guilt and suffering, because the rhythms of his story are

Catholic, wherein freedom hinges on self-abnegation. But the imagery in *Belinda* diverges from the Catholic, reflecting Rice's belief that sexuality offers genuine salvation more readily than do restrictive doctrines.

Rice was raised Catholic, and despite shedding her religion in college, despising its view of sexuality, and even considering atheism, she recognized the mythical power of the Catholic symbols and rituals. Whether writing about vampires, witches, or devils, she uses the imagery of her faith to endow the most intense moments with greater energy, particularly moments of transformation. Spirituality for her means heightened sensation and transcendence, so applying this experience to sexuality gives both additional power. Right from the start, Jeremy's experience with Belinda is highlighted with religious paraphernalia. When Belinda disguises herself in Catholic garb, her white blouse and pleated skirt remind Jeremy of the innocence he knew during his parochial education. Yet, on a deeper level, Jeremy responds to Belinda's facade because he himself is still enveloped in pretense. When she introduces herself falsely, she bypasses the guard he uses against honesty and so gains entrance into his world.

Even when Belinda's obvious intentions dissolve his impression of her as an innocent Catholic schoolgirl, Jeremy clings to that image. Belinda continues to evoke his most powerful boyhood memories, which emerge from a religion that had once immersed him in transcendent possibilities. One evening, he dresses her in a white nightgown, and her girlish mien reminds him of the Catholic May Procession, "the little girls in white lace and linen up in the cloister outside ready to go in."[6] When he envisions the blessed sacraments and the ephemeral light of the Holy Communion, his retrospection urges him toward something so potentially blasphemous that he can barely imagine doing it. Yet, like the rats-and-roaches paintings that nudge him from within, he cannot resist the force that propels him, the meeting of spirituality and sexuality, each joined to enhance the other. Jeremy wants to dress Belinda as the young girls were dressed for their First Communion, yet with more prurient intentions; he desires sex with her in the guise of the little girls that once had excited more exalted sentiments.

With a sense of both shame and vigor, feeling connected to something that keeps swelling within him, Jeremy shops for a white dress (substituting a linen nightgown), a veil, socks, gloves, and shoes. He leaves these items, along with his mother's rosary and pearl-encrusted prayer book, for Belinda to find, then decorates her room with candles and white flowers. "The effect was as I had imagined it: the church at mass."[7] Still, it seems to him insane, contrived by a madman. He fears that Belinda will balk at his profane vision. But she is ready to indulge him. She allows Jeremy to make love to her in her virginal dress and veil. Symbolically, he pours wine into her vagina and drinks it, entangling the erotic with Christianity for a highly potent climax. When he asks if anything scares her, she insists that there is nothing to fear. At that moment, she is his inner self, tolerant of the seeming contradiction of religion and forbidden sex, and letting him get close to this transgressive juxtaposition. Later, she drinks wine in a communion glass and says in echo of Christ at the Last Supper, "This is my Body. This is my Blood."[8]

According to Catholic doctrine, the sacrament of Holy Communion involves sharing in the body, blood, soul, and divinity of Christ as a way of contacting God through the Holy Spirit. It perpetuates the sacrifice of the cross and provides nourishment to Christians through Christ's own self so that they become capable of greater love. It also anticipates the messianic banquet of the coming kingdom of God. To partake of the wine and bread, the essence of which has been mysteriously "transubstantiated" into the actual body and blood of Christ, one must be purified of sin. God's righteousness cannot tolerate unlawful acts. Through penitence, confession, and forgiveness, the participant can be cleansed (sanctified) and thus enabled to receive with reverence the consecrated host. People who cannot physically participate in the service engage in a "spiritual communion," which is simply the desire to receive it, expressed through acts of love.[9]

Jeremy and Belinda engage in a form of spiritual communion, in which their sexual relationship is considered the highest act of love possible. Indeed, another name for the Eucharist is the Sacrament of Love or the Sacrament of Unity. While Jeremy's interpretation is not what the Church had in mind—the Church may in fact view it as the ultimate degradation of holiness—Rice uses her characters to reform the meaning of the sacred and transfer it to a new context. To honor the erotic life force, she cloaks it in the symbolism of the highest blessedness she knows. To her, the sexual union of two people is just as lofty and edifying as the spiritual union of a person with God.

Later, Jeremy paints Belinda in the veil and wreath of flowers, without clothing, but holding the rosary and prayer book. In echo of God's creation of the world, he takes six days to paint it. As background, he uses the illusion of a cloister to disguise the four-poster bed and calls the painting *Holy Communion*. This becomes a phrase that he and Belinda use to affirm their rebirth together as a couple. Jeremy understands that this painting is the breakthrough of his career. "Everything I know about reality and illusion is there"[10]—although the real illusion is that he believes he knows the difference between the two. Until he spiritually dies and experiences renascence, he abides by his old rules of perception.

Jeremy fully immerses himself in the forbidden: Diving headlong into sacrilege in order to come out on the other side, he finds within a sexual experience the same power he once had found within the spiritual. The more he indulges in the flesh, the more "real" he becomes. He rips spirituality away from naive rituals of obedience in order to link it to his more immediate generative power as a man and an artist. Just as the divinity of Christ transubstantiates the wine and bread of the Eucharist, so Jeremy's sexual indulgence transubstantiates his body into a source of greater creative spirituality. The union of body and soul via sex feels dangerous to him, yet also mysteriously vital. The nude paintings of Belinda undermine a whole lifetime, potentially destroying all that he has accomplished. Yet he realizes that if he does not risk this, if he does not die to his former self, he will never be anything, despite his superficial fame.

Just as his rats-and-roaches paintings have invaded his artistic sensibilities, so too has Belinda's overt, unashamed sexuality. Both represent a repressed childhood, the contents of which scare him. But Belinda's apparent freedom entices him, and he boldly draws out the covert sensuality of the white-garbed girl at her First Communion. If he can touch the forbidden in this experience, he may open other psychological doors.

Each large painting of Belinda gets more daring than the last. Jeremy feels more expansive, yet these paintings seem to him dark and frightening. Whatever power he taps in himself to do them clearly disturbs him. Nevertheless, he continues. Belinda is the part of himself he needs to explore, and as long as she is there to emphasize a new reality, she compels him.

Eventually, Jeremy takes Belinda to New Orleans, where he has preserved his mother's mansion. The stagnancy of her house parallels the stale art of his children's books. He does not realize it, but this return to his roots takes him deeper into the shadowed side of himself, whence his darker paintings had sprung. With Belinda, he traverses the city of his childhood and paints several more canvases, including one of Belinda nude in his mother's bed. Belinda—the voice of his inner self—insists that what his mother asked of him has annihilated him, and he acknowledges that truth. Getting close to his secrets, however, continues to provoke tension and fear. His bid for freedom must take him through yet another phase.

The full Christian story of redemption involves betrayal; like Christ, Jeremy must suffer and die a spiritual death. Both he and Belinda have withheld information and indulged in deceit: After Belinda realized that Jeremy had surreptitiously investigated her identity, she gave her mother access to Jeremy's house—including the attic, where he kept his secret paintings. He viewed this act as supreme betrayal, although his own lies had set him up for it. Still he blames Belinda, hitting her and driving her from his house. Symbolically, with his paintings of Belinda he had approached his inner self so closely that it scared him, so he deflected it. But when he feels the life force leave him with Belinda's departure, he knows he must accept all that she represents. He has lost what is most precious to him and he cannot continue without her. Thus, he resolves to do what she most wanted: show the paintings and admit to the power of his relationship with her. In forgiving her, he moves into communion with the part of his soul that can grant him a Godlike ability to truly create—not just art but transcendent love. Jeremy's feelings for Belinda transform him, and, just as the Holy Eucharist is meant to do, his change of heart delivers them both from darkness.

He paints more canvases and then puts them on public display. To Jeremy's surprise, this show is the breakthrough of his career. Dying to his former self—deadened as it already was—and affirming his sexuality via Belinda, he captures the attention of the most prestigious art collectors. Despite a social outcry and an attempt to criminalize him, Jeremy quickly triumphs. His art also grants Belinda substance and brings her back into his life. They marry, and Jeremy gains new talent. "For the first time, I could do anything I wanted."[11] By creating honest art via honest love, he slips off his former facade. Just as the true believer gains God's grace through Christ's Body and Blood, so Jeremy experiences the grace bestowed from his own body through sexuality and art.

NOTES

1. Anne Rice, *Belinda* (New York: Arbor House, 1986), 39.
2. Alice Miller, *The Drama of the Gifted Child*, rev. ed. (New York: Basic Books, 1994), 43.
3. Rice, *Belinda*, 78.
4. Ibid., 29.
5. Ibid., 40.
6. Ibid., 106.
7. Ibid., 114.
8. Ibid., 119.
9. *The Catholic Encyclopedia*, ed. Robert C. Broderick (New York: Thomas Nelson, 1987).
10. Rice, *Belinda*, 129.
11. Ibid., 496.

Visions, Dreams, Realities

THE PROBLEM OF IMAGINAL REVELATION

Leonard George

Why have the novels of Anne Rice proven phenomenally popular among such a diverse and devoted readership? The quality of her writing is necessarily part of the answer; but it's not a sufficient explanation. Not all fine writers attain the stratosphere of success. Compelling art of any sort fascinates on a variety of levels. It may be amusing, or sublime, or intriguingly grotesque—in a readily accessible way—but it also must resonate with desires or meanings that lie beneath the surface awareness of most of the audience. Much of my personal fascination with Rice's works comes from the "insider's view" of the supernatural realms she portrays. These are worlds where other dimensions teem with strange life, where spells and ceremonies have real punch, where "the blood *is* the life"—and where visions and reality are sometimes one. These occult plot elements stir intuitions, vividly felt but often only dimly articulated, about who, and where, I truly am.

What deep and secret relevance is glimpsed in these experiences, attested by the legions of Rice readers? Exploration of these topical elements opens a rich spectrum of associations, beyond the scope of a single essay. Here, I have chosen to focus on the topic of visions. I feel that visions are linked to core features in our culture's attitude toward reality itself. Following the thread of visions through the historical development of the Western world view, we might attain some understanding of the intuited relevance of visions. In the Anne Rice corpus, the greatest range of visionary phenomena can be found in the Mayfair trilogy, so I draw my examples from those works.

In the Mayfair series, visionary events repeatedly have fateful consequences for the main characters. The most frequent visionary phenomenon noted among the Mayfair witches is the dream. These visions of the night bring knowledge and power to the living and serve as a conduit of influence from the sphere of the dead. *Precognitive dreams*—those containing knowledge of future events—abound. For instance, the witch (and neurosurgeon) Rowan Mayfair's sleep is disturbed by a series of weird dreams: She is operating on a body that is part child, part man, containing organs that are too small. She realizes that she needs a special form of DNA to expand the organs. The dream proves to be a glimpse of the future in symbolic form—when she brings the supernatural being Lasher into fleshly existence, she must use her powers to stimulate his genetic material in order for him to survive.

Also found in the Mayfair trilogy is the *clairvoyant dream*. This experience reveals hidden truths about the present. Dreaming, Ryan Mayfair encounters his departed wife, Gifford. She tells him the identity of the father of Mona Mayfair's unborn child, Morrigan. This dream also symbolically hints that the child is no ordinary human, but a member of the mysterious and powerful Taltos species.

The *telepathic dream* is another form of nocturnal revelation. "Telepathy" refers to the direct exchange of knowledge between minds, and Anne Rice portrays it occurring among the living as well as across the divide of death. In the case of

Mona and Morrigan, the child's memories of an ancient Taltos existence leak into her mother's dreams even before she is born.

The waking state is also suffused with visions in the Mayfair trilogy. Take *apparitions*, for example. An apparition is a sensory (typically visual) appearance of a being or an object that is not physically present, at least in the ordinary manner. Lasher appears and vanishes in a typically apparitional fashion. Ghosts of the departed pop up on occasion in the Mayfair saga. Stuart Townsend's shade is observed by Arthur Langtry, who infers that Stuart's corpse is somewhere in the house. Julien Mayfair seems to have a knack for apparitional appearances—his first ghostly visit (to Evelyn Mayfair) happens even before his death. Postmortem, he shows himself to Michael Curry and to Mona Mayfair. Indeed, his ghostly matchmaking brings them together.

Julien's visionary tour de force is the creation of a totally apparitional environment for the couple's love nest—a house interior of a bygone era, complete with period furniture, velvet draperies, carpets, candle-decked chandelier, and the fragrance of the candle wax. (Encounters with total visionary environments are known technically as *metachoric experiences*.)

The *near-death experience*, or NDE, lies between the states of waking and unconsciousness. In the world of the Mayfairs, the NDE is linked with visionary awareness. After Michael Curry almost drowns in the Pacific Ocean, his visionary eye is opened, and he develops the ability to practice psychometry—the gaining of knowledge about an object and its owner by touching it. In Michael's psychometrizing, the information from an object comes to him as images. The *out-of-body experience*, or OBE, consists of the feeling (usually accompanied by a visual awareness) that one is somehow outside of one's skin. It is often, although by no means always, associated with the NDE, as in Michael Curry's case.

Given the power and knowledge available through visions, it is unsurprising that characters in the Mayfair novels would deliberately seek them out. Ashlar the Taltos, for instance, consumes a weird brew and waits alone in the Witches' Cave for a vision of his lost love, Janet. Several Mayfairs—Julien, Cortland, and Mary Beth—demonstrate the ability to induce OBEs at will.

But the possibility is also raised in Rice's work that visions can be false or even hazardous. When visions are used as a channel to connect the living and the "beyond," there are no guarantees that the intentions of everyone—or every*thing*—involved are strictly benign. Whether the experiences that follow Michael Curry's NDE are truth or are Lasher's diabolical illusions long remains a nagging question for him. And, even when knowledge gained through visions is accurate, Michael senses the harmful effects of occult knowledge on the mortal personality. He says of visionary powers, "They destroy the human in us."[1]

The conventional world view of today—built and maintained by the scientific, legal, and mental-health professions—is untroubled by the allure and danger of the realm of visions. The official map of the cosmos has a province marked off for such things as spirit encounters, voices from beyond, out-of-body journeys, and near-death glimpses of other worlds. The name of this region is *imagination*. The associated adjective is *imaginary*, which connotes "unreal."

Those empowered to define reality have excluded the imagination from their blessing; psychiatrists, police, and editors of scientific journals patrol the border for violations of sanity/legality/rationality. Anyone who suggests that reality might have a different shape—that the border between real and "imaginary" is not as fixed as we have been taught—is suspected of suffering from a muddled map.

Despite the dismissal of the "imaginary" by today's reality elites, surveys show that many still take seriously the occurrence of what is, by conventional definition, "unreal." One person in five admits to having had an OBE—*if* the survey guarantees respondents' anonymity. Up to one in three claims to have seen an apparition. Among those who have been close to dying, estimates of NDEs often fall at around 40 percent. Several surveys have found a majority of respondents claiming ESP experiences—precognition, clairvoyance, and telepathy. And, as among the fictional Mayfairs, in our lives the "true dream" is the most commonly reported form of vision. The metachoric experience is not often noted by researchers. It may be more frequent than we think, however. Perhaps we can slip into and out of a visionary enfoldment seamlessly and unaware. How can you be sure that it's not happening *right now?* . . .

Modern culture is thus marked by an underlying tension at the boundary between sensory and visionary experience. As no amount of education or discouragement seems able to bar the intrusion of these haunting "figments," eventually the illicit question begs asking: *Is the imagination, at least sometimes, a doorway to the Real?*

The question is openly addressed only in the margins of our culture—by devotees of New Age and other occult movements, Jungian therapists, parapsychologists, and, occasionally, by philosophers. More commonly, the tension surrounding the possibility of "real imagination" is probed in the safe guise of fiction—including, as we've seen, in the novels of Anne Rice.

Who decided to mark the mental divide between real and unreal where it currently lies? Has it always been there, or has its location altered over time? The answers lie in the remote past, at the roots of Western civilization. In the following pages, let's review the drama of how the imagination came to be merely "imaginary." (Instead of this prejudicial adjective, I will use the word *imaginal* to refer to the experiences now included under "imagination"—dreams, visions, voices, apparitions, out-of-body awareness, as well as everyday fantasies and "mental images.") This drama has five acts.

ACT ONE: *TRUE MYTHS*

In the beginning was . . . the Image, not the Word. The earliest surviving traces of imaginal activity are depictions of things that could never have been perceived with the senses. Deep in the caves of southwestern Europe, artists painted the forms of the creatures with which they shared the Ice Age landscape. There is no evidence that carcasses of bison or horses—and certainly not woolly mammoths—were hauled into the murky depths to serve as models for the paleo-painters. A number of the images are located in such cramped nooks that the artist could not have viewed an animal corpse no matter where it was placed. But there are signs that the creatures on the cave walls were not entirely based on memories of animals seen above ground, either. Although they are clearly intended to be seen as animate—and appear to move when viewed under the original lighting conditions, a flickering torch—the feet of many of the beasts are portrayed in such a way that they seem to be floating in the air.

Researchers say that such foot positioning would never have been seen in a living animal, even during the leaping frenzy of the hunt. Animate creatures, floating through the air . . . The eye with which the artist spied such things was not of the flesh, scanning the forests and plains of the surface world. It was the eye of vision, surveying an imaginal ground where dwelled the *spirits* of the animals that were so central to the life and death of early humanity.

And what are we to make of one of the oldest artifacts of our species, a sculpture in mammoth ivory from the German site of Hohlenstein-Stadel, dating back nearly thirty thousand years? Clearly portrayed is a being with the body of a man and the head of a lion. The feline head seems too close-fitting to have been severed from a lion and worn as a mask. Again, the model can only have been a visitor from the realm of imagination.

The exact meaning of the old Stone Age images, and the uses to which they were put, are still debated by scholars. It is certain that they were not purely decorative. Scholars guess that the images were used in initiation rites, hunting magic, or divination. Evidently, the imaginal domain was not stamped "unreal" on the cosmic maps of the Paleolithic age; rather, it was a spirit land, populated by entities that had great consequence for the course of human life.

This impression is confirmed by the tradition that most directly links today with those primordial times. Shamanism has been practiced in hunter-gatherer societies around the globe. The shaman is a specialist in contacting the spirit land and harnessing its might and wisdom for human benefit. Generally, this contact is made in an altered state of consciousness. The experience may be triggered by taking psychedelic drugs, drumming, singing, dancing, or severely stressing the body. Such manipulations produce vivid visual displays called "entoptic phenomena." Brilliant flashes of color, spirals, and glowing geometric shapes are most common. In the mind of a shaman, these striking sensations unfold into a sequence of visions depicting a voyage through the world of ghosts. No impotent fantasy, the shamanic journey yields precious gifts—stories and songs from the other side, and confidence in being part of the cosmic Whole that often brings healing and tenacious survival despite adversity.

The first literate civilizations—Egypt and Mesopotamia—inherited the belief in "real imagination." For them, myths were not entertainments or allegories but living truths. Prior to the unification of Egypt around 3100 B.C., the Nile Valley was a chain of independent societies, each with its own divine pantheon and cosmology. When Narmer, the first pharaoh, conquered the valley, one might have expected him to impose the worldview of his town on the entire valley. Instead, it appears that *all* the diverse reality models of the regions were officially embraced; none was discarded or suppressed. For more than thirty centuries of ancient Egyptian culture, this acceptance endured unbroken. Novel gods and rites did not supplant the old, but simply formed a new layer of imagery that served to access and celebrate the lushness of Reality. This tolerance of contradiction is hard for us to understand; Western culture is geared, philosophically and scientifically, to discern the One Truth about the world; but, for the Egyptians, Truth is Many. Historian Henri Frankfort summarized the Egyptian view thus:

> The ancients did not attempt to solve the ultimate problems confronting man by a single coherent theory;. . . Ancient thought—mythopoeic, "myth-making" thought—admitted

> side by side certain *limited* insights, which were held to be *simultaneously* valid, each in its own proper context, each corresponding to a definite avenue of approach.[2]

The Egyptian attitude is reflected in their Book of the Dead. Unlike the scriptures of the Jews, Christians, and Moslems, this text does not tell a story of revelation, from beginning to end; rather, it is a patchwork of spells and prayers, accreted over the centuries, referring to diverse afterworlds, souls, and deities, without any effort to create a linear order or narrative. Indeed, in some copies of the book, if the scribe ran out of room at the edge of the papyrus, the text simply ends in midsentence. Reality, the book's structure implies, is like that. In such an interpenetrating universe, there would seem no place for zones of absolute unreality ("mere imagination"); the sensory and the imaginal worlds are two sides of the same cosmic coin.

ACT TWO: *MISTRUSTING THE MIND*

Among antique Mediterranean societies, the concepts of "imagination" and "fantasy" as we define them today were unknown. There was a broad understanding that dreams and visions are types of perception—glimpses beyond the veil of the senses, into an alternate reality. But in two of these cultures, mythmakers and thinkers sensed a negative side to the imaginal; over time, the imagination became the object of mistrust, and even of banishment from the camp of the Real. These two exceptional societies happened to be those that laid the foundations of the Western worldview—the Greeks and the Hebrews.

The story of Prometheus was the central Greek myth of

cultural origins. Prometheus conveyed to humanity the fire he stole from the gods. He was also esteemed as the one who taught us how to create everything that distinguishes us from other animals. In other words, Prometheus led the human race from nature to culture. But this act outraged Zeus. The fire of creation was the exclusive property of the gods—its wielding by humans was a pathetic mockery. Zeus chained Prometheus to a rock, where an eagle eternally tears at his liver. The crime of Prometheus thus had a double-edged result: It endowed humanity with a power of creation, but it also alienated us from harmony with the divine.

Who—or what—is Prometheus? His identity lies in his name: In the Greek tongue, *pro-metheus* literally means "fore-sight"; or, as philosopher Richard Kearney put it, "the power to anticipate the future by projecting an horizon of imaginary possibilities."[3] It was the *imagination* that evoked such ambivalence in the Greek mythic mind.

This primordial tension around the imaginal became more clearly manifest among the great philosophers of classical Greece. Foremost among these was Plato. His early life was one of turmoil, in which Athens was defeated in war, and his beloved friend Socrates was executed by his own people. Confronted with the injustices of the world around him, Plato felt that perfection belonged to another domain—the realm of the Ideal, of Being. The things of the ordinary world are but crude copies of their Ideal Forms, which can only be grasped by abstract reason.

Plato admitted that mental images can accompany thinking. They are by no means necessary for thought, however, and their presence signals that the thinking is imperfect; the thoughts that carry us in the direction of the Ideal are entirely cleansed of imagery. Dreams fared little better in Plato's account; he had them originating in the vicinity of the navel, from the part of the soul that is "bound down like a wild animal."[4]

Plato had a generally dim view of the artistic products of imagination. While art connoisseurs today marvel at the naturalism of classical Greek sculpture, Plato was contemptuous—if a body in the realm of the senses was an imperfect copy of an Ideal Form, then a marble imitation of that body was even further removed from perfection, "a poor child of a foster parent."[5] Artificial images, he thought, could be downright dangerous—their power to excite the viewer drew the soul down into the blindness of passion, rather than up to the serene, imageless domain of Truth.

Plato was the leader of the cognitive elite of his time. But most ordinary folk still believed that the imaginal was a gateway to the Otherworld, and eagerly studied dreams and visions for signs of divine and daemonic will. Plato could not entirely escape this heritage of belief. Grudgingly, he admitted that images entering the mind unbidden can sometimes be sent by gods, and contain truths. But human reason was still needed to sort the revelation from the imaginal spoor of our animal nature.

The other giant of Greek thought was Aristotle. His world view differed from Plato's in many ways. Unable to solve the puzzle of how the radically different realms of Being and physicality could be related at all, he rejected the notion of a world of Forms separate from the world of sense. He also held that purely abstract thinking is impossible; every thought—and every perception—is accompanied by a mental image. But, if anything, he was even harsher in his verdict concerning dreams and visions than was Plato. Aristotle taught that, for the most part, involuntary images arise from bodily states rather than divine inspiration, a sort of mental flatulence. In any case, whether waking or sleeping, the imagination must not serve as a guide; rather, the image must kneel for judgment before its lord—Reason.

The central myth of origin for the Jewish people was the account of creation in Genesis. In this myth, too, an original harmony between Holy and human is upset by a human gesture—the eating of the forbidden fruit. But this act had a consciousness-expanding effect on Adam and Eve. They became aware of ethics (the choice of good or evil), and of time, indeed being exiled from the eternally static Garden into the cascade of past, present, future.

What aspect of the first man enabled him to make his fateful choice, leading to the curse/blessing of alienation/consciousness? In Hebrew tradition, when God created Adam "in His own image,"[6] He installed a faculty called the *yetser*. This Hebrew term, closely related to *yotser* ("creator"), refers to the human ability to imitate God by creating forms—and is customarily translated into English as "imagination." The serpent tempted the first couple by inviting them to *imagine* what the banned fruit might reveal. In the Genesis account, the Lord is not amused by the use to which the gift of *yetser* had been put:

> And God saw that the wickedness of man was great . . . and that every imagination (*yetser*) of the thoughts of his heart was only evil continually. And it repented the Lord that He had made man on the earth, and it grieved Him at his Heart.[7]

As in the myth of Prometheus, here, too, our capacity to imagine disobeying God lifts us above brute animality—but also away from the divine embrace.

Not surprisingly, the human feature that led to the Fall was in for rough treatment in later Jewish tradition. Many commentaries declare the imagination to be an enemy: "To him who kills his *yetser* . . . it is as if he would have honoured the Holy One"[8]; "one who obeys his *yetser* practices idolatry."[9] One text suggests that the custom of circumcision symbolizes the righteous desire to amputate the imagination. The medieval Jewish philosopher Maimonides went so far as to equate the imagination with the satanic snake itself.

The imaginal was not consistently damned by the ancient Hebrews. Indeed, many of the Old Testament prophets received revelations via dreams, visions, and voices, usually while "the hand of the Lord was upon me"—thought by some scholars to refer to an altered state like the shaman's trance. And a number of Hebrew writings hint that the *yetser*, defiled since the first sin, would one day be redeemed. But the tilt of opinion is definitely toward suspicion, if not outright hostility, of the imaginal. The Hebrews were struggling to retain their monotheism in a sea of pagan cultures that practiced visionary contact with their "false gods"; in this context, worries about the idolatrous possibilities of a free imagination make sense.

ACT THREE: *THE IMAGE STRIKES BACK*

Alexander the Great, a pupil of Aristotle, conquered the vast region from Macedonia to Egypt to India, seeding the worldview of the Greeks throughout. The Romans in turn conquered much of this "Hellenistic" territory; but the newly captured Greek culture proved to be a sort of "Trojan Horse," as it converted the Roman civilization to its own patterns of thought. The Promethean tension surrounding the imagination thus became a general feature of the Roman reality map.

The followers of Plato and Aristotle, as well as the followers of the other important school of thought, Stoicism, agreed that the imagination could not be trusted and that it was vastly inferior to reason as a path to Truth. The intellectual elite had become somewhat united in its belittling of the imaginal; but, deep in the collective soul, a response was brewing.

By the first century before Christ, around the Mediterranean, there were signs of a widespread eruption of fascination with visions and dreams. This imaginal renaissance continued for the next few centuries. In fact, among the common people, this interest had never fully departed; the denizens of the ivory tower have always overestimated their impact on popular thought. But now, it seemed, people from every level of society were reporting encounters with visitors from hidden dimensions of the cosmos. As one ancient inscription attests, "the gods have been appearing in visitations as never before, to the girls and women, but also, too, to men and children. What does such a thing mean?"[10]

Imaginal experiences were not only arising uninvited but were being pursued, and with renewed intensity, during this time. In the mid-second century A.D., a father and son, both named Julian (rumored to be from Chaldaea, a Mesopotamian region associated in the Roman mind with magic and mystery), wrote a text known as the *Chaldaean Oracles*. The work claimed to provide a direct revelation of the gods through the power of special ceremonies, in a process that today we would call "channeling." The immense popularity of the *Oracles* throughout the Empire fueled the idea that the divine world, and even the Platonic realm of Being, was accessible through mind-altering rituals.

The movement that grew out of the *Chaldaean Oracles* was known as Theurgy. It became the last great spiritual influence in the ancient pagan world. During the brief reign of the last pagan emperor of Rome (again, a Julian) in the mid-fourth century, Theurgy was the favored imperial religion.

Theurgic methods created a state of awareness that was akin to the visionary condition of the shaman. Practitioners would chant or make sounds; visualize divine images; meditate on statues until they saw them move, or heard them speak; or mesmerize themselves with a kind of spinning top called an *Iynx* (the original meaning of this term was forgotten, but it kept a supernatural flavor and eventually deformed into the English word *jinx*).

Iamblichus, a prominent fourth-century Theurgist, explained how the techniques worked. He wrote that the rites washed the soul. Invisible light radiating from the gods could stir patterns in a purified person's aura, which would be seen as visions. Direct perception of the divine light itself was a high spiritual attainment, known as *autopsia*.

The rising value of the imagination can be seen in the artistic, as well as the religious, sphere. In the first century B.C., Cicero described how a great sculptor used as his model "a surpassing vision of beauty"[11] within his mind, and hinted that such inner images are connected with the Ideal Forms of Plato. Two hundred years later, this elevation of mental imagery from its lowly status as a sign of inferior thought to a perception of highest Reality was complete; according to Flavius Philostratus, the imagination of an artist is a *direct* awareness of the Forms.

What provoked this return of the imaginal? Modern writers offer various answers. J. M. Cocking notes the resurgence of "more primitive ways of thinking, inherited from the

East, notably Babylon and Egypt"[12]—in other words, a reawakening of the mythic mind. If this primordial mentality had been kept alive in Eastern lands, perhaps it was enabled to spread at this time by the uniquely efficient communication system uniting Mediterranean cultures that characterized Roman rule. Alternatively, Robin Lane Fox implies that educated Romans needed no outside impetus to seek direct experience of the hidden worlds:

> Their visions were not a passive escape but a positive search for knowledge. People wanted to know the secrets of higher theology . . . because the schools and philosophers had raised so many more questions than they had been able to answer.[13]

The status of the imaginal was also rising among the Hebrews around this time. Again, scholarly fingers have pointed at the Babylonians as a possible triggering influence. Around the third century B.C., a new type of literature, known as "apocalyptic" or "pseudepigraphic," appeared in Jewish communities. These texts featured descriptions of bizarre visions and out-of-body journeys, often attributed to famous Old Testament figures (hence the term *pseudepigrapha*, or "false writings," as the authorities viewed the authorship claims as spurious). In many of these writings the author recounts trips to otherworldly planes; he describes the layers of heaven and the angels he met along the way. The only text of this visionary period to be accepted as scripture was the Book of Daniel. The rest, although officially rejected, remained very popular, and gave rise to a host of beliefs that later found their way into Christianity; most significant was the tale of the Fallen Angels.

ACT FOUR:
WAR FOR THE IMAGINATION

As on treasure maps, so in history: X marks the spot. In the case of history, the X is the cross of Christ, and the spot—the birth of the Christian religion—is where the great Greek and Hebrew worldviews intersect and blend. The surge of imaginal energy in both the root traditions sets the stage for the new faith's rise; the old Greek and Hebrew dance of ambivalence regarding visionary experience was now joined by the Christians. Indeed, the beginnings of Christianity can be understood, in large part, as a struggle for control of the imagination.

The orthodox version of early Christian history resembles a tree. Jesus Christ's time on earth is, of course, the seed. Rising straight out of this sacred source, the tree trunk is the Catholic tradition, the doctrines of which were transmitted from the Founder by a process called "apostolic succession." The apostles received the eternal Truth about Salvation from Christ, and passed it to their successors, the priests and bishops; generations of Catholic clergy have preserved this Truth to the present day. From the beginning, there were those who distorted or lost Christ's revelation. These heretics and their schools form the branches of the tree, experiments in falsehood that deviate from Truth's trunk until they dead-end in midair.

Many historians disagree with this view of Christian history. In fact, the "tree" was more like a tangled thicket. An observer during the first two centuries A.D. might have been hard-pressed to predict which of the dozens of versions of Christ's teaching then circulating would eventually emerge as "orthodoxy." The range of ideas gradually narrowed, as some

Christian groups acquired political power and suppressed their competitors. The grand winner was finally declared only in 381 A.D., when the emperor Theodosius outlawed all faiths except the Catholic brand of Christianity.

The various Christian schools, along with their pagan and Hebrew contemporaries, did have something in common—a fascination with visions. The New Testament itself features several visionary tales: Christ's Transfiguration in front of three of his disciples; Jesus' postmortem appearances to his followers; the conversion of Paul (when he encountered "a light from heaven, brighter than the sun"[14]); Paul's ascent to the third heaven ("whether in the body or out of the body, I know not, God knows"[15]); and the psychedelic experiences recorded in Revelation (classic apocalyptic writing with a Christian twist), among others.

Unexceptionally, the early Catholics were enamoured of visions. One of their favorite texts was the *Shepherd*, composed by Hermas toward the end of the first century. Hermas recounts his trance experiences, in which he journeyed to a spiritual land and took instruction from a mysterious woman, who symbolized the Catholic Church. Catholic communities revered traveling "prophets"—who were visionaries as well as teachers—and offered them the best wines and oils when they visited. And Catholic martyrs often received waking visions and dreams of the heaven to which they would shortly depart.

The strongest Christian competition to the Catholics came from a religious movement known as Gnosticism. The Gnostics were so called for their belief that salvation is reached through a type of knowledge called *gnosis*. Unlike the knowledge of ordinary things—books, birds, bodies—gnosis is an awareness of one's own true nature. The core of the self, said the Gnostics, is a spark of divine light. Dazzled by the spectacle of the physical world, we have lost sight of this inner glow, and forgotten who we really are. When we reawaken to our identity as light—in other words, when we attain gnosis—we are freed from all evil, and have no further need of religious guidance. As the Gnostic *Gospel of Philip* puts it, the enlightened Gnostic "is no longer a Christian, but a Christ."[16]

How is this divine self-recognition achieved? The Gnostics themselves were divided on this question. Advice from elders and study of scriptures were often recommended. But centrally important in many accounts were visionary revelations. Unlike the tradition of apostolic succession, Gnosticism held that Christians could receive the salvific instruction from Christ *directly*—through visionary visitations, just like the first apostles. Or the devotee could connect with Jesus at His place, via an OBE. What need, then, for bishops and priests? Why support a church with tithes? And why "bear witness" for the faith through martyrdom, when you could be chatting with the Lord?

In the hands of the Gnostics, personal visions undermined the development of an *institution* of Christianity by removing its reason for existence—as an ark for preserving God's once-only revelation to Jesus' followers in the early first century. In Catholic circles, it was clear—the subversive potential of visions was too great. The imaginal had to be discredited, or controlled; if possible, even harnessed against their Gnostic competitors with their tempting offer of "becoming a Christ." Catholic spokesmen needed to resurrect the negative, untrustworthy connotations of imagination from their Hebrew and Greek heritage.

Around 180, Irenaeus, bishop of Lyons, issued the first

Catholic theology text. In it, he attacked the Gnostics and mocked their revelations. According to Irenaeus, there are only four authentic gospels—Matthew, Mark, Luke, and John. But Gnostics, through their visions, were proclaiming new gospels every week. How could eternal Truth be found in the ever-shifting fantasies of the Gnostics, which contradicted one another as well as the "Faith once delivered to the saints"[17] (and forever after preserved and monopolized by the Catholic Church)?

This opening salvo was followed by other Catholic attacks. In the early third century, Cyprian of Carthage urged the Church to adopt the structure of an authoritarian government. Power was vested in the bishops; the role of the laypeople was to obey. For the believing Catholic, it would be foolish not to—after all, the bishops had inherited, by apostolic succession, the *only* keys to the gates of heaven.

The Catholic Church, with its strict chains of command, proved an effective recruiting machine. It gradually attracted more important citizens of the Roman Empire. With prestige came power; and with power came the chance for the Church to back up its written assaults on visionary "heretics" with fist, sword, and firebrand. After the proclamation of Theodosius, Catholic thugs could attack unorthodox Christians, as well as pagans such as the Theurgists, with relative impunity. Some Catholics were still reporting visions—but their content was in strict accord with the opinions of the bishops.

By the early fifth century, the Gnostics were a fading memory in the Mediterranean world. This was the era of Augustine of Hippo, whose writings formed the basis of the Catholic worldview of the Middle Ages. He revived, in Christian philosophical guise, the subjugation of imaginal to rational that had dominated classical Greek thought. But for Augustine, reason was itself not free; rather, it was governed by the dogmas of the Catholic Church. The priestly conquest of the Christian imagination was officially complete. The imaginal revival that had bloomed in ancient pagan and Jewish society was over.

ACT FIVE: *THE LEGACY*

We've tracked the play of imaginal reality through ancient times: the notion of imaginal experiences as contact with a hidden, but real, dimension, which dominated archaic thought and the cosmology of the first civilizations; the tension between dismissal and reverence for the imaginal, found among the two seminal cultures of the Western vision; the flowering of interest in "real imagination" in late antiquity; and the fight over control of the imaginal life of the earliest Christians. What was the legacy of the Catholic victory in the war for the imagination?

Part of this legacy was the rupture of the mainstream Christian Church into the Roman Catholic and Eastern Orthodox branches. This rift, the greatest disaster in the history of the faith, remains unhealed today. Especially after Augustine, the Latin-speaking Western church highlighted the likely demonic origin of spontaneous experience in general, and visionary revelation in particular. The Greek-speaking Eastern church, less impressed by the saint of Hippo, remained more mystical and visionary. The Easterners had greater interest in church fathers like Gregory of Nazianzus. For Gregory, the task of the Christian is to polish the mirror of the soul through piety, so that the images seen within are clear reflections of the divine; eventually, the speckless soul of the saint can attain "the Beatific Vision where images dissolve into Truth."[18] This difference in attitude between West and East, expressed in many ways, deepened over the centuries; by the eleventh century, each branch of Christian orthodoxy viewed the other as virtually heretical.

The Western ambivalence about the imaginal, built into the foundation of our culture from Jewish and Greek sources, has continued ever since. During the Middle Ages and the Renaissance, some visionaries (Catherine of Siena, Teresa of Ávila, John of the Cross) were so respected—and so unveeringly obedient to the Church—that they were declared saints. But others—most notably, the religious genius Meister Eckhart—were judged to have strayed beyond the fence of dogma and into the devilish domain of imaginary falsehood. These errant imaginers were lucky to get off with only their writings condemned, as did Eckhart. Heretics preaching a freer imagination more commonly ended up in bonfires.

The rise of modern science was connected to the idea that reason and observation are the best ways to comprehend reality. The imagination was at best a source of ideas to be investigated by the more reliable methods of knowing, and at worst a morass of "hallucinations" and "delusions." But the uninvited guests—the visions and dreams and weird visitations—have refused to stay away. The visionary adventures of the Mayfair witches, and other creations of Anne Rice, are but the latest expressions of a primordial need—the attempt to compass this mystery in human terms. These interlopers from the "unreal" intrude, more and more, into our favorite fiction and our lives. As the old inscription asks, "What could such a thing mean?" Are the borders of the Real on our received maps of the cosmos about to shift? It's happened before. Imagine what might happen next. Just imagine . . .

NOTES

1. Anne Rice, *The Witching Hour* (New York: Ballantine, 1990), 780.
2. H. Frankfort, *Ancient Egyptian Religion* (New York: Columbia University Press, 1948), 4.
3. R. Kearney, *The Wake of Imagination: Toward a Postmodern Culture* (Minneapolis: University of Minnesota Press, 1991), 80. This point was originally made by Northrop Frye in *The Anatomy of Criticism* (New York: Atheneum, 1969).
4. Plato, *Timaeus* 70d–71d.
5. Plato, *Timaeus* 29–31.
6. Genesis 1:27.
7. Genesis 5:5–6.
8. Sanhedrin 43b.
9. Jer Nedarim 41b.
10. Quoted in R.L. Fox, *Pagans and Christians* (San Francisco: HarperCollins, 1986), 102.
11. Cicero, *Orator* 2:7–3:10.
12. J. M. Cocking, *Imagination: A Study in the History of Ideas:* (New York: Routledge, 1991), 26.
13. Fox, *Pagans and Christians*, 125.
14. Acts 26:13.
15. 2 Corinthians 12:2–3.
16. W. Barnstone, ed., *The Other Bible* (San Francisco: HarperCollins, 1984), 94.
17. Jude 3.
18. Quoted in A. H. Armstrong, ed., *The Cambridge History of Later Greek and Early Medieval Philosophy* (Cambridge, England: 1967), 443.

FURTHER READING

Bundy, M. W. *The Theory of Imagination in Classical and Mediaeval Thought.* Urbana, IL: University of Illinois Press, 1927.

Cocking, J. M. *Imagination: A Study in the History of Ideas.* New York: Routledge, 1991.

Collins, J. J., and M. Fishbane, ed. *Death, Ecstasy, and Otherworldly Journeys.* Albany, NY: State University of New York Press, 1995.

Davenport, G. *The Geography of the Imagination.* New York: Pantheon Books, 1981.

Dodds, E. R. *The Greeks and the Irrational.* Berkeley: University of California Press, 1951.

Engell, J. *The Creative Imagination: Enlightenment to Romanticism.* Cambridge: Harvard University Press, 1981.

Erickson, C. *The Medieval Vision: Essays in History and Perception.* New York: Oxford University Press, 1976.

Fox, R. L. *Pagans and Christians.* San Francisco: HarperCollins, 1986.

George, L. *Crimes of Perception: An Encyclopedia of Heresies and Heretics.* New York: Paragon House, 1995.

———. *Alternative Realities: The Paranormal, The Mystic and The Transcendent in Human Experience.* New York: Facts on File, 1995.

Kearney, R. *The Wake of Imagination: Toward a Postmodern Culture.* Minneapolis: University of Minnesota Press, 1988.

Kirk, K. E. *The Vision of God: The Christian Doctrine of the Summum Bonum.* Harrisburg, PA: Morehouse, 1991.

Le Goff, J. *The Medieval Imagination.* Chicago: University of Chicago Press, 1988.

Lindblom, J. *Prophecy in Ancient Israel.* Philadelphia: Fortress Press, 1963.

Lossky, V. *The Vision of God.* Crestwood, NY: St. Vladimir's Seminary Press, 1983.

Merkur, D. *Gnosis: An Esoteric Tradition of Mystical Visions and Unions.* Albany: State University of New York Press, 1993.

Pagels, E. *The Gnostic Gospels.* New York: Random House, 1979.

Watson, G. *Phantasia in Classical Thought.* Galway, UK: Galway University Press, 1988.

White, A. R. *The Language of Imagination.* Cambridge, MA: Basil Blackwell, 1990.

Wolfson, E. R. *Through a Speculum That Shines: Vision and Imagination in Medieval Jewish Mysticism.* Princeton: Princeton University Press, 1995.

Anne Rice's Pastiche of the British "Thriller"

COMPARING *THE MUMMY* TO SIR ARTHUR CONAN DOYLE'S "LOT NO. 249"

Gary Hoppenstand

Several of today's most successful authors of best-selling horror fiction—including Stephen King, Clive Barker, and Anne Rice—have demonstrated not only a masterful ability to entertain their legions of devoted readers but a willingness to include in their work conspicuous literary allusions to earlier popular fiction classics. Stephen King, for example, updates Bram Stoker's classic vampire novel *Dracula* (1897) in his horror epic *'Salem's Lot* (1975), and Clive Barker reworks Christopher Marlowe's *Doctor Faustus* (1604) in his novel *The Damnation Game* (1985). Not to be outdone, Anne Rice, with her 1989 best-selling horror novel *The Mummy or Ramses the Damned*, has written a modern-day pastiche of the traditional British thriller. Rice borrows a number of significant motifs from the thriller and incorporates them as part of her story. A comparison between Anne Rice's *The Mummy* and Arthur Conan Doyle's late-Victorian thriller, "Lot No. 249," in particular, reveals Rice's great success at imitating a tremendously popular genre. As does Doyle in "Lot No. 249," Rice investigates in *The Mummy* the mystical and mythic connection between our knowledge of our certain mortality and our desire for immortality. Then, after borrowing those narrative elements required to place *The Mummy* firmly within Doyle's British thriller tradition, Rice transforms the thriller formula into an entertaining adventure story in which she critiques such things as modern technology and contemporary sexual practices. Political or social satire may have never surfaced in Arthur Conan Doyle's thrillers, but they make for lively reading in Anne Rice's wonderful homage to the thriller.

Rice does not hide her sources of inspiration for *The Mummy*. To make apparent the genre from which *The Mummy* originates, she includes as part of her novel's dedication the names of several writers and their stories—including H. Rider Haggard's *She* (1887) and Doyle's "The Ring of Thoth" (1890) and "Lot No. 249" (1892)—thus providing her readers with a clear literary trail. In his book *Snobbery with Violence: Crime Stories and Their Audience*, Colin Watson defines both the social and historical context of the British thriller.

> [The thriller] was fiction that pandered to the "non-serious" public by offering vicarious experience in contrived and self-resolving situations—a sort of literary fairground ride. This was the reading matter that subsequently would be categorized as "escapist" literature. It was fated never to become quite respectable, and although by the turn of the century the tradition of regarding all but expressly educative or morally improving books as time-wasters was virtually dead, censure was still reserved for those novels of sensation whose theme was crime and for which the handy term "thriller" or "shocker" had been coined. Like most things that excite disapproval, the thriller was popular.[1]

Arthur Conan Doyle (1859–1930) offers perhaps the simplest (yet most obvious) definition of the thriller in the preface to his 1908 short-story collection, *Round the Fire*

Stories. This type of story, Doyle states, is "concerned with the grotesque and with the terrible—such tales as might well be read 'round the fire' upon a winter's night."[2]

The thriller evolved from the Victorian "penny dreadful" (which was the British equivalent of the American dime novel or pulp magazine) and the Edwardian serial-fiction magazine. Basically, it championed escapist storytelling. During the late Victorian period, the thriller featured pure adventure fiction, as seen in the novels of H. Rider Haggard (1856–1925) and Rudyard Kipling (1865–1936), or suspense, as in the novels of E. W. Hornung (1866–1921) or Guy Boothby (1867–1905). The thriller often contained elements of horror, romance, or intrigue. It became the literary foundation for a number of popular modern-day fiction formulas, including the spy story and the action/adventure story.

Professional writers frequently exhibited great skill in their effective thrillers, yet this great skill was directed almost totally at simple entertainment. The fundamental intent of Bram Stoker's *The Jewel of Seven Stars* (1903) or Sax Rohmer's *The Insidious Dr. Fu Manchu* (1913)—two representative examples of the British thriller—was not to proclaim some aesthetic philosophy of literature, but instead to transport readers to exotic lands and engage them in exciting adventure. The thriller was a proven commodity in the popular books and magazines of its time, but only if its author could maintain a breakneck narrative pace that combined with breathtaking imagination. The fiction of competing, yet critically respectable, genres—like the novel of social protest or the novel of personal introspection—was anathema to the thriller's audience.

One of the most popular authors of the thriller was Sir

Arthur Conan Doyle, a prolific author who wrote a wide variety of fiction. He was best known, obviously, as the author of the Sherlock Holmes stories. Although Doyle's published adventures of the "world's most famous detective" earned him a great deal of money and international fame, Doyle generally felt coerced into writing about Holmes. He even tried, unsuccessfully, to kill his famous detective in "The Final Problem," only to be forced, following much reader protest, to resurrect the character.

Doyle was also one of the earliest authors of science fiction. His Professor Challenger adventures, in particular, helped to establish a number of significant narrative motifs—such as the "lost world" and the "end of the world" stories—that were later imitated by other popular science fiction authors. In addition, Doyle wrote lurid tales of adventure and the supernatural. "Lot No. 249," for example, is considered by many readers and critics to be one of the finest examples of the mummy horror story ever published.

In his autobiography, *Memories and Adventures*, Doyle expressed his admiration for the cultural accomplishments of the ancient Egyptian empire; he especially respected Egypt's seemingly eternal quality. However, he also condemned ancient Egyptian culture as being "petrified." "Their arts seem to have been high," Doyle wrote, "but their reasoning power in many ways [is] contemptible."[3] Doyle's sense of revulsion surrounding ancient Egyptian burial practices is revealed in the following excerpt from his autobiography.

> The recent discovery of the King's tomb near Thebes—I write in 1924—shows how wonderful were their decorations and the amenities of their lives. But consider the tomb itself. What a degraded intelligence does it not show! The

> idea that the body, the old outworn greatcoat which was once wrapped round the soul, should at any cost be preserved is the last word in materialism. And the hundred baskets of provisions to feed the soul upon its journey! I can never believe that a people with such ideas could be other than emasculated in their minds—the fate of every nation which comes under the rule of a priesthood.[4]

Doyle's racial and imperialistic prejudices found a convenient outlet in "Lot No. 249." Doyle considered himself a zealous spiritualist (sometimes to his own professional embarrassment), and his frequent attacks against so-called materialism found their way into the thematic underpinnings of "Lot No. 249." The Egyptian mummy featured in the story is evil, according to Doyle, because it represents the ancient Egyptians' love of physical excess. The body is of no importance to Doyle the ardent spiritualist, and thus when Edward Bellingham reanimates a mummified body of an Egyptian nobleman, the act reveals in Bellingham's character an unnaturally grotesque fascination with the world of the flesh. That world is thus defined as profoundly immoral.

"Lot No. 249" remains a compelling tale of suspense, despite the fact (or perhaps because of the fact) that the macabre elements in the story occur just out of the reader's sight, in much the same way as the reader never sees the horror lurking behind the closed door in W. W. Jacobs's "The Monkey's Paw." Set at Oxford University, "Lot No. 249" recounts the bizarre adventures of Abercrombie Smith, a freshman studying medicine. Smith's apartment is located above that of fellow student Edward Bellingham, the story's villain. Bellingham's expertise is in Eastern languages, but his scholarly interests also include the dark arts. The repugnant

Bellingham is the owner of a mummy, labeled as "Lot 249," and when he recites the incantations written on a papyrus scroll, he is able to animate the mummy to do his vile bidding.

Doyle's tale is structured somewhat like a detective story, with Smith acting as the detective to investigate the mystery surrounding Bellingham and the mummy. When Smith does solve the mystery and confronts his neighbor ("You'll find that your filthy Egyptian tricks won't answer in England," Smith proclaims), the sinister Bellingham sets his monster after Smith himself, and the plot swiftly becomes an adventure story. The scene in which Smith is pursued by the mummy down a darkened Oxfordshire road is particularly exciting. Smith eventually triumphs over Bellingham and his mummy. In his final confrontation with Bellingham, Smith forces Bellingham to dismember the mummy and burn its remains in Bellingham's fireplace.

One of the things that makes Edward Bellingham such a repulsive villain in "Lot No. 249" is his obesity ("It seemed to Smith . . . that he had never seen Nature's danger signals flying so plainly upon a man's countenance," Doyle informs us about Bellingham). Yet there is more to Bellingham's evil than mere outward appearance. Early in the story when Abercrombie Smith's old school chum, Jephro Hastie, is visiting him, Hastie tells Smith that there is "something damnable" about Bellingham. Hastie then goes on to report Bellingham's knowledge of Eastern languages and recounts a tale about Bellingham's uncanny ability to command respect from the Middle-Eastern natives ("when they [the natives] saw this chap Bellingham, before he said five words they just lay down on their bellies and wiggled," states Hastie). Both Hastie and Smith—as upstanding public-school English gentlemen—find Bellingham's aptitude with foreigners repugnant.

Smith, as the story's hero, is little more than a thinly disguised version of Doyle himself. Smith is training to be a doctor, just as Doyle had done before he became a full-time professional writer. Smith and his friend Hastie are described as being "open-air men—men whose minds and tastes turned naturally to all that was manly and robust," just as Doyle had thought of himself as an open-air man who was fond of sports and other manly activities. Smith's views regarding Bellingham and the wickedness that Bellingham represents are intended to depict Doyle's own views, we may assume. Smith also embodies at a larger level Doyle's perception of the moral values inherent in British culture.

Doyle houses within the dramatic conflict between Abercrombie Smith and Edward Bellingham the larger contrast between Western (i.e., wholesome, noble, English) culture and Eastern (i.e., unwholesome, ignoble, foreign) culture. Patrick Brantlinger calls this type of fiction "imperial Gothic," which he defines as the combination of the "seemingly scientific, progressive, often Darwinian ideology of imperialism with an antithetical interest in the occult."[5] Brantlinger goes on to say: "The three principal themes of imperial Gothic are individual regression or going native; an invasion of civilization by the forces of barbarism or demonism; and the diminution of opportunities for adventure and heroism in the modern world."[6] "Lot No. 249" falls under Brantlinger's second category of imperial Gothic; Doyle, in fact, intends his thriller to be an attack against that brand of imperialism—the ancient Egyptian variety—which is not resoundingly British. Thematically, "Lot No. 249" functions as Doyle's expression of inflexible cultural ethnocentricism; it is a popular fiction that declares its author's (and perhaps its Anglocentric audience's) fear of foreign customs and foreign black magic.

In this sense, then, his tale achieves a resolution profoundly different from Anne Rice's *The Mummy*. Doyle's "Lot No. 249" was consistent with popular thrillers of the period in that narrative elements of horror and adventure were employed exclusively to reinforce the status quo. Good and evil were defined in the thriller by their proximity to British middle-class values. Doyle would have never dreamed of critiquing in his thrillers the accepted social customs and beliefs of his readers. Unlike Doyle and his contemporaries, Rice employs the thriller formula in *The Mummy* to burlesque a number of contemporary social conventions, to attack the status quo by challenging such concepts as traditional gender roles and modern-day assumptions about the value of unfettered technological progress. Good and evil in Rice's variant of the thriller are relative concepts, finding their definition in the actions of individuals rather than in social expectations. As does Clive Barker in his Books of Blood, Rice employs Doyle's thriller formula to provide initially a familiar context for her readers, and then, after establishing this context, she addresses issues that articulate her personal views about various problems in postmodern society.

Katherine Ramsland reports in her biography of Anne Rice, *Prism of the Night*, that the immortality elixir that plays such a crucial role in *The Mummy* also appeared in a story written by Rice when she was in the seventh grade.[7] Years later, Rice wrote her first version of *The Mummy* as a television miniseries. Rice says:

> I had long wanted to do my own version of *The Mummy* . . . But I'd never gotten around to it. Then two producers from Hollywood approached me to do something for television. I pitched the idea of *The Mummy*—his being romantic and

> beautiful when he popped out of the wrappings, and falling in love with the archaeologist's daughter—you know, exactly my kind of thing. *Interview with Ramses* so to speak. To my utter amazement, the producers liked it.[8]

Rice quickly wrote a script for *The Mummy*. But she was so upset with the way Hollywood abused her "script bible" that she pulled the project and submitted the story to Bob Wyatt at Ballantine Books. She reworked the television script into a novel, with the intent of publishing the book as a trade paperback.[9] Ramsland quotes Rice as saying:

> I really wanted to do *The Mummy* in paperback . . . I'd like to do a whole series in paperback where I go back to the themes of the B-movies I loved as a child. It was fun evoking that atmosphere and doing outrageous things that I wouldn't do in other books.[10]

Rice states that she wrote *The Mummy* "in usual white-hot passion," and that it subsequently became, to her surprise, one of her most popular books.[11]

Rice incorporated two of the most notable personalities from ancient Egyptian history as the central protagonist and antagonist of her story—Ramses II, the most famous of Egypt's pharaohs, and Cleopatra, the most infamous of Egypt's queens. Rice also assimilated elements of the legend surrounding the famous 1922 discovery of King Tutankhamen's tomb. Part of that discovery involved a mythical curse that was rumored to have killed Lord Carnarvon, one of the archaeologists responsible for "violating" King Tut's tomb. Even Sir Arthur Conan Doyle, who deemed himself an authority on occult matters, became involved in the debate concerning King Tut's so-called curse, claiming that a "malevolent spirit may have caused Lord Carnarvon's fatal illness."[12] From such legends the groundwork of popular culture was established, and King Tut's curse quickly became fictionalized, retold time and again in the thriller formula in popular fiction, story radio, film, and television.

Rice's *The Mummy* still reads like a television screenplay. The scene transitions, for example, appear similar to the scene shifts in a movie. Early on, they occur casually and are not hurried, but as the plot progresses toward its adventurous climax, Rice enhances her story's suspense by frequently "cross-cutting" from one scene to another, a strongly visual, typically cinematic technique. (In fact, *The Mummy* begins with an episode reminiscent of the opening scene in the Universal Pictures 1932 horror movie of the same name, which starred Boris Karloff.) As the novel opens, archaeologist Lawrence Stratford has just discovered the tomb of Ramses the Damned. While he examines Ramses' mummy and the other contents of the tomb (including Ramses' own autobiographical writings), he is poisoned by his greedy nephew, Henry Stratford. The poisoning is witnessed by the immortal Ramses himself, since the sun had partially reanimated him as it shone into his newly opened tomb.

Ramses (along with the valuable contents of his tomb) is later transported to London and placed on temporary exhibit in Lawrence's home before being moved to a permanent exhibit in the British Museum. When Lawrence's headstrong daughter, Julie Stratford, who has assumed responsibility for the Ramses exhibit in her father's library, is attacked by the unscrupulous Henry, Ramses springs to full life to defend Julie. Henry's murderous plans are thus temporarily thwarted, and as Ramses investigates his new world—1914 London—a romance develops between the beautiful Julie and the charismatic Ramses. The reader learns that Ramses, during his mortal life as Egypt's greatest pharaoh, drank a magical elixir that granted him immortal life. Although he knows the secret to preparing this immortality elixir, he is compelled to keep it from the world, because, as Ramses is painfully aware, the gift of immortal life is in reality a dire curse.

Ramses—employing the manufactured identity of Reginald Ramsey, an Egyptologist—and Julie travel by ship to Ramses' ancient homeland, Egypt, accompanied by the villainous Henry (whom Ramses keeps under a suspiciously watchful supervision), and by the Earl of Rutherford—Elliott Savarell—and Elliott's son, Alex, who harbors his own romantic hopes for Julie. While visiting the Cairo museum, Ramses discovers the mummy of his past love, the notorious Cleopatra. Ramses attempts to revive Cleopatra but is interrupted as he is giving her the immortality elixir, and Cleopatra awakens from death deformed, both physically and mentally. She assumes a monstrously psychopathic personality and engages in a killing spree. Among her male victims is Henry Stratford, who is forced to account for his many crimes. Rice's story draws to a riveting climax when Cleopatra, after she has been made entirely whole by drinking more of Ramses' elixir, becomes romantically involved with the naive Alex Savarell. A suspenseful encounter at the Cairo Opera House (reminiscent of Gaston Leroux's 1911 thriller, *The Phantom of the Opera*) is followed by Cleopatra's apparent fiery destruction when, in swift flight from Ramses, she drives across a train's path. The novel concludes with Ramses offering his magical elixir as a type of reward to Elliott Savarell, which he accepts (one of the novel's subplots involves Elliott Savarell's dogged pursuit of the truth behind Ramses' immortality), and then with Ramses finally persuading the reluctant Julie to drink the elixir and become his eternal lover. Cleopatra, unknown to Ramses, has survived her accident intact, the elixir swiftly repairing her damaged body while she recovers under a doctor's care.

In several significant ways, Rice's *The Mummy* honors the British thriller formula. For example, she cuts her cast of characters from the fabric of the thriller, and her episodic plot is thick with cliffhanger action typically found in the yellowing pulpwood pages of popular turn-of-the-century serial-fiction magazines. Rice "borrows" from H. Rider Haggard's *She* the story of an immortal romance between an exotic queen and her noble lover that is doomed in spite of its eternal passion. From Arthur Conan Doyle's "Lot No. 249" and his "The Ring of Thoth," Rice takes both the idea of an ancient Egyptian mummy as a living monster and the use of an immortal Egyptian as a protagonist. However, once she establishes her tribute to the literary and cinematic thriller, she goes on to develop several ideas that are not part of the traditional formula, ideas that reveal her work to be a sophisticated attempt to wrestle with complex social and moral issues.

The Mummy, first of all, provides Rice with a critical political metaphor for modern, technological society. Employing both Ramses and Cleopatra as her narrative voice, Rice portrays technology in an ambivalent fashion. When Ramses is fully revived in Lawrence Stratford's home, he swiftly becomes enamored with 1914 London society. Rice tells us in chapter 7 (part 1) that Ramses passionately loved the motorcars and the typewriters that were presented to him as Rice's representations of technological advancement. But Rice also establishes during this moment in the story an interesting thematic conflict that arises when the magic of the old world (the immortal Ramses) confronts the magic of the new world (modern-day London). Despite humanity's apparent great strides regarding the acquisition of science and knowledge, the social ills that have plagued humanity since Ramses' ancient times still fester in modern times, corrupting the gilded foundations of Julie Stratford's refined Edwardian world. When Ramses sees a beggar woman and questions Julie about poverty ("But cannot all this wealth help these people?" Ramses asks), her reply is a type of veiled indictment of the social failings of post–Industrial Revolution society ("Some things don't change with time," she tells Ramses). Ramses, the immortal, is appalled by the cursed immortality of poverty.

Rice implies during this episode that the economic system that created the wonders of modern technology also failed to achieve general social welfare. In addition, Julie Stratford's environment has become polluted (physically and intellectually) by industry. Rice's descriptions of Ramses' perceptions of London's wonders reads more like a description of his perceptions of London's horrors:

> And how did *he* [Ramses] perceive it—this overgrown metropolis, with its towering brick buildings, its rumbling trams and belching motor cars, and hordes of dark horse-drawn carriages and cabs choking every street . . . What did he make of the little shops where the electric lights burned all day long because the streets themselves were too smoky and dark to admit the natural light of the daytime sky?[13]

This passage is somewhat reminiscent of the conclusion in Edward Bellamy's utopian fantasy, *Looking Backward* (1888), and as Bellamy's novel attacks the social failings of nineteenth-century American capitalism, so, too, Rice's message in *The Mummy* is profoundly socialistic. Her argument that objects—or the products of people's labor—possess more value than people themselves do is a socioeconomic philosophy that simply never existed in Doyle's fiction.

In addition, *The Mummy* provides Rice with a dark metaphor for contemporary sexual values. The eroticism that is such an integral component of The Vampire Chronicles is also an important narrative ingredient in *The Mummy*. The evolving sexual relationship between Ramses and Julie Stratford is framed by a breathless passion adopted directly from the "bodice-ripper" variant of the contemporary paperback romance novel.

But Rice's more interesting use of eroticism occurs when the reanimated mummy of Queen Cleopatra procures naive young men to satisfy her immense sexual appetites, and then when they no longer interest her, she kills them by breaking their necks with her inhuman strength. As it did with Ramses, the immortality elixir elicits in Cleopatra a ravenous appetite. She voraciously consumes both food and sensual experiences. She murders a young Englishman and a young American, after she rapes them. The Englishman she kills because he can no longer adequately pleasure her, the American because, during their lovemaking, he sees her physically deformed leg and foot.

Rice carefully juxtaposes in her story these horrifying scenes of explicit sex and violent death, treating the relationship between the two in a way typically unknown in the British thriller. If *The Mummy* is a monster story, then the only real supernatural monster is Cleopatra, whose evil is defined on the one hand by her disregard for proper sexual conduct, and on the other hand by her blatant sociopathic disregard for human life. She says to Lord Rutherford: "I will tell you a secret . . . You are weak, all of you. Strange beings! And I like killing you. It soothes my pain to watch you die."[14] At one level, Cleopatra becomes for Rice an extrapolation of the femme fatale stereotype that gained popularity as a stock character type in both the traditional thriller (beginning with Haggard's immortal Ayesha) and in American film noir following World War II. Rice's Cleopatra is the supernatural equivalent of Barbara Stanwyck's "man-eater" antagonist, Phyllis Dietrichson, in Billy Wilder's *Double Indemnity* (1944). At another level, Rice's Cleopatra serves as an elaborate symbol for the dangers associated with sexual practices in contemporary society, ranging from date rape to sexual predators to virulent sexually transmitted diseases (such as AIDS). Even though *The Mummy* is set in 1914 London and Cairo, the author's portrayal of Cleopatra's shocking actions in which her wanton sexual intercourse directly leads to the death of her lovers is, in actuality, very current in its message to the reader. Rice seems to underscore Cleopatra's serial murders with an implied warning to today's sexual partners.

Ultimately, *The Mummy* provides Rice with the opportunity to explore the larger question of human morality. "There is a strong moral overview in all the books I write," Rice states in a 1989 *Lear's* interview. "I believe that even if we live in a godless world, we can search for love and maintain it and believe it. 'Make love not war' is the most important cliché of our century, when we are finally shaping a secular morality we can live with as ethical and moral beings even if we don't believe in a divinity."[15] Rice has remarked that she wrote *The Mummy* to create an engaging, adventurous "romp" for her reader. She obviously succeeds, but along with the romp, Rice has created a fairly sophisticated moral allegory, in which she explores both religious and secular notions of ethical responsibility. There does exist a subtle Judeo-Christian subtext in *The Mummy*; Rice, in a sense, is rewriting theology. Ramses, for example, is described several times as resembling Old Testament characters ("[Ramses] looked biblical, larger than life"[16]). Ramses is compared to Cain at one point in the story ("A wanderer on the face of the earth like the biblical Cain, marked by his great eternal vigor which separated him from all humankind forever"[17]). Certainly, Ramses' character is Christlike. His miraculous rebirth via his exposure to sunlight offers an interesting play on the Christian phrase "Son of God." Cleopatra, as Ramses' immortal antagonist, can be viewed as a Satan figure, but Rice also describes this character's behavior within a mythological context ("Oh, he [Alex Summerfield] was so much sweeter than the others, and when a strong man is sweet, even goddesses [like Cleopatra] look down from Mount Olympus"[18]). By depicting Ramses and Cleopatra as being godlike, because both of them have mortal origins and all-too-human flaws, Rice is suggesting to us that divinity may be found within each of us.

If Ramses and Cleopatra are godlike immortals, they are flawed gods with human responsibilities and moral obligations. They are very much like us in that they need to abide by a standard of moral conduct. Through her characters, Rice is espousing the existential philosophy that argues that people should be responsible for their own individual actions, whether good or evil. "All of the major characters in my novels have fallen from grace, in the religious sense," says

Rice, "but they can't stop living a good life, even without religion, even without belief in God."[19] Rice suggests in *The Mummy* that gods and devils do not necessarily dwell in a mythical heaven or hell, but that they instead exist in our actions, in our daily behavior with one another. Such a notion would have had heretical implications in Doyle's version of the thriller, which basically followed a socially conservative formula that advocated obedience to God, Queen, and Country, in that order. A typical Doyle protagonist (such as Abercrombie Smith) would have never directly challenged religious order or social class in his adventures, but Rice does not limit her protagonists in such a way. Characters like Ramses are used by Rice to challenge such things as cultural expectations of an individual's moral behavior, or sexual preferences.

In her pastiche of the traditional British thriller, Rice has entirely redefined the conventional role of the monster. For Doyle, Bellingham's mummy embodies nothing more than the unwholesome product of an immoral ancient Egyptian society. The creature in "Lot No. 249" has no personality other than that of a mindless evil "tool" given direction by the diabolic Bellingham. Neither Doyle nor his readers would ever have considered viewing this less-than-human bogeyman who terrorizes society as the thriller's protagonist. The hero's role was always reserved for the square-jawed, intrepid, British public-school adventurer. Even Bram Stoker's vampire king, Dracula, the most famous monster of late-Victorian and Edwardian popular fiction, is little more than a blood-sucking animal in human disguise. But for Rice, Ramses is not a monster at all. He is a larger-than-life romantic figure, a charismatic lover who is immensely attractive to the opposite sex. He is Rudolph Valentino incarnate, charming, elegant, beautiful, a creature of the sun; he is not the charnel-house ghoul of Doyle's thriller. Ultimately, what Rice has accomplished in *The Mummy* is to invert the conventions of Doyle's thriller, to turn the formula on its head by making heroes out of monsters who search for life's meaning in a morally ambivalent universe.

NOTES

1. Colin Watson, *Snobbery with Violence: Crime Stories and Their Audience* (New York: St. Martin's Press, 1971), 22–23.
2. Sir Arthur Conan Doyle, "Preface," *Round the Fire Stories* (San Francisco: Chronicle Books, 1991), ix.
3. ———, *Memories and Adventures* (London: Hodder and Stoughton, 1924), 130.
4. Ibid.
5. Patrick Brantlinger, *Rules of Darkness: British Literature and Imperialism, 1830–1914* (Ithaca: Cornell University Press, 1988), 227.
6. Ibid., 230.
7. Katherine Ramsland, *Prism of the Night: A Biography of Anne Rice* (New York: Plume, 1994), 40.
8. Teresa Simmons, "The Queen of the Chroniclers," *The Vampire Companion* 1, no. 3 (1992): 5. Wheeling, West Virginia: Innovation Corporation. (Not to be confused with Ramsland's *The Vampire Companion*.)
9. Ramsland, *Prism*, 314.
10. Ibid., 320.
11. "The Queen of the Chroniclers," 5.
12. Arnold C. Brackman, *The Search for the Gold of Tutankhamen* (New York: Mason/Charter, 1976), 113–14.
13. Anne Rice, *The Mummy or Ramses the Damned* (New York: Ballantine, 1991), 105.
14. Ibid., 305.
15. W. Kenneth Holditch, "Interview with Anne Rice," *Lear's*, October 1989, 155.
16. Rice, 301–2.
17. Ibid., 343.
18. Ibid., 329.
19. Holditch, 155.

More than Kin, Less than Kind

THE MAYFAIRS AND THE TALTOS

Kay Kinsella Rout

In the Mayfair trilogy, which includes *The Witching Hour*, *Lasher*, and *Taltos*, Anne Rice lets her imagination run back to prehistoric Britain and creates a complex and detailed history of two unusual groups of outsiders. The destinies of these two, a hitherto unknown and now nearly extinct species called Taltos and a family of human witches named Mayfair, intertwine from the creation of the first witch in the middle of the seventeenth century. The secret organization called the Talamasca, younger than the Taltos but older than the Mayfair dynasty, comprises a third strand braided into the destinies of the two principals. The Mayfairs, descended from an illegitimate line of Scottish lords, are related to the nonhuman Taltos; an aberrant, giant double helix marks both groups and makes it possible, on rare occasions, for a Mayfair to reproduce a Taltos. Not only has the Talamasca known both groups, but through one of their investigators has shared in the genes of the Mayfairs from the first.

While all three groups live more or less outside the conventions of mainstream Western culture for different reasons, the most extreme is the nonhuman Taltos. The Mayfairs are wealthy, amoral, and, in some cases, possessed of paranormal abilities; the members of the Talamasca live like upper-class monks in pursuit of the study of the occult and the strange. The tall and childlike Taltos are exploited, persecuted, and finally almost exterminated for both their appearance and their behavior. But to be a true outsider means not merely to be strange or idiosyncratic; it means to remain apart from and unmoved even by those whom one has known most intimately. While this coldness in the Taltos might be attributed to their nonhuman identity, Rice also makes them an emblematic group that comes to represent the Other, the rejected and isolated ones, the descendants of the oppressed whose blood is inextricably mingled with the blood of the oppressor, but whose identity remains intact. At the end of the third volume of the trilogy, the surviving Taltos are pledged to destroy the human race.

The first volume of the trilogy is dominated by the Mayfair family history; the second details the events in the sixteenth-century life of Lasher as background for his reincarnation in the twentieth century. It is only in the final volume that the reader learns the long history of the species to which he belongs—the Taltos.

The Witching Hour, the first volume, introduces the Mayfair dynasty of witches in Donnelaith, Scotland, and follows them through many generations with Lasher, a disembodied being variously thought to be a demon, a monster, or the Devil himself, functioning as their familiar. Here we learn of the beginning of the line in the person of the beautiful half-witted woman, Suzanne of the May Fair, and of her calling Lasher by chance in 1660. When Suzanne was burned at the stake in 1665, her twelve-year-old daughter, Deborah, was flogged and forced to watch as the burning took place. Deborah, a "merry-begot" who had been conceived during the fertility rituals on the first of May, was probably the daughter of the local lord, who was destroyed by Lasher along with his eldest son and his grandson on the day Deborah was burned as a witch in Montcleve, France. Although Lasher's role is only assumed, it seems that he avenged Deborah's death because he believed that if she had been acknowledged by the Scottish laird, she would not have been burned. It may also be that Lasher felt he had no need of the clan at Donnelaith any longer, since Deborah had produced a female child who could in turn produce a witch. At the least, the destruction of the clan points to a connection between the lord and Suzanne, which is important in Rice's ultimately establishing a genetic bond between Deborah and Lasher in *Lasher*.

In Lasher's account of his life, he spoke of his birth to Queen Anne Boleyn in 1536[1] and of his awareness that this was not his first birth, that "things had greatly changed."[2] His father, Douglas of Donnelaith, who identified him immediately as the legendary "Ashlar, who comes again,"[3] saved him from death at the hands of Henry VIII and spirited him away to Scotland. This lord was a direct ancestor of the one who fathered Deborah in the same village more than one hundred years later, in 1653. This fact clarifies Lasher's motive for selecting the Mayfair family down through the ages; although Suzanne had called him by accident, her child's father was a carrier of the giant helix, which meant in turn that Deborah could produce females who could one day make a Taltos, just as Lasher himself had been born to Queen Anne. Anne, reputed to be a witch, had cried out at Lasher's birth that he was the product of "a witch coupling with a witch,"[4] the error she had committed in her eagerness to give Henry a son. Upon Lasher's return to Donnelaith after twenty-three years as a Franciscan priest in Italy, his sister Emaleth denounced him as the Taltos: "The curse of this valley since the dark times, the curse that rises without warning in our blood."[5] The knowledge of this genetic secret is what made Elizabeth I, the half-sister of Lasher, afraid to bear a child, Emaleth insisted.

The Talamasca has also been genetically linked to the Mayfairs from the birth of the third witch, although the family itself has forgotten this fact along with the rest of its history. Rice allows the reader to know only as much as the family knows of "the man" (Lasher) throughout the centuries, and only as much as the Talamasca has known about the family history. Mary Beth had once mentioned that the family history was "all lost in the dust,"[6] and Stella told the Talamasca investigator Arthur Langtry that the Mayfairs did "not have any Scottish ancestors. We were all French."[7] Until Rowan, the last witch, and her husband, Michael, are allowed to read the files, no one outside the Talamasca has been aware that the blood of one of their investigators has also flowed in Mayfair veins from the first, ever since Petyr van Abel, a Talamasca investigator, and Deborah produced the witch Charlotte of Saint-Domingue. Thus, unknown to the Mayfairs, their family is related to both the Talamasca and the Taltos.

Petyr of the Talamasca became connected to the Mayfairs when he visited Donnelaith to investigate the burning of Suzanne as a witch and saved Deborah and brought her to Amsterdam. Soon he became her lover, and thus obtained for the Motherhouse Rembrandt's portrait of Deborah. Later, he produced both Charlotte from Deborah and Jeanne Louise from Charlotte, concentrating the "witch potential"; Petyr himself possessed strong mental powers. From the beginning, Petyr understood that Lasher's nature was not satanic, but probably evil, and certainly as deceitful as Satan was ever said to be. He warned Deborah, "Do not believe what it tells you of itself and its intentions."[8] It is he who introduces the idea that Lasher grows stronger from the attention Deborah pays to him.

The Talamasca remains almost completely passive toward the Mayfairs after Petyr's death; while investigators arrive in New Orleans, they study the Mayfairs simply as witches. No one understands who Lasher really is or what his relationship to the Taltos may be. The Talamasca became aware of the Taltos very early, but there had never been any reason to link the Mayfair familiar with those unusual beings. Lasher, though, knows what he is and how to manipulate the Mayfair witches into helping him escape his spirit realm and take a place among the living again.

In *Taltos*, the original Ashlar, still alive and now a modern businessman, tells the story of his people. The Taltos resemble human beings enough to blend with them ("pass") in most circumstances, but they differ in a number of vital, unique ways. A single prolonged act of intercourse produces within hours a large offspring that grows to adult height almost immediately, able to reproduce its own kind right after birth. They also have a strong sex drive combined with high physical vulnerability to the hazards of childbirth among the women; as a result, their cultural practice allowed for sexuality without vaginal sex: foreplay that included nursing at length, and homosexual or lesbian sex "just for fun" as opposed to heterosexual sex for the purpose of procreation, which was indulged in rarely and then only at designated times. These occasions, kept secret from humans, were characterized by public intercourse within the holy circles of stone followed by the immediate birth and maturity of the new offspring.

Unfortunately, the winter solstice was usually selected as the time for the birth ritual; the coincidence of that fascinating spectacle with the birth of Christ led the Celts, as soon as they were Christianized in the late sixth century, to assign Christmas Eve after Midnight Mass as the time when they would depart from the church to a secular setting and offer newborn Taltos captured in the "Sacred Hunt" as their animal sacrifice while the Yule log burned and the evergreen, holly, and mistletoe filled the hall. Either Taltos tradition or an ironic recollection of the Christmas sacrifice has impelled Lasher to choose for his own modern nativity the witching hour on Christmas Eve; this time, though, the birth will be directed by a Taltos for his own ends.

The foundation of Lasher's long-term plan for reincarnation is also revealed in *Taltos*. Ashlar left Donnelaith on a long pilgrimage in the sixth century. When he returned in 1228, he found a great cathedral containing a shrine to the memory of himself as Saint Ashlar and a new Taltos he had never met functioning as the celibate priest. Knowing he had left behind only males, Ashlar was stunned to understand that this creature had been born, as had three others over the six centuries since his departure, from a human couple of the clan of Donnelaith. "How could it be? A wild Taltos, born to humans who had no idea they carried the seed in their blood? No. It could not have been."[9]

It is clear from the reference to rare but not unheard-of cases of a Taltos being born to two human beings in Donnelaith that the giant double helix had implanted itself in a few people, emerging only rarely. Occasionally such creatures had been born before Lasher's sixteenth-century incarnation, all descended from the original Taltos who had built Stonehenge four thousand years before Christ, and perhaps even from Ashlar himself. Thus, the assumption of Lasher's father that his new son is Ashlar reborn is explained, and the technique Lasher hopes to use to accomplish his twentieth-century rebirth is revealed.

In *Lasher*, researchers analyze the tissue and blood specimens Rowan Mayfair was able to take from Lasher and herself. They discover through DNA analysis that the fetal Chris, Rowan and Michael's baby, was probably never human at all, but "the product of a separate and complex evolutionary process,"[10] a creature resembling a human in some ways, but "a different sort of placental primate."[11] Only 40 percent of these creatures' genes overlap with those of humans, far fewer than among chimpanzees, whose DNA is 97 percent identical with that of human beings.[12] Chris's spirit was replaced by Lasher's at the moment of Lasher's Christmas nativity, but his body was Taltos all along, as was Morrigan Mayfair's (the child of the witch who succeeds Rowan, Mona). The father of both, Michael Curry, has the ninety-two chromosomes of a true Mayfair witch. From Rowan's or Mona's standpoint, that means a "trigger" could cause the DNA in their dormant extra genes, those that linked them to the Taltos, to create a "wild" Taltos.[13] Michael's alternate genes were that DNA trigger.

The question of Michael's ancestry is solved when Rice reveals that he is an illegitimate descendant of the promiscuous and unprincipled Julien, whose affair with a young O'Brien girl (Rice's maiden name) created the child Michael O'Brien and led to the mother's retreat into a convent as Sister Bridget Marie. Two generations later, Michael Curry, a carrier of the dormant Taltos genes as surely as any lord of Donnelaith,[14] was born in the Irish Channel of New Orleans. It would seem, then, that only luck kept a Taltos from being born sooner than it was; if Julien carried the correct DNA, and the Mayfair women did as well, then Mary Beth or Stella could have given birth to (or could have *been*) the Taltos, and Lasher, already able to embody himself, could have seized that child's soul instead of Chris's.

Julien guesses before his death that Lasher is not the Devil, as Carlotta had always believed, but rather the spirit of a dead man named Ashlar. This theory is closer to the truth than any other, but it still does not grasp at the reality of an unknown species. Lasher kept the truth from the Mayfairs because of the fantastical nature of his plan, with its dependence upon the production of a Taltos, and its deadly agenda—destroy the human race. He revealed things to the witches as needed, which is to say, not openly or clearly at any time, but "through a glass, darkly," so to speak. In spite of his vow that the Mayfairs will be "upheld," Lasher undoubtedly intended to kill them just as he had eliminated the Scottish branch of the family in 1689. No non-Taltos would be allowed to survive; the historical record was too bloody for them to be trusted. As he tells the unborn Emaleth, Rowan's child by him, "Sad and sorrowful the weakness of humans and the tragedy of the little people, and is it not better that all be driven from the Earth?"[15] As she well understands, his intent is to return to Donnelaith with her and to live with their "hundreds of children" in their Bethlehem. "And that would be the beginning of all time."[16]

The genetic relationship of the Taltos and the Mayfairs has a serendipitous bonus from Lasher's point of view: the Mayfair females, or those, at least, in whom the giant double helix is found, also manifest the concupiscence of the Taltos. Their sex drives are so unusually strong that even females barely past puberty are aggressively sexual, and their judgment and morality are hopelessly clouded by this drive, so that it was an easy matter for Lasher to arouse and stimulate the witches as his ability to materialize increased. Thus he was able to pacify and corrupt all the witches and to seduce Rowan.

The corruption of the witch by both sex and money is in the contract from the beginning. Petyr and his Talamasca mentor, Roemer Franz, surmised that Suzanne had thought herself evil; they assumed that she did so only because she was a healer, unjustly condemned by the superstitious, but her hut was full of gold and there is no reason to doubt that the lure of the incubus worked with her, as well. Roemer foreshadows Rowan's battle when he expresses worry for Deborah, who is very soon in possession of the huge Mayfair emerald. "This is always the mistake of the sorceress . . . to imagine her power is complete over the unseen forces that do her bidding, when in fact, it is not. And what of her will, her conscience, and her ambition? How the thing does corrupt her!"[17]

The next strong reinforcement of the Mayfair potential for producing a Taltos came when Julien initiated, through multiple incest reminiscent of Petyr's in the seventeenth century, the strongest witches that had ever been known in the family: Mary Beth, Stella, and Antha, mother of Deirdre. Julien, like Petyr, produced his own granddaughter from his own daughter, fathering Mary Beth from his sister Katherine and Stella in turn from her; unknown to almost everyone, including himself, he also fathered the great-grandmother of Michael Curry. Carlotta, sister of Stella, understood Julien's intent perfectly. In her recounting of the Mayfair history to Rowan, she condemns the female witches down to Deirdre, and "that evil despicable Julien" most of all: "Incest, my dear, was the least of their sins, but the greatest of their schemes, incest to strengthen the line, to double up the powers, to purify the blood, to birth a cunning and terrible witch in each generation, going so far back it's lost in

European history."[18] Since neither she nor anyone else knows about the Taltos strain in the blood, Lasher's real plan is not clear to her in all its details; she understands only that his "ends" were "to be alive, as we are alive. To come through and to see and feel what we see and feel."[19]

Among the Mayfairs, Lasher promotes the idea of a plan, a design according to which all human beings associated with the Mayfairs have been subordinated to divine will. Even members of the Talamasca have believed that the family fate was "all planned," though not by Lasher. In the current generation, encouraged by images Lasher placed in their minds as they talked, Rowan and Michael fell in love and married. Lasher did everything he could to create a "sense of destiny"[20] in Michael, sending visions to him during his near drowning and later suggesting what he was to do for the "beings" that had spoken to him. Lasher kept alive in Michael thereafter, once he had met Rowan, the "idea of a magnificent pattern and purpose that served some higher value,"[21] a "dark mandate"[22] that would coexist with his growing love for her. Michael, however, refuses to accept the concept that he and the others have never had more than the illusion of free will, that the sequence of events has occurred solely according to Lasher's plan and not because of human decisions or even blind fate.

Certainly a family tradition would be a strong counterpressure to individual reluctance or disbelief. In fact, a sense of fate is exactly the lure that overbalances Rowan's skepticism once she arrives in New Orleans and is surrounded by her family and its awareness of its place in history as especially "chosen" to have a pact with a familiar. Lasher can convince people that there is no alternative but his will, even when they wish to do otherwise, because he knows them and their weaknesses so well. Hence, he is able to manipulate Rowan in the same way as he has all the other highly sexed Mayfair witches, through his services as an incubus, and also through flattery. Rowan is a talented neurosurgeon. She is proud of her skills and also of her willpower; Lasher adds to the usual lures the Faustian appeal of research science: himself as a newly created being, a Taltos formed, or so she thinks, from a normal human fetus, a creature from which to learn more than anyone else knows about DNA, a source of fame. Rowan expects, just as Franz had said of Deborah three hundred years before, that she will be able to control her familiar through intelligence and determination. Her pride blinds her to his strength and to the extent of her own corruption. She tells her daughter Emaleth, as she believes herself to be dying in childbirth with her, "I made an error, a terrible error. The sin was vanity. Tell Michael this."[23]

It is clear that in working for the realization of his plan, Lasher has no concern for the consequences of his involvement with the family, as long as he has been able ultimately to be "made flesh." Some of these consequences, which began with the burnings of Suzanne and Deborah at the stake and have continued through the years, include the deaths of various Mayfair women as he tries to impregnate them with as many Taltos fetuses as possible. He is even willing to sacrifice the witch who gave him birth, his own mother, Rowan, to this end. Michael's recognition of Lasher's ruthlessness and his desire for revenge motivate him to use a tool of his trade, the hammer, to administer justice like Thor and eliminate the Taltos (or so he believes) forever. But in fathering a child with Mona, Michael has unknowingly kept the Taltos alive.

Morrigan, child of Michael Curry and Mona Mayfair, is born of two witches with Mayfair blood and the requisite giant double helix; she is the Taltos daughter of Mona, who has already been named the legatee by Rowan (in lieu of her own Taltos daughter, whom she killed). Thus, Morrigan is the sole heir of the Mayfair billions. The Other has become a member of the human family and Lasher, in a manner not foreseen by himself, has apparently won after all. Morrigan expects that Rowan and Michael will opt for her execution, and it is with this fear in mind that she has solicited the loyalty of her mother and her cousin Mary Jane, knowing that they are completely ignorant of the possible long-term consequences. It is Morrigan's matter-of-fact understanding that if she can find a mate, Lasher's plan will still be put into effect, and then "the world will crumble."[24]

The history of the Taltos species and its unfortunate contact with human beings makes it more than clear that this time the Taltos will take into consideration the mistakes that led to their near extinction in the past. It seems inevitable that a clash will result, leading to an Armaggedon. Ashlar's story of his life as told to Rowan and Michael in *Taltos* emphasizes the impossibility of two species living together in the same world where human races "battle endlessly," and people slaughter one another in the name of religion. There the "gentle people," as he designates the Taltos, would not long survive. His realization that the Taltos would have to exterminate the humans if they wanted to be free led him, back in the sixth century, to choose to annihilate all Taltos who would not swear themselves to celibacy. He has resigned himself to solitude, but as he tells his story to Rowan and Michael he plants the fear in the reader that will come to mind when he rides off with the newborn Morrigan: "Within the space of one night, a pair of Taltos could breed a battalion of adults, ready to invade the citadels of human power, ready to destroy the weapons which humans know how to use so much better, ready to take the food, the drink, the resources of this brimming world, and deny it to those less gentle, less kind, less patient, in retribution for their eons of bloody dominance."[25]

As Morrigan and Ashlar depart for the glen at Donnelaith to mate, the Mayfairs stand confounded. Rowan and Michael assent, though fearfully, to this development; they have sworn to protect Morrigan, their own flesh and blood. Possessed of the knowledge of an inevitable future conflict, Rowan nonetheless regrets having killed Emaleth, her Taltos daughter by Lasher. Ashlar's manner seems to have moved her to identify with him and Emaleth, and by extension all Taltos past and future, as misunderstood outsiders, those whose freedom, identity, and even right to life have been unjustly denied by dominant human beings. If so, then her nod of permission to Ashlar may be her attempt at reparation; neither she nor Michael will take on the responsibility of deliberate murder again, for any reason. The revulsion she felt against fetal research and her lifelong vow to protect life, along with Michael's sympathy for his own offspring—ideas that had bound them together when their relationship was young, in San Francisco—now motivate their acceptance of the future.

In Rice's work, the outsider has been variously mulatto, homosexual, vampire, or witch. From time to time she has blended these characters, creating androgynous figures, mixed-race figures, vampire-human blends (as when Lestat, full of nostalgia for his days as a human being, exchanges bodies with a man in *The Tale of the Body Thief*), and now Taltos-human blends in the persons of Emaleth and Morrigan. To some extent, each of these is an analogue of the others. Just as Michael saw many then-current horror films, from

Eraserhead to *Alien*, as reflections of society's collective guilt over abortion, the reader may perceive in the Mayfair trilogy and other works the fear of a white postindustrial society toward the dark masses of outsiders who were once exploited for their labor but are now nearly useless. The various untouchables hover along the edges of society, picking off prey, like the vampire, or manipulating individuals from the master class to their own ends, like the quadroons in *The Feast of All Saints*. Some, like those light-skinned "colored" people, or homosexuals, pass themselves off as white and/or straight, maintaining all the while a counterculture outlook on the majority of society and its flaws, just as various Taltos throughout history, including both Lasher and Ashlar, have presented themselves as human. Always, like Lestat and other (once human) vampires, like the disembodied Lasher, like the lower-caste "people of color" or even the blue-collar Irish, like the ostracized homosexuals or the mutilated and exploited castrati of *Cry to Heaven*, they crave admission into full humanhood, full equality.

The ultimate threat at the end of the third volume, then, reflects the fears of a conquest, even annihilation, by the Other, the outsider, the "ethnic" in the full and original sense of the term, third-world people. It is tempting to examine the idea that the Taltos, the sleeping giants that always had the latent power to take over, represent the upwardly mobile and vengeful minority races that could arise and change the world their way. In its single-mindedness this new "race" could be no less ruthless than Lasher himself. The "otherness" of a group of offbeat, privileged, and well-educated Caucasians like the Mayfair dynasty or the Talamasca pales into irrelevance by comparison. In contrast with the victims of genocide, these two groups are merely eccentric.

On the unconscious level, Rice is expressing her awareness, perhaps, that through modern racial amalgamation and upward social mobility there may arise a future in which there are no longer whites and blacks in the United States, but a mixed breed that looks white, even as Morrigan exactly resembles her mother, Mona, but is "in fact" black, especially in self-identification. Or it may be that Rice sees moving among "regular" Americans and Western Europeans the enemies of the values and standards that are defined as normal. The parallels of Taltos and Native American or African American are clear in the terminology of genocide, cultural or otherwise, that is freely employed by some, and in the talk of retribution. Even the assumption that the Taltos lack souls is an echo of past racist arguments of Christians favoring conquest, subordination, and even genocide of various indigenous pagans. In this context, the assent of Rowan and Michael to the Taltos victory has its counterpart among liberal and radical whites who reject white hegemony, although in their cases there is no commitment to future race warfare; rather, it is their idea to avoid conflict and the resultant guilt by recognizing the equality of oppressed groups. What will end, it is assumed, is not white people themselves, but the concept of white supremacy, along with the class structure, racism, and exploitation that have always accompanied it.

Rice's trilogy provides, on one level, an exciting story of the occult centered on three unusual and related groups for more than three hundred years, since the establishment of the Mayfair line of witches. On a deeper level, however, Rice comments on the lure of sex and money in corrupting people, and on the ruthlessness of those who will use for their own ends creatures they think of as outsiders, beings who are perceived as less than fully human: fetuses, nonwhites, nonheterosexuals, or members of other species, animal or Taltos. When people are able to choose, they often select the option labeled Might Makes Right: the stronger and more aggressive dominate the weak and the diffident, the greater in number the fewer, and the adult the child. To many, power and wealth are the spurs; to others, the motive is simply, as Rowan says when she kills Emaleth, "survival," interpreted as broadly as possible. It is this morality that has characterized the relationship of human beings toward the Taltos from the beginning of their awareness of them, and that Rowan and Michael refuse to embrace at the end of *Taltos*. Disregard for the rights of others is the essence of evil; those who labeled Lasher a "devil" in the past were as close to correct as possible, given what they knew. Perhaps it is Rowan's and Michael's opinion that Mayfair collusion with Lasher over the centuries was enough in itself to warrant the family's destruction at the hands of the Taltos branch of the Clan of Donnelaith.

NOTES

1. Anne Rice, *Lasher* (New York: Knopf, 1993), 526.
2. Ibid., 486.
3. Ibid., 487.
4. Ibid., 485.
5. Ibid., 533.
6. Anne Rice, *The Witching Hour* (New York: Knopf, 1990), 399.
7. Ibid., 495.
8. Ibid., 288.
9. Anne Rice, *Taltos* (New York: Knopf, 1994), 418.
10. Rice, *Lasher*, 52.
11. Ibid., 55.
12. Ibid., 53.
13. Ibid., 54.
14. Ibid., 221.
15. Ibid., 4.
16. Ibid., 5.
17. Rice, *The Witching Hour*, 289.
18. Ibid., 649.
19. Ibid., 647.
20. Ibid., 189.
21. Ibid., 201.
22. Ibid., 204.
23. Rice, *Lasher*, 314.
24. Rice, *Taltos*, 457.
25. Ibid., 422–23.

Forced Consent and Voluptuous Captivity

THE PARADOXICAL PSYCHOLOGY BEHIND ANNE RICE'S EROTIC IMAGINATION

Katherine Ramsland

Inner conflict can amplify the sensuality of any experience. Tension adds intensity. Anne Rice's most provocative literary descriptions rely strongly on this intimate mind/body bond, and she works hard to locate sources of psychophysical friction. One source that she has returned to over and over again is the notion of forced consent. "The delicate balance between force and consent is hard to find," says Rice of her erotic fiction. "I wanted to maintain that balance." From her earliest stories this paradoxical coupling of opposites has attracted her attention, and she has developed it in a variety of forms ever since. By examining her early erotica, we can better understand how this particular theme influences her later, more famous work.

Combining force with consent seems confusing—even contradictory—yet the complexity of the human psyche makes it work. We all have the capacity to initiate some activity and then immerse ourselves in it to such a degree that we can actually "forget" we set it in motion; we can thus believe we had no choice in the matter. This is how Rice's description of sexual bondage operates: Masochists, or "slaves," willingly surrender to a "master," who can then force them into an extremely physical sense of their bodies, enabling them to explore capacities for pleasure and surrender which they might resist on their own. Rice typically describes the experience of forced consent from the masochist's perspective, experimenting with variations on its key ingredients: masked intention and covert collusion between cooperative partners. As such, it requires at least two people who recognize the way the scenario works. Both of them play with the *illusion* of force, yet both also realize that willingness is an essential ingredient. Consent makes the relationship happen, but once things are in motion, all memory of the act of consent recedes. The intense role-playing produces a sort of altered state of consciousness, in which the captive *feels* forced. That is, under the auspices of "having no choice," one person gains erotic benefits from becoming forcefully enslaved to another's will. If the captive is fully satisfied, this experience becomes "voluptuous captivity": As long as there is no risk of serious harm, the slave agrees to be dominated in unpredictable ways so that fear in the right measure can produce the most intense sexual stimulation.

Whenever Rice had read descriptions of this kind of relationship in other books, she found them exciting. She wanted to get as close as possible to the experience herself through language and fantasy. She first tried writing erotica in the mid-sixties after encountering Nabokov's *Lolita*. Rice appreciated its elegant eroticism and cinematic language, and was particularly drawn to the way Nabokov portrayed the devotion of Humbert Humbert to the young Lolita. That such a controversial story could be published to great acclaim inspired her. "*Lolita* has had an influence on everything I've written," Rice claims. "[Nabokov's] way of writing erotic scenes so eloquently and elegantly had a huge influence."

Rice also read Pauline Reage's *The Story of O*, an explicit novel about a female photographer who becomes a sexual slave in a chateau near Paris. The photographer, O, is repeatedly humiliated, whipped, and violated, and—masochist that she is—she submits to it all. In one version, when she senses that she no longer serves her masters' purposes, she begs for death. This part of the story disturbed Rice. She failed to understand why, even in fiction, sexual pleasure and masochistic thrills should be mortally punished. "There was something frightening about the way the book took itself seriously," she says. Yet she still appreciated the fact that novels with such graphic imagery were becoming available to the general public. She, too, wanted to write about erotic captivity, albeit with the finer, more subtle elements of *Lolita*, raising the sexual temperature without inviting the brutal consequences.

Long acquainted with her own sensuality and affinity for extremes, Rice decided to explore a more congenial form of dominance and submission. For much of her life, her daydreams had played out her personal obsessions. These were like prime-time soaps and often involved masochistic elements. Yet they always involved tenderness, too. One of her fantasies was set in a slave market in ancient Greece; the closest she has come to revealing its details is in Elliott Slater's sexual fantasy in *Exit to Eden*.

Elliott imagines himself as one of seven boys whom the priests select to serve as sexual slaves. He becomes an object of both scorn and veneration, not considered fully human. Tormented for the amusement of his master and paraded naked in front of people, he is nevertheless secretly cherished. Harshness combined with affection is key to the eroticism of this fantasy, with Elliott uncertain how much of either he will get. Elliott claims that for the scenario to work sexually for him, there must be a sense of coercion without actually being forced against his will. He needs to be constrained and anxious, but not terrified. Consent must be a factor, because it is the very act of consent that makes it provocative. The extreme humiliation of knowing he *wants* to be treated this way creates inner tension: It pits one part of himself against another. "The ultimate degradation is that you consent and grow to like it."[1]

For Rice, the idea of being punished into something one both fears and craves sparks a fierce kind of tension that draws body and mind together in a heightened state of arousal. She believes that the body teaches the most concrete form of wisdom—that pleasure is life's prize—and that true spirituality should reinforce that notion. Whatever engages the senses and makes one feel *alive* should be actively employed (within a safe framework), even if it involves some degree of pain. Going even further by applying restrictions to the body in the form of bondage or discipline brings attention to its capacity for extreme sensation. This is the central element in what Rice terms voluptuous captivity—absolute surrender to the full impact of the flesh. Straining together, body and mind merge, defying the boundaries of an individual ego to flow into something larger. Sexual captives use feelings of resistance and helplessness to tap inner resources for a powerful transcendence.

Fired by the need to express her desires fully and encouraged by the social atmosphere of the sixties, in which erotic material was tolerated and even sought, Rice initially wrote several novellas for a small group of friends. The first was "The Sufferings of Charlotte." Set in the nineteenth century, it is a masochistic fantasy in which the heroine is given a choice: be prosecuted for a murder of which she is accused or avoid arrest by joining a sexual cult. The circumstances more or less compel her to opt for the latter, but it is in fact what she secretly wants. Although to admit her desire would prove too humiliating, Charlotte is glad to be "forced" into sexual slavery. Her consent is "reluctant" merely for the sake of appearances (even to herself). It is a game and both she and the cult know it, yet both preserve the illusion of coercion so that Charlotte can experience the additional charge of her own defiance.

Right from the start Rice preferred to write from the masochist's perspective, believing her attraction to it echoed that of most people. "I'm almost never writing from the point of view of the dominant one," she states. "I have no interest in it. I think those who love porn generally love writing that is from the masochist's point of view." Unfortunately, her first novella was lost when she loaned it to friends, but her experience in writing "The Sufferings of Charlotte" motivated subsequent stories about the tension inherent between the masochists' submission to things they *claim* to fear and resistance to what they *genuinely* fear. Rice continued to try to articulate the sensation of being trustingly brought to the edge.

Psychologists who study masochism affirm many of Rice's instincts. Rosemary Gordon views masochism as an aspect of the universal need to venerate and surrender to a higher being,[2] while Roy Baumeister describes it as a flight from self. The two interpretations go hand in hand. Reducing one's identity to the body via pain, Baumeister claims, is a carefully choreographed activity that can provide intense, immediate pleasure with little danger of harm. Pain deconstructs the ego, and "when the self is taken apart, people cease to be reluctant to perform actions inconsistent with the self."[3] The masochist may go through a wholesale identity change, from powerful to powerless. Loss of control and a feeling of humiliation appear to be key factors in enhancing the degree of intensity of sexual experiences, while being absolved of responsibility for one's actions facilitates participation in activities the person might desire but would not freely choose. If pleasure results, the masochist is likely to repeat the activity.

Another erotic novella that emerged from Rice's early period was "Nicholas and Jean." For years, Rice had been interested in the image of a sexually precocious, beautiful boy held captive and exploited by older men. Her enigmatic young Jean had violet eyes and dark hair, and she wrote many stories in which he was a central character. Jean is coerced into sophisticated sexual relationships, yet he also experiences love from his captors. "Love between dominants and submissives is just about the only thing that interests me in my porn," says Rice. "I've written scenes in which the love complicates and heightens the experience for both people. *Thrall* is the key word. The dominant and submissive hold each other in thrall. Love between them totally shapes the experience."

The first chapter of this novella was published in 1965 in *Transfer*, a college literary journal. (It appears in this collection, on p. 84.) A photographer named Nicholas encounters Jean at an isolated castle on an island. Jean confesses that he has been a sex toy since the age of ten for lascivious older men, although he has run away from all of them. Nicholas is attracted to Jean and decides to take care of him, but Jean runs from him as well. He tracks Jean to a sleazy New Orleans sex club where the boy has been drugged and abused, and rescues him. They make a commitment to each other. The published chapter ends with their embrace.

Although Jean complains of being a sexual captive, he has continually placed himself in positions where men will desire and enslave him. He wants it, flees from it, and then wants it again. This is the mechanism that operates here: Jean pretends he does not want something that in fact he craves, so to get it without admitting it, he allows the *fact* of his desire and his pretense concerning it to ebb from his awareness. He can complain only if he can make himself (and others) believe that he really doesn't want to be a captive. By his actions, he consents to be "forced."

The bulk of "Nicholas and Jean" no longer exists. A few years later, Rice developed Jean's secret indulgences more fully in her 1972 master's thesis, "Katherine and Jean."

Katherine is an innocent girl from New Orleans who encounters the enigmatic Jean. Through him, she glimpses the underground world of sexual hustling. Jean only vaguely hints at his escapades, but one night Katherine discovers him dancing naked for an older man. She understands little about his shadow life until he takes her to an S&M club whose members are pursuing him. Since Rice had little familiarity with such places, she was unable to provide much detail. Instead, she focused on Jean's erotic character—the vulnerability that made him submissive to men and the fantasy life he developed to adapt to S&M situations that simultaneously attracted and frightened him. Turmoil and inner resistance like Jean's became a central element of masochistic characters such as Tristan and Beauty, whom Rice later developed in the Roquelaure series.

Rice also wrote a revealing novella about sexual captivity told from the perspective of a female masochist, "The Tales of Rhoda," around the time she was developing "Katherine and Jean." Similar to *The Story of O* but revealing another side of such female fantasies, the story featured a twenty-five-year-old college student so bored with life that she is nearing despair. Even Rhoda's ventures into erotic novels are disappointing. She senses that male writers know little about what a woman really wants, and she dislikes the way female desire is often punished with death, as if there is something wrong with it. The humiliation of total surrender flavors her own fantasies, and she thinks that extreme erotic suffering could make a more enhanced sexual experience possible, although she is unsure what that experience might be. She only senses the possibilities.

One day Rhoda encounters a man from a secret organization that trains women to be sexual slaves; he believes Rhoda would be an excellent candidate. To ease her fears, he lays out the terms: no harm, no cuts, no risk of death, nothing physically unhealthy, and no pain aside from that produced by the blows of a flat or flexible object. She will be paid a large sum of money for a year of consensual captivity, but once involved, there is no escape. Rhoda must learn to trust her captors and relax in her captivity to derive the most sensation possible from surrendering to another's discipline. In this way, she can employ her most intense emotions—rage, anxiety, shame, excitement, and desire—to work herself into a state of total abandonment to her body. The goal is to push her to the point of being incapable of thought or language—of losing self-consciousness—so she can experience a sort of "death" that enables a spiritual rebirth, the larger experience she seeks.

The idea of captivity frightens Rhoda but also entices her. It affirms her fantasies of surrender, and the man's proposal is the most interesting event to come her way in a long time. Because despair threatens to engulf her, she feels she has no choice but to agree to the terms, although of course she is actually free to accept or reject them. This is the fine balance Rice describes: boredom forces a decision to be forced into something one wants to do. Once Rhoda joins, she is told that she belongs to the organization. This means her masters will work her until she loses herself. They will ensure that the experience is frightening enough to stimulate her into a high pitch of excitement and thus compelling enough to override her fear so she can contact the deepest and most complex parts of herself that respond to power.

Rhoda signs the contract. Then, as their "captive," she immediately resists, protesting "too late" that she has made a mistake. This is one of the pivotal moments of forced consent: The slaves agree to submit, then test the bonds, secretly hoping there is no escape and pushing awareness of their consent out to the margins of consciousness until eventually it dissolves as they become immersed in their roles. Such resistance heightens the emotional pitch and enhances erotic sensation. Rhoda's master understands the scenario all too well. He laughs at her resistance and tells her she only protests because she thinks she should. He "sees more deeply" into her soul and recognizes a born flagellant.

Rhoda's first humiliating experience—which she both dreads and craves—is a thorough physical evaluation. Close scrutiny of one's nakedness is a feature common to all of Rice's erotic fiction. She believes that being the object of such concentrated attention is a source of great pleasure. "It intensifies the relationship," she explains, "because the master is so interested in the slave. Masochists occupy center stage always in my pornography. All eyes are on them. I do think being treated as a specimen, being spoken of as if you were there 'for sale' or for pleasure is very sexy." Rhoda feels vulnerable and exposed in her nakedness, but those who examine her praise her attributes.

She soon learns that her master is the sole source of her pleasure and satisfaction; the only release allowed from tension will come at his command. Her initiatory session involves being corseted (a symbol of captivity), probed, pricked with needles, humiliated, displayed, and paddled—all actions calculated to make her aware of her skin, the source of sensation. She is forced into humiliating postures—on her knees, eyes down—in which her subservient body is meant to influence her soul: As she relaxes and becomes attuned to her punishments, her physical pliability, helplessness, and readiness should make her spirit soften and yield. Body and soul work toward perfection, translated as absolute obedience to a greater power. Toward this end, Rhoda's master exposes her to constant anxiety to raise her sense of anticipation without satisfying her curiosity. She is never bored, never complacent, constantly on edge. And yielding promises the possibility of experiences she has never known.

Her master's attention is focused on her erogenous areas, particularly those usually ignored or unappreciated. In one game, for example, the master commands Rhoda to fetch flowers, which he then pokes into her anus, humiliating but exciting her. She is surprised that although she hates this experience, she also likes it: "She looked forward to it with misery."[4] Even worse, her master forces her to become a plaything for other slaves, so she is made subservient even to her equals in debasement. Contrary to what she expects, they seem more sadistic than her master. They are relentless because they know what Rhoda needs to be made more malleable.

Rice never did anything with "The Tales of Rhoda" except

read it to friends; she failed to finish it, but its themes emerged years later in her published erotica.

She continued to investigate male masochism in another unpublished story, "The House." This story opens with a young man, Alex, embarking on a weekend of sexual subservience at a place known simply as "the house" (later incorporated into *Exit to Eden*). It is a charming Victorian wherein masochistic fantasies of all kinds are encouraged. Alex wants to be dominated despite his anxiety about exposing his shameful desires. Yet, instead of starting cautiously with only one night, he requests a stay of a whole weekend, ensuring his total immersion. Voluntarily blocking escape allows him to resign himself fully to being "forced."

Alex understands that once he makes this choice—"forced" by his obsession—he is at the mercy of his appointed master. He agrees to allow the master to determine what he needs, within the limits of health and safety, but the thought of such total surrender still frightens him. The master tells him that fear is what one feels when one is trying to control what will happen and adds that when Alex realizes he has no control, he will learn valuable erotic lessons: "You're in the hands of men who are skilled at training you," Alex is told, "molding you, bending you and breaking you slowly according to your needs."[5] Via rounds of discipline and affection, the master gradually strips Alex of dignity, fusing his utter humiliation to the keenest pleasures he has ever known.

According to the rules, Alex is to take no initiative save to kiss the master's feet, and he is never to talk unless invited or to try to sexually relieve himself. Thus Alex controls to some degree the intensity of the punishment he will receive: Disobedience draws more discipline and greater pain and humiliation for longer periods of time. As much emphasis as there is on surrendering one's will to the master, the slave can still demonstrate his desire for more, and a good master responds. Both master and slave realize that the power locus lies not with the master but flows back and forth between them in the delicate balance that their interaction maintains.

Since the slave desires to reach his own ideal of perfection, the master's role is pivotal. His job is to discern what it will take to reach that goal with a particular individual. The best masters are people who have played the submissive role, but such experience is not necessary to do the job right. If the slave needs a genteel master who can nevertheless exercise power, as in Alex's case, then such is the image the master must evoke. (Alex's master dresses as a sophisticated Englishman in a smoking jacket and speaks to him in gentlemanly tones.) Because such fantasies involve exposing secrets, the relationship becomes deeply intimate: The master validates that which might otherwise embarrass the slave by playing it out to the slave's satisfaction. Only those who fully understand the fear and eroticism of surrender can dominate *well*. The master fulfills the slave's desires through the ordeals to which the slave is subjected, so there is no need for the slave to exercise self-restraint. The slave can let go and simply *feel*. And in Rice's scenarios, the master must balance discipline with tenderness, mimicking the potent rhythms of tension and release.

Playing with imbalances of power through risk and surrender involves spiritual stretching. Forced into their deepest anxieties and shame, captives must draw on inner strength to endure and overcome their fears. Often they gain a more heightened sense of life and self: They become stronger, wiser, and more self-aware. Self-enhancement via forced consent became a central factor in Rice's development of many of her fictional characters.

One such character is Tonio Treschi in Rice's third novel, *Cry to Heaven*, a story about the castrated opera singers in eighteenth-century Italy. A boy of the Venetian nobility, he has been forcibly castrated and then entered into voice training at a Naples conservatory. Tonio did not choose this mutilated mode of life and at first he allows it to diminish his sense of self. He is not a man. However, he comes to realize that he can either feel sorry for himself and live in despair or work to reshape his identity. Reluctantly, he chooses the latter, straining against the implications of the choice even as he develops his singing voice into a tool of utter perfection. He strives to overcome what was done to him. Eventually Tonio learns that a life spent suspended between the genders frees him from the restrictive social roles that strap normal people. Within the blurred boundaries of these roles, he discovers the fuller possibilities of ambiguity, that an "abnormal" life can be as rich or even richer than a normal one. Although Tonio's creative potential still emerges from a situation of forced consent, ultimately he chooses to immerse himself so thoroughly in his ambiguous identity that he is able to use it as a source of power. He becomes a star onstage with great range and diversity and also finds enough peace within himself to engage in a loving relationship.

Even in Rice's supernatural novels the framework of forced consent provides erotic tension and inner enhancement for her characters. *Interview with the Vampire* presents Louis, who suffers interminably over his decision to become a vampire. Although his maker, Lestat, ostensibly had offered him a choice, Louis had felt compelled to accept the offer. Deep in grief over losing his brother, Louis had wanted to die. Lestat's invitation had seemed a magical way out, so he had grabbed for it, only later realizing the ghastly consequences. Louis is a true submissive: He craves domination by someone as enchanting as Lestat, so he gives his consent—forced into it by his personality as much as by his desire to escape pain. Rice has admitted, "I was Louis," when she wrote this novel, so perhaps he echoed her masochistic leanings and thus was deeply attracted to his excruciating fate. Although he complains about his need to kill and the guilt he suffers, he stays with Lestat for decades, compliant and aware that immortality provides the most intense experience possible. "My vampire nature has been for me the greatest adventure of my life."[6]

The vampire is an embodiment of the complex relationship between surrender and power, threat and rapture. Years after she wrote them, Rice realized how similar her vampire novels were to her pornography: "I am writing about the same themes, dominance and submission, and there's an erotic tone to everything." Louis may be not so much a victim as a person maneuvered by a clever subconscious to reach for more. He admits that as a mortal, he never really knew the richness of life. In fact, vampirism is so intense that the human sexual experience is but a pale shadow in comparison. Certainly what he describes of his immortal existence is charged with sensuality and a tension that seeks no release. As a result, he feels everything more fully and intimately. "It was as if I had only just been able to see colors and shapes for the first time."[7] Even as Louis becomes disenchanted with Lestat, he falls under the spell of the child vampire, Claudia, who torments him with an intense blend of love, hate, and the threat of abandonment—all the fixtures of a masochist's vision of voluptuous captivity.

And Louis is not the only one. Although he presents Lestat as a sadistic master who makes slaves of his vampire children, Rice wrote the other Vampire Chronicles from Lestat's point of view, revealing *his* desire to be dominated. After she wrote *Interview*, she did more complex work with dominance and submission, so she was able to make Lestat a new type of character: the person who can play the dual role of master and slave. Seeking trancendence by merging the two, but gravitating toward masochism, Lestat forces himself into extreme experiences: He wants to be engulfed. Although Magnus, his vampire maker, supposedly forced him into vampirism, in fact Magnus made Lestat ask for it. Lestat struggled, but inevitably gave in to his own craving. The experience was too great for him to refuse. Thus, force and consent merged in his transformation. He claims he had no choice but to become a vampire, and that he wants to become mortal again—but given the opportunity to do so two centuries later, he recognizes that it is not really what he wants.

In other ways, too, Lestat reveals his desire for total surrender to something larger than self, typical of masochism. In *Lestat*, when he describes how he became enamored of various humans, he indicates his need for a friendship that will dominate his soul: "In this dark fairy tale I would pass right into my mortal lover."[8] He seeks such obliteration variously with Nicolas, Marius, Akasha, Louis, Gretchen, and David. In the final book in the series, when Memnoch the Devil takes Lestat to Heaven and Hell, he also loses himself in the experiences he has there. He is laid waste, intellectually and emotionally, by the spiritual demands, and at least for a while, the idea of captivity by an overpowering personality loses its allure. Yet there is every reason to believe that Lestat will eventually recover and seek this experience again. Such is the rhythm of compulsive desire.

A stronger description of supernatural erotic enslavement occurs in Rice's twelfth novel, *The Witching Hour*. Detailing the lives of thirteen generations of a family of witches, the Mayfairs, Rice introduces their familiar, an incubus-type spirit named Lasher. His sexual skills and promise of eventual immortality enthrall even the most powerful members of this clan. Some of them believe they can master him, but others simply seek the heightened experience he delivers and become enslaved: "With every passing year [Marguerite] became less interested in men, more addicted to the fiend's embrace, and altogether less coherent."[9] Even some of the males, such as Julien and Cortland, engage Lasher in relationships involving dominance and submission. They freely pursue the benefits of such coupling, yet they also feel a certain compulsion to do so, not the least of which is the fear of harm or death should they resist him. Although via music and other charms they gain a transient mastery over Lasher, power is never clearly in their hands.

As stated earlier, certain elements must be present for relationships to be erotic to Rice: a degree of coercion, inner struggle with resistance, being in thrall to a dangerous power countered by fear of it, the possibility that such danger offers enhancement, and fluctuations in the locus of control between master and slave. As a sensual occult entity with a sinister agenda, Lasher represents an alluring figure to the witches. They wish to get as close as possible to his mystery and power, but hovering over his irresistible invitation is a potent threat: He may offer the most intense experience they could ever have on their way to annihilation. The potential is there for either or both. This is the heart of voluptuous captivity. The simultaneous stimulation of fear and desire pushes those who venture into it closer to their Dionysian potential for either expansion or destruction. The greater the risk, the greater may be the payoff, and the interplay of resistance and momentum can be quite exciting, despite its dangers.

What Rice has done here is to exploit a complex erotic impulse: Whatever inhibits desire can also, under certain circumstances, enhance it. For example, arousal raises one's pain threshold, so that what may otherwise hurt can actually increase pleasure. What we fear or abhor may be exactly what makes us hot. Voluptuous captivity means pushing the boundaries to explore painful or frightening experiences for whatever emotional or physical energy they might provide.

Of course, when Lasher acquires human form, the women have no recourse against his onslaught. Against their will, he couples with them and thus murders them one by one. Yet without the element of choice, he no longer holds them in thrall. This is force without consent and there is nothing erotic about it.

The most explicit and detailed descriptions of forced consent leading to voluptuous captivity occur in Rice's pseudonymous novels. As Anne Rampling, she wrote *Exit to Eden* and *Belinda*, and as A. N. Roquelaure, she penned the three Beauty books. Only *Belinda* fails to explore this theme. The four others were written to satisfy Rice's desire to make available a certain type of elegant pornography that she could not find anywhere. She wanted to write about people who could submit to extreme degradation yet retain their integrity and dignity, and who could find within the trauma a way to transcend. "Good porn teaches you something," Rice believes. "It takes you someplace in the imagination, and when you return, you know something more."

The first book in the Roquelaure series was *The Claiming of Sleeping Beauty*. In style and theme, this novel picked up where Rice had left off with her earlier erotica. Wanting the fairy-tale heroine, Beauty, to experience shocking and forbidden pleasures, Rice sends the young princess into a training program for love slaves. The prince who awakens Beauty takes her there to master her and make her pliable. He forces her to accompany him, spanking her and exposing her nudity to strangers along the way, but she finds herself unexpectedly aroused: "there was in her, even in her helplessness, a sense of power."[10] She soon discovers what her captors expect of her and how their safety measures against real harm provide a sort of container for overly extreme experiences. Under the guise of force, the masters grant Beauty license to experience fully her most debased sexual desires. They command her to do things she actually wants to do but which shame and fear prohibit, such as look at naked men and indulge in orgasmic pleasures.

At first Beauty fails to realize the setup. Since her masters and mistresses tell her constantly that her will is not her own, she believes she has no choice in the matter. However, as she hears stories from other slaves, she realizes that they can run from the castle and reach a land where slaves are given safe passage. Therefore, anyone who stays is consenting to remain. Yet those slaves with a clear understanding of their masochistic nature assure Beauty that there is no point in trying to escape, because she'll never find the heated adventure and feeling of energy that she has right there. For example, the slave Tristan ran from a weak master to set himself up with a harsher one. Although he fears such hardship, he embraces it. By viewing the pain in sacred terms, he transforms his loss of physical power into greater psychological resilience. When he finds the master whom he trusts to take him to the ultimate edge, his experience becomes more vital as well as more spiritual.

"Putting people under the jeopardy of restraint," says Rice, "sets up conditions for them to feel incredibly alive under limitations. It has to do with being constricted and bound. Knowing your limitations allows you to be totally free."

Eventually Beauty realizes how much she actually craves extreme humiliation and punishment, even going so far as to disobey to make it worse for herself. She loves it when her mistress spanks her hard. By *pretending* she has no choice, she forgets that she does, and this allows her to go as far as possible into the erotic intensity.

The slaves who accept their nature and do what they can to be thoroughly tested have the most powerful experiences. One slave, Alexi, tells Beauty about the series of debasing things the Queen put him through. She exposed all of his bodily secrets to common villagers and pressed gold balls that he had fetched for her into his anus. Yet, he claims, he found a source of great strength through his ability to rise above it all. By being "forced" to perform embarrassing acts and submit to humiliation, slaves are given the opportunity to break down walls of resistance created by social taboos that had veiled their best sources of arousal. "In the midst of the worst humiliations," Rice explains, "they can attain the feeling of freedom and power because they went through it. It's similar to the saints and mystics. Their bodies were no longer important. They transcended the physical to become one with Christ."

Laurent is the slave who best understands what it means to consent to being forced into humiliating postures and behaviors. He experiences tranquillity and potency in suffering: "in those moments I had known the full power of my captors, but I had also known my own power—that we who are bereft of all privileges may yet goad and guide our punishers into new realms of heat and loving attentiveness."[11] The discipline that most frightens him—being put on the Punishment Cross, for example—is what he does his best to bring on himself. He knows what it means to dominate as well as to submit, so he craves the type of master who can force him into the most intense sensations. In the end, he winds up harnessed to carts with a horsetail dildo strapped in his anus.

"There are moments in the Roquelaure books," Rice states, "where the most profound feelings about exposure and sexual revelation are being examined. I experience them as a gradual transcendence and opening up. You get out of yourself, you're turned into something else, you become the thing that is happening to you. I'm very happy that I went all the way with them, making them fairy tales of erotic detail which are outrageous really. That's what I wanted: to go deep into the fantasy, no matter how childish or embarrassing it might seem to someone else. I'm proud of them. I believe the Beauty books have as much or more significance than anything I've ever done."

While writing the Roquelaure novels, Rice took the erotic experience in a new direction in her 1985 novel *Exit to Eden*. The story of Lisa Kelly, a dominatrix, and Elliott Slater, a slave at her exclusive resort known as The Club, is set on a luxurious island. Members of The Club can safely act out their sexual fantasies with the slaves who serve them. These slaves are beautiful young men and women who compete to be chosen, but once accepted, they have no choice in what they will be commanded to do.

At The Club, no serious pain or damage is ever inflicted. What might have adverse effects in reality can be safely acted out in fantasy. There is no risk of disease, rejection, psychotic episodes, or abuse. Mutual satisfaction is the goal. Ostensibly, the slaves exist to please the masters, but the masters are all too aware that they have to live up to the slaves' expectations for a grand experience of domination. Elliott Slater signs up to be a slave for the full two years because he wants to be totally immersed in an experience that may prove too much for him. "I'm doing it for pleasure, the word made flesh but also for . . . some harrowing of the soul, some exploration, some refusal to live on the outside of a dark and heated inner world that exists beyond the civilized face I see in the mirror."[12] His passion for danger and for getting close to what frightens him compels his choice. He volunteers to go to The Club because his psychological need makes it impossible for him to do otherwise. He consents to be forced, but in a way he is also forced to consent.

In two chapters that were cut before the novel was published, Elliott discovers just how extreme the trainers can be. They force him into submissive postures, command degrading tasks such as cleaning bathrooms with a scrub brush held in his mouth, and sexually use him from one end to the other until he believes he can endure no more. He nearly reaches the breaking point, yet, despite his horror, he craves to be pushed that far again. To be so possessed and controlled by others is nearly orgasmic to him. "S&M in this novel," Rice insists, "is a type of exotic love, as sex play, not as something sick." As nasty as the masters get, they also show great affection for the slaves.

Elliott's worst fear is to be dominated by a woman, someone he considers weaker than himself, yet that is exactly what he gets with Lisa, and it has the effect of drawing him into a new experience: love. He feels even more vulnerable, but decides to move toward it. Lisa, however, is too fearful of such intimacy to surrender easily. Nevertheless, after a great deal of agonizing, she finally agrees to join Elliott in marriage, the riskiest captivity of all. Both are "forced" by powerful feelings into a commitment that is equally based on choice. Yielding to love and all its rewards is the epitome of voluptuous captivity.

The strongest sensations occur within the tension between passion and satisfaction. The goal of desire is fulfillment, but satiation then quenches all momentum. The key to maintaining heightened arousal, then, is to find a personal rhythm that sustains desire. For some people, surrender to captivity—consensual force—proves highly exciting and offers long-term stimulation. The master may draw out pleasure by prohibiting release. Challenge, restraint, or threat may induce potent feelings, so people who need these elements set up conditions that maximize one or more of them. Too great a threat may diminish the experiences, so conditions of safety provide intensity without a debilitating fear of harm. Yet fear can help stimulate sexual excitement, so these same safety issues must recede from awareness. In the experience of forced consent, they must be simultaneously remembered and forgotten.

On a conceptual level, this seems contradictory and thus impossible, but in actual experience, the psyche opens up into many dark pockets. Consciousness is partially focused and partially diffused, which means that sharp awareness of one thing can blur when focusing on something else. Thus, knowledge of safety conditions and acts of agreement can dissolve into the immediacy of the experience. Enslaved souls who yield as if they have no choice—be they vampires, witches, or sexual captives—become more pliable. A skillful master or mentor can guide them toward breaching barriers, erasing boundaries, and defying taboos, thus contacting their own most powerful source of stimulation. The goal of forced consent is to use another person's assistance to safely surpass personal limits for greater openness to euphoria, heightened sensation, connection, and deep satisfaction. To have no choice but to go all out for what you want is voluptuous captivity indeed.

NOTES

1. Anne Rice, *Exit to Eden* (New York: Arbor House, 1985), 24.
2. Rosemary Gordon, "Masochism: The Shadow Side of the Archetypal Need to Venerate and Worship," *Journal of Analytic Psychology* 32 (1987): 3.
3. Roy F. Baumeister, *Escaping the Self* (New York: Basic Books, 1991), 124.
4. Anne Rice, "The Tales of Rhoda" (unpublished), 12.
5. ———, "The House" (unpublished).
6. ———, *Interview with the Vampire* (New York: Knopf, 1976), 82.
7. Ibid., 20.
8. ———, *The Vampire Lestat* (New York: Knopf, 1985), 338.
9. ———, *Lasher* (New York: Knopf, 1993), 286.
10. A. N. Roquelaure, *The Claiming of Sleeping Beauty* (New York: Dutton, 1983), 32.
11. ———, *Beauty's Release* (New York: Dutton, 1985), 15.
12. Rice, *Exit to Eden*, 32.

FURTHER READING

Apter, Michael J. *The Dangerous Edge: The Psychology of Excitement.* New York: The Free Press, 1992.

Morin, Jack. *The Erotic Mind.* New York: HarperCollins, 1995.

Ramsland, Katherine. *Prism of the Night: A Biography of Anne Rice.* New York: Dutton, 1991.

———. *The Vampire Companion: The Official Guide to Anne Rice's The Vampire Chronicles.* New York: Ballantine, 1993.

———. *The Witches' Companion: The Official Guide to Anne Rice's Lives of the Mayfair Witches.* New York: Ballantine, 1994.

———. *The Roquelaure Reader: A Companion to Anne Rice's Erotica*, New York: Plume, 1996.

Rice, Anne. *Interview with the Vampire.* New York: Knopf, 1976.

———. *Cry to Heaven.* New York, Knopf, 1982.

———. *The Claiming of Sleeping Beauty* (as A. N. Roquelaure). New York: Dutton, 1983.

———. *Beauty's Punishment* (as A. N. Roquelaure). New York: Dutton, 1984.

———. *Beauty's Release* (as A. N. Roquelaure). New York: Dutton, 1985.

———. *Exit to Eden* (as Anne Rampling). New York: Arbor House, 1985.

———. *The Vampire Lestat*. New York: Knopf, 1985.
———. *The Queen of the Damned*. New York: Knopf, 1988.
———. *The Witching Hour*. New York: Knopf, 1990.
———. *The Tale of the Body Thief*. New York: Knopf, 1992.
———. *Lasher*. New York: Knopf, 1993.
———. *Memnoch the Devil*. New York: Knopf, 1995.

About the Contributors

JOHN BEEBE, M.D., a Jungian analyst in San Francisco, writes frequently about film for the *San Francisco Jung Institute Library Journal*, of which he is founding editor. Coeditor of the *Journal of Analytical Psychology*, he is the author of *Integrity in Depth* (Fromm International) and the editor of C. G. Jung's *Aspects of the Masculine* (Princeton University Press).

LEONARD GEORGE, PH.D., is a psychologist, writer, and broadcaster in Vancouver, British Columbia. He is the author of *Alternative Realities: The Paranormal, the Mystic, and the Transcendent in Human Experience* (Facts on File) and *Crimes of Perception: An Encyclopedia of Heresies and Heretics* (Paragon).

W. KENNETH HOLDITCH is a research professor emeritus of English at the University of New Orleans, where he taught for thirty-two years. He is founding editor of *The Tennessee Williams Journal*. In addition, he was one of the founders of the Tennessee Williams/New Orleans Literary Festival, the Faulkner Literary Festival, the Pirate's Alley Faulkner Society, and the annual Tennessee Williams Festival in Clarksdale, Mississippi. A specialist on southern literature, Holditch has published numerous articles on Williams, Faulkner, Lillian Hellman, George Washington Cable, and Richard Ford. He has also published several articles on Anne Rice, including an interview in *Lear's* magazine. He lives in New Orleans and has run literary walking tours through the French Quarter since 1974.

GARY HOPPENSTAND is associate chairperson of the Department of American Thought and Language at Michigan State University. He has published numerous articles on topics ranging from nineteenth-century American literature to popular-culture studies. He has edited or written eight books, including an anthology of W. W. Jacobs's horror fiction *The Monkey's Paw and Other Tales of Mystery and the Macabre* (Academy Chicago Publishers) and *The Gothic World of Anne Rice* (Bowling Green University Popular Press). He published *Clive Barker's Short Stories: Imagination as Metaphor in the Books of Blood and Other Works* in 1994 (McFarland). Addison Wesley Longman will publish his college textbook, *Popular Fiction*.

KATHLEEN MACKAY is a journalist and the author of three books. Her articles have appeared in *Time*, *People*, the *Los Angeles Times*, *The Washington Post*, *Rolling Stone*, *Redbook*, *Working Woman*, and many other publications. Her books include *Relax and Enjoy Your Baby* (Norton, 1986), and she is currently working on a novel. She lives in the Boston area.

ROBIN MILLER has been a journalist for twelve years, working for newspapers in Louisiana and Mississippi. She has written extensively on Creoles and the Creole community of Isle Brevelle. Her articles have won numerous state and regional Associated Press awards. She lives in Louisiana.

RICHARD NOLL, PH.D., is a clinical psychologist and a postdoctoral fellow in the history of science at Harvard University. He has written five books, including *Bizarre Diseases of the Mind* (Facts on File) and *The Jung Cult: Origins of a Charismatic Movement* (Princeton University Press). He has written extensively on the psychiatric syndromes of vampirism, lycanthropy, and possession; he also studies shamanism. His most recent book is *The Aryan Christ* (Random House). He currently lives in the Boston area.

KATHERINE RAMSLAND, PH.D., teaches philosophy at Rutgers University and has written eleven books, including *Prism of the Night: A*

Biography of Anne Rice; *The Vampire Companion: The Official Guide to Anne Rice's The Vampire Chronicles*; *The Witches' Companion: The Official Guide to Anne Rice's Lives of the Mayfair Witches*; *The Anne Rice Trivia Book*; and *The Roquelaure Reader: A Companion to Anne Rice's Erotica*. She lives with her husband in Princeton, New Jersey.

BETTE B. ROBERTS teaches courses in composition, British and Victorian literature, and the novel at Westfield State College in Massachusetts, where she recently completed her six-year term as Chair of the English Department. She has published two studies on the gothic, her dissertation *The Gothic Romance: Its Appeal to Women Writers and Readers in Late Eighteenth-Century England* (Arno) and *Anne Rice* (Twayne's U.S. Authors Series), along with many essays on gothic fiction and Charles Dickens. She and her husband live in Belchertown, Massachusetts.

KATHLEEN KINSELLA ROUT has been interested in witches ever since she saw *Snow White* as a child. Various aspects of the occult, especially vampires, have occupied her mind since, along with the academic study of literature and psychology. This fascination became focused and legitimized when she was able to produce scholarly articles on vampire films and novels. In 1993, she read a paper on Anne Rice's Mayfair novels at the Popular Culture Association Conference in New Orleans. Dr. Rout has written a book on Eldridge Cleaver and teaches in the Department of American Thought and Language at Michigan State University.

MICHELLE SPEDDING holds degrees in journalism and counseling. She is vice president of management information systems for a marketing services company and lives with her husband, Ben, in New Jersey.

CLAUDIA VARRIN is a former professional dominatrix who began her career in 1991. She has enacted more than three hundred fantasy sessions with supplicants from around the world. Being much in demand, she has appeared on *The Joan Rivers Show*, *Geraldo*, *The Maury Povich Show*, and *Real Personal*, discussing such topics as dominance/submission, sexual role-playing, fantasy, aggressive women, and exhibitionism. *New York Magazine* has featured her in an article titled "Mean Sex," and she has written *Going from Vanilla to Raspberry Swirl: A Beginner's Guide to Dominant and Submissive Play in the Bedroom*. She is also working on an erotic novel.

S. K. WALKER is a creativity specialist living in Bucks County, Pennsylvania, and couldn't resist the coincidence of sharing a last name with Jeremy Walker.

GAIL ABBOTT ZIMMERMAN has worked in television production for more than twenty years. From 1993 to 1995 she produced and wrote stories for ABC News *20/20*. She currently produces for *CBS News 48 Hours*. She has also produced, written, and directed ABC News *Business World*, *Good Morning America*, *Entertainment Tonight*, and other programs. She was nominated for an ACE award for the documentary *Woodstock Stories* for MTV Networks, and she has won Emmys for her participation in two of the four Olympics that she has covered. She was associate director of several soap operas and one Movie of the Week. One of her favorite assignments was a profile of Anne Rice for ABC News *Day One* in 1993.

Index

Ben Vieyetes

ABOUT THE EDITOR

KATHERINE RAMSLAND has a Ph.D. in philosophy. Her articles have appeared in *Psychology Today*, *The Writer*, and numerous professional journals. In addition to *The Vampire Companion: The Official Guide to Anne Rice's The Vampire Chronicles*, *The Witches' Companion: The Official Guide to Anne Rice's Lives of the Mayfair Witches*, and *The Anne Rice Trivia Book*, she is the author of eight books including *Prism of the Night: A Biography of Anne Rice*. Dr. Ramsland lives in Princeton, New Jersey.